PENGUIN BOOKS

THE FRIENDLY JANE AUSTEN

Natalie Tyler has been a devoted Jane Austen scholar and lecturer for more than a decade. She is currently a professor at Ohio State University.

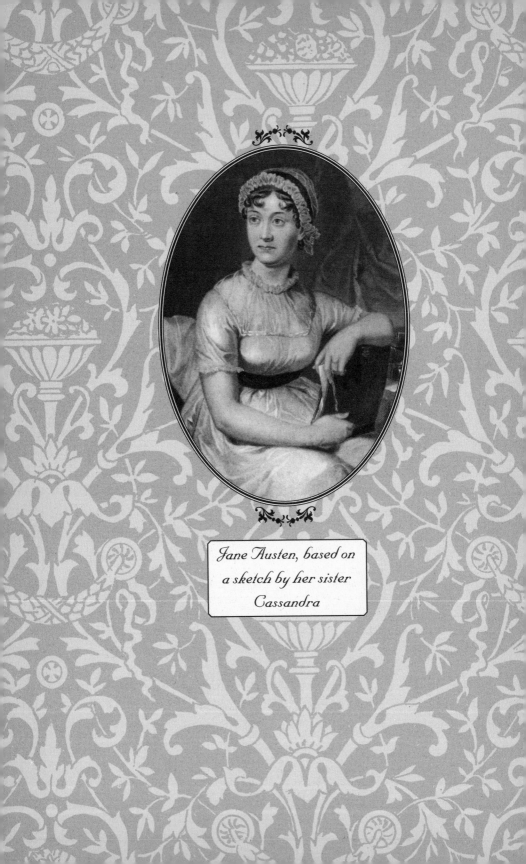

Jane Austen, based on
a sketch by her sister
Cassandra

THE FRIENDLY

Jane Austen

A Well-Mannered

Introduction

to a Lady of

Sense & Sensibility

Natalie Tyler

A Winokur/Boates Book
PENGUIN BOOKS

PENGUIN BOOKS
Published by the Penguin Group
Penguin Putnam Inc., 375 Hudson Street,
New York, New York 10014, U.S.A.
Penguin Books Ltd, 27 Wrights Lane,
London W8 5TZ, England
Penguin Books Australia Ltd, Ringwood,
Victoria, Australia
Penguin Books Canada Ltd, 10 Alcorn Avenue,
Toronto, Ontario, Canada M4V 3B2
Penguin Books (N.Z.) Ltd, 182–190 Wairau Road,
Auckland 10, New Zealand

Penguin Books Ltd, Registered Offices:
Harmondsworth, Middlesex, England

First published in the United States of America by
Viking Penguin, a member of Penguin Putnam, Inc., 1999
Published in Penguin Books 2001

1   3   5   7   9   10   8   6   4   2

THE LIBRARY OF CONGRESS HAS CATALOGED THE HARDCOVER EDITION AS FOLLOWS:
Tyler, Natalie
The friendly Jane Austen: a well-mannered introduction to a lady
of sense & sensibility / Natalie Tyler.
p.   cm.
Includes biographical references and index.
ISBN 0-670-87425-6 (hc.)
ISBN 0 14 10.0192 5 (pok.)
1. Austen, Jane, 1775–1817 Handbooks, manual, etc.—2. Women
novelists, English—19th century—Biography Handbooks, manuals, etc.
I.Title
PR4036.T95   1999
823'.7—dc21
[B]   99-27609

Printed in the United States of America
Set in Century Old Style
Designed by Jessica Shatan

To the Memory of my sister,
Andrea Hale Tyler (1954–1975) ♡

With love forever ♡

You could not shock her more than she shocks me;
Beside her Joyce seems innocent as grass.
It makes me most uncomfortable to see
An English spinster of the middle class
Describe the amorous effects of "brass",
Reveal so frankly and with such sobriety
The economic basis of society.
—W. H. AUDEN,
Letter to Lord Byron, Part I

Acknowledgments

I have always suffered from a supercilious derision of authors who acknowledge a cast of thousands. I was hubristic. Although my debts may look like the cast listing of a Cecil B. De Mille epic, the reality is that it would be unthinkable of me not to mention the following people; each has contributed, sometimes very substantially, to my understanding of Jane Austen or of life in general (and a life without Jane Austen is unthinkable).

I am fortunate to have an exceptional triumvirate of people, "without whom" this book would never exist. First I must thank Norrie Epstein, who got me started, who kept me excited, and who has given me more than twenty years' worth of some of the best conversations of my life. And David Riede: "thou, O wall, O sweet, O lovely wall. . . . Thanks, courteous wall. Jove shield thee well for this!" He has been the wall "without whom" the scaffolding would have crumbled and *il miglior fabbro* in every sense. Finally Kris Puopolo, an incomparable editor whose "coruscating" wit and certainty have won my complete admiration and gratitude. *Benedicite!*

Thanks especially to all those people who generously gave of their time and their patience in providing me with ideas, interviews, and quotations for the book. Your insights, your intelligence, and your delight in Jane Austen are really the substance and the spirit of this book. Jane Austen's works and her letters are my primary sources, but I would be more than remiss were I not to acknowledge the excellent material I have scrounged and filched from Austen's biographers, those valiant people who did all the real research while I have reclined and read. Without the works of J. E. Austen-Leigh, Richard Arthur Austen-Leigh, Douglas Bush, Jan Fergus, J. David Grey, John Halperin, Park Honan, Deborah Kaplan,

Deirdre Le Faye, Valerie Grosvenor Myer, Nigel Nicolson, David Nokes, Brian Southam, Claire Tomalin, and George Holbert Tucker I would have had but a very limited understanding of what was indeed important to Jane Austen.

And many thanks to all the members of the Jane Austen Society of North America and the members of the Jane Austen Mailing List who patiently answered my questions and provided me with many intelligent and ingenious ideas. I am especially grateful to Joan Austen-Leigh, Shirley Gershen, Mary Hardenbrook, Julia Braun Kessler, Edith Lank, Elsa Solender, and Joan Vredenburgh. They all have contributed to this book's virtues; I alone am responsible for its faults or infelicities.

I am much indebted to my friends, advisers, and necessary provocateurs and provocatrices who populate that checkerboard of mirth and misery, enigma and enchantment that makes up my life. They are Reid and Karen Boates, Diane Brounstein, bsb and nkn, Jennifer Ehmann, Barbara Fisher, Charles Flowers, Blynn Garnett, Dee Goodman, The Killerbees, Ellis Perlswig, who gave me my first copies of Jane Austen's novels when I was sixteen years old, Sidney Oliver, Lindsay River, Gillian Speeth, Helen Spier and her excellent family, Gray Standen and *Gli Amici*, and Jon Winokur.

A particularly deep debt of obligation and gratitude goes to those friends and teachers who have joined the majority. I will always remember them with enormous fondness for their infectious gusto for art, language, and literature: Marilyn Sibley Fries, George Healey, Marjorie Jacobs, Arthur Mizener, James Rieger, John Arthur Sellers, James Leo Spenko, Karin Margaret Strand, and Clarence Tyler.

I can never appreciate sufficiently my family (does any of us?): my mother, Natalie Tyler, who never has tolerated a bookless home or a dull moment; my dear siblings, John, Carol, Cynthia, and Elizabeth; those young men Benedict and Austin Riede, who amaze and delight me with their wit, their banter, their startling sensitivities, and all those rich, moist, dense moments of Infinite Jest; the presence of Susanna Wolf; Joe and Cindy Jacobs, impresarios of my heart; that generous woman of mystery Betty Jane Riede; a wonderful, delightful generation of young nieces, nephews, and cousins: Chris, Margot, Tyler, Mallory, Alex, Jacob, Alison, Catherine, Bram, Bonny, Molly, Anna, Susan, Norah, and James; and lastly I bow low before those farouche bons vivants Doulton, Myra, Face, Oslo, Blixa, Bongo, Wolfie, and a certain superannuated gerbil.

All quotations from Jane Austen's six major novels, from *Lady Susan*, *The Watsons*, and *Sanditon* are from the Penguin Editions. Quotations from *Volume the First*, *Volume the Second*, and *Volume the Third* are from R. W. Chapman's edition of *The Oxford Illustrated Jane Austen*. Material quoted from Jane Austen's letters is gleaned from Deirdre Le Faye's third edition (1997) of the letters.

Contents

� PART I: EARLY LIFE AND JUVENILIA 15

❧ PART II: MAJOR WORKS 63 ❧

❧ Part III: The Legacy 235 ❧

Preface

I have loved Jane Austen since I was a teenager too innocent in the ways of the world to know that there is a great divide between crude sarcasm and delicious irony. Learning how first to discern and secondly to cross that division is part of learning how to understand and appreciate Austen's sensibility.

I had my earliest lessons in that fine art when I first read *Pride and Prejudice* at age sixteen. Initially I came to some of the following conclusions: that Mary Bennet was the most intelligent and potentially the most interesting Bennet sister; that Mr. Collins expressed himself very prettily indeed and I would love to have such a well-spoken suitor; that Mrs. Bennet's maternal enthusiasms were wonderful and that my mother was very lacking in her failure to scout the neighborhood for a suitable match for me. Upon more reflection, I realized that perhaps some subtleties had been lost on me. Had Austen been crudely sarcastic about her characters, I would have understood at once. But she demanded that I explore the nuances in her characters. I read another Jane Austen novel, this time *Emma*, and in a flash of illumination I understood the delicacies and the delectations of Austen's irony. I reread *Pride and Prejudice* with gusto then, realizing that Mary Bennet was a parody of pseudointellectual show-offs, that those "well-spoken" words of Mr. Collins revealed that he was a ludicrous nerd, and that Mrs. Bennet was a more tiresome mother than my own could be on her worst days.

Rereading Jane Austen has taught me how to read the world and has given me more guidelines and examples on how to behave than the combined efforts of Emily Post, psychoanalysis, and a lengthy stay at the Betty Ford Clinic possibly could. With each rereading I gradually realized that Jane Austen was teaching me something that was not on the curriculum of my high school.

Many years later, in graduate school, I was thrilled to have the opportunity to enroll in a seminar on the works of Jane Austen. At last my love for Austen's novels would be married to academic discipline. I would become a Jane Austen scholar, which promised to be the harmonious denouement of my love of literature and my desire to teach. My desires were thwarted. The professor approached Jane Austen the way Wagner's Brunnhilde and her warrior Valkyries approached Valhalla. She was dressed in academic armor and rode on stallions of critical theory. Her battle cries seemed too fierce for what I had thought of as the always amusing and gratifying act of reading Jane Austen. The professor drilled us in the arcane metalanguage of academic theory. We galloped through *Sense and Sensibility* dutifully noting "tagged indirect discourse," "untagged direct discourse," "free indirect discourse," or "free direct discourse." As if this were not sufficient to dampen my delight in Austen scholarship, she flew on, with great zeal, to Lacanian Austen, poststructuralist Austen, Todorovian and Bakhtinian Austen, and Austen under the pendulum of Foucault. I was still wondering why Elinor Dashwood found Edward Ferrars so appealing and whether or not Jane Austen was endorsing the decision of Charlotte Lucas to marry Mr. Collins. The novel is a *text*, I was reminded, and it was naive to treat the characters, those verbal constructs, as though they were real people with whom I could interest myself.

When my aunt Marjorie had an eye operation and was forced into a fortnight of blindness, she asked me to read *Pride and Prejudice* to her. It was a redemptive experience after my graduate school seminar. Virtually every page gave us cause to howl with laughter. Marjorie and I were captivated by the Bennet sisters, and between chapters we eagerly discussed the characters and their actions, much as we talked about our own families. It became easier to see how we could cope with our boorish brothers, crude cousins, indecorous in-laws, and surly sons after the tonic effect of Jane Austen's wit.

Austen became our lodestar. We vowed to be civil to the officious, the maladroit, the impolitic, and the insincere. Having worshiped at the tabernacle of Jane Austen, we were better people for it. If we could not actually be Elizabeth or Jane Bennet, then we could certainly identify and exorcise any traces within us of a Miss Bingley, a Lydia or a Mary Bennet, and we could learn how to stand up to any Lady Catherine de Bourghs rampaging about the neighborhood. In reading Jane Austen, we had in fact become better people. We had learned how to read the characters of others, how to discern those people made of gold from those pyrite puppets of humanity.

I think that people today hunger for the kind of experience I had with my aunt, and that accounts for the explosion of Jane Austen onto the best-seller list of the *New York Times* (with such strange bedfellows as Danielle Steel, John Grisham, and Robin Cook) and the multiplying television and film productions of her novels in recent years.

In *Mansfield Park*, Jane Austen says that she would "Let other pens dwell on guilt and misery. I quit such odious subjects as soon as I can, impatient to restore every body, not greatly in fault themselves, to tolerable comfort and to have done with all the rest."

As for *The Friendly Jane Austen*, my plan is to let other pens dwell on Lacan, Derrida, Foucault, political correctness, and cultural diversity. *The Friendly Jane Austen* is for the uninitiated as well as more serious Austenites. In short, I promise unalloyed adoration of Austen's works.

On Jane Austen

*J*ane Austen is weirdly capable of keeping everybody busy. The moralists, the Eros-and-Agape people, the Marxists, the Freudians, the Jungians, the semioticians, the deconstructors—all find an adventure playground in six samey novels about middle-class provincials.
—Martin Amis

*W*hen I think of Jane Austen I think of opulence and sophistication.
—Beatrice Arthur

*T*he oddest yet by no means inapt analogy to Jane Austen's art of representation is Shakespeare's—oddest, because she is so careful of limits, as classical as Ben Jonson in that regard, and Shakespeare transcends all limits. . . . Like Shakespeare, she gives us figures, major and minor, utterly consistent each in his or her own mode of speech and being, and utterly different from one another.
—Harold Bloom

Jane Austen . . . always invites us to rise to precisely her own masterful level of inference about moral relations. She presents the signs of moral and intellectual strength and weakness; we make a stab at the correct inferences; she then gently corrects our misreadings.
—WAYNE BOOTH

She was naturally exuberant. Her power came as all power comes, from the direction and control of exuberance. But there is the presence and pressure of that vitality behind her thousand trivialities; she could have been extravagant if she liked. She was the very reverse of a starched or a starved spinster; she could have been a buffoon like the Wife of Bath if she chose. . . . Jane Austen may have been protected from the truth but precious little of the truth was protected from her.
—G. K. CHESTERTON

There are some writers who write too much. There are others who write enough. There are yet others who wrote nothing like enough to satisfy their admirers, and Jane Austen is certainly one of these. There would be more genuine rejoicing at the discovery of a complete new novel by Jane Austen than any other literary discovery, short of a new major play by Shakespeare, that one can imagine.
—MARGARET DRABBLE

Jane's specialty is the knowing smile. Jane is perhaps the greatest tour guide to the affections of men and women, a guide who knows how to reveal the delicate conversational dance without making her own presence obtrusive. The chief reason that I have returned to her works repeatedly is that I love her style (her "smile style" as it were). If style is to writing as grace is to dancing, then Jane is most graceful on her feet. She does not opt for a "grand jeté" when a pirouette is best.
—MICHAEL FISCHER

Jane Austen's works used, fondly, to be thought of as the spontaneous effusions of a vicarage parlour: as little systems of light and energy, full of delicate, decisive love comedy and miraculously independent of any hampering local circumstances. If these are classics, we thought, then classics are fun. Their nature encouraged us to feel about them somewhat as we might feel about lyric poems conceived in the same way—the song of a witty skylark perhaps. It is a mistake to sneer. Such a response is a response to some perennially fresh quality in the novels which if we miss we miss everything.
—ROGER GARD

I've always thought of Austen as a miniaturist. If you look at miniatures, particular Elizabethan miniatures by Hilliard, and Oliver, you can see that she does much the same thing by creating an entire world in a very small place. Hilliard's miniature portrait of Francis Drake, although tiny, captures all of Drake's vanity and arrogance. I think Austen does much the same thing. Her universe is small, but within it you see everything that needs to be seen.
—Blynn Garnett

There is a time to be born and a time to die, and a time to be middle-aged and read Miss Austen. Some men are born middle-aged, some achieve middle age of their own preference, others have it thrust upon them.
—H. W. Garrod

Some years ago I was participating in a voir dire for a criminal trial. The judge asked me, "Who is your favorite author?" When I replied, "Jane Austen," she said, "In thirty years on the bench, no one has ever given that response to me." I responded, "More's the pity," and she agreed. I was seated on the jury.
—Gene Gill

Miss Austen is an inimitable painter of quiet life. . . . Common, workday life, with here & there a suit of best for Sundays. Yet there is nothing trivial. It is what Alfred [Tennyson] calls in one of his unfinished poems "most ideal unideal, most uncommon commonplace." Dignity in the sentiments, dignity in the style . . . —none but a woman & a lady could possess that tact of minute observation & that delicacy of sarcasm.
—Arthur Henry Hallam

If there is a mature man incapable of being infatuated with Mary Crawford, or in love with Anne Elliot, he must be a dull fellow.
—William Hamilton

An artist without artistic temperament and a feminine woman with a masculine mind. That's what I call a double-barrelled blessing.
—Florence King

There are those who think Jane Austen tea-tablish, as there are those who think that Mozart tinkles.
—LOUIS KRONENBERGER

Among the writers who have approached nearest to the manner of [Shakespeare's characterizations] we have no hesitation in placing Jane Austen.
—THOMAS BABINGTON MACAULAY

At first sight, Jane Austen's manner and matter may seem to be old-fashioned, stilted, unreal. But this is a delusion to which the bad reader succumbs.
—VLADIMIR NABOKOV

Jane Austen. Based on the watercolor sketch by Cassandra, this slightly glamorized picture gives Jane more embonpoint and a backdrop of books.

Jane Austen is not an opera, she's a string trio or quartet—clear and direct and uncompromising.
—NANCY PANNIER

In Miss Austen there is, though a restrained and well-nuanced, an insatiable and ruthless delight in roasting and cutting up a fool.
—GEORGE SAINTSBURY

That young lady had a talent for describing the involvements and feelings and characters of ordinary life, which is to me the most wonderful I ever met with. The Big Bow-wow strain I can do myself like any now going; but the exquisite touch, which renders ordinary commonplace things and characters interesting, from the truth of the description and sentiment, is denied to me. What a pity such a gifted creature died so early!
—SIR WALTER SCOTT

Reading Austen has led me to read texts with much more scrutiny, to catch potential glimpses of irony. Now I read everything—novels, newspapers, cereal boxes—for the subtext, which is a bit paranoid. I blame Austen.
—DARYL SNG

For reading Jane Austen, to those who love her, is like mounting with wings as eagles; we cannot tire.
—G. B. STERN

A full appreciation of the genius of Jane Austen is the nicest touchstone of literary taste . . . Jane Austen, Jane Austen and life, which of you two copies the other?
—MONTAGU SUMMER

Once we have comprehended her mode of judgment, the moral and spiritual lessons of contemporary literature are easy—the metaphysics of "sincerity" and "vulgarity" once mastered, the modern teachers, Lawrence and Joyce, Yeats and Eliot, Proust and Gide, have but little to add save in the way of contemporary and abstruse examples.
—LIONEL TRILLING

Jane Austen wrote about situations that are repeated today—the driving scenes in Northanger Abbey *are so similar to those on a date with a boy who drives too fast. There are Lydias, Emmas, Bingleys of the same age today. Adopting Austen's eyes to see people and situations as amusing rather than infuriating does wonders for one's blood pressure.*
—SALLIE WADSWORTH

Much of America lives by the process of manipulation, and nobody renders it more brilliantly than Austen.
—HARVEY WEINSTEIN

She is not a gentle writer. Do not be misled; she is not ignorant, merely discreet; not innocent, merely graceful.
—FAY WELDON

Her cool silence on the wherefore of the why is a million times more evidential of an interest in the fundamental things of life than "Brother, brother, how shall I know God?" sobbed Alyosha, who by this time was exceedingly drunk, or any such sentence from those Russians.
—REBECCA WEST

—How did I feel about Jane Austen? [Somerset Maugham] asked.—I said that . . . I thought her one of the six greatest English writers (the others, as I did not say, are Shakespeare, Milton, Swift, Keats, and Dickens). We spoke of Jane Austen a moment. Why did the people who didn't like her dislike her so much? I asked.—Oh, because she didn't care about public events, didn't mention the Napoleonic wars.—
—EDMUND WILSON

How Do We Love
Jane Austen?
Let Us Count the Ways

Jane Austen is a writer like Shakespeare and Dickens who is read and understood on multiple levels. There is no one Jane Austen and no single reason to love her. But there are at least four good reasons and thus four essential types of passionate reader of Jane Austen. The following multiple-choice test will help you determine into which school of readership you fall.

SELF-EVALUATION QUIZ

Answer the following multiple choice questions honestly.

1. Your favorite Meg Ryan movie is:
   A: *Sleepless in Seattle*
   B: *You've Got Mail*
   C: *When a Man Loves a Woman*
   D: *Courage Under Fire*

2. Your favorite planet is:
   A: Venus
   B: Jupiter
   C: Mercury
   D: Saturn

3. Your favorite Shakespearean comedy is:
   A: *Taming of the Shrew*
   B: *A Midsummer Night's Dream*
   C: *As You Like It*
   D. *The Twelfth Night*

4. After a long absence, Reginald, the man whose marriage proposal you still regret declining, reappears in your life. You:
   A: Can only blush and silently implore him to forgive you. You embark upon a program of good deeds.
   B: Tell the beloved Reg that you made a mistake and that you are sorry.
   C: Arouse his jealousy by flirting with the wealthy but doltish owner of your nearest equivalent to a country estate.
   D: Act indifferent. You can be happy without Reginald.

5. Your favorite Beatle is:
   A: Paul
   B: George
   C: John
   D: Ringo

6. Your favorite Dickens novel is:
   A: *Oliver Twist*
   B: *The Old Curiosity Shop*
   C: *Bleak House*
   D: *Dombey & Son*

7. You identify most with which of the following maxims:
   A: Life is a glass of blessings.
   B: The glass is always half full.
   C: We see life through a glass darkly.
   D: The glass is always half empty.

8. Your half sister Jonquil wants to put on a home performance of *No Sex Please, We're British,* and she begs you to participate. You:
   A: Are shocked and pray for the safe deliverance of her soul.
   B: Are shocked and immediately condemn such folly.
   C: Are appalled at her vulgar taste. Why can't Jonquil read Pinter and Beckett?
   D: Insist that she put on *Hamlet*; you will take the lead à la Sarah Bernhardt.

10. You like most the tenor voice of:
    A: José Carreras
    B: Luciano Pavarotti

C: Placido Domingo

D: k. d. lang

11. To comfort your acutely sensitive friend Primrose, who has just been jilted by her love, you first have a cozy chat about Jane Austen and reflect upon what Lizzy Bennet would do in similar circumstances. Next you make her a bracing cup of tea and then you:

A: Read the poetry of Cowper and Crabbe to her.

B: Show her your photos of Colin Firth as Mr. Darcy.

C: Play your disc of Gorecki's *Symphony of Sorrowful Songs*.

D: Rent videos of *Thelma and Louise, Bound,* and *The Piano*.

12. For hors d'oeuvres you prefer to serve:

A: Gateaux and chocolate-covered strawberries

B: Cucumber and watercress tea sandwiches

C: Martinis, shaken not stirred, hold the vermouth

D: Alfalfa sprout sandwiches; sliced kiwi fruit

13. You are signing up for a free course at the local community college. You choose:

A: Petit Point, Quilting, or Embroidery

B: Calligraphy, Determining Your Fashion Color Season, or Folk Dancing

C: Bereavement Counseling, Current Events Discussion Group, or Studies in Flannery O'Connor

D: Self-Defense, Tai Kwon Do, Vegetarian Cooking

14. You most appreciate the sensibility of:

A: Martha Stewart

B: Heloise (she of the Hints)

C: Miss Manners

D: Susie Bright

15. You have a date on a wintry Friday evening. You decide to:

A: Cook at home and rent *Love Story* or *Doctor Zhivago*. Snuggle and cuddle.

B: See if you can find a place where you can enjoy moonlit ice skating or cross-country skiing; bring along a thermos of Irish coffee.

C: Go first to a concert and then to a coffeehouse with a blazing fire and discuss the music.

D: Go to a poetry slam and then go home for sexual aerobics.

16. The artist who most exemplifies the American spirit in your opinion is:

A: Norman Rockwell

B: Gilbert Stuart

C: Diane Arbus

D: Annie Liebowitz

17. Your therapist asks you to react to the letter *O*: You say:
    A: Oatmeal, Oahu, organza
    B: Orchid, Orion, oregano
    C: Oblomov, Orwell, osso buco
    D: Orgasm, organic, O'Keeffe

18. Your idea of good medicine for a cold is:
    A: Chicken soup, brownies, chamomile tea
    B: Nyquil, vitamin C, aspirin, rest
    C: Prozac, Midol, Courvoisier, low-tar cigarettes
    D: Ginseng tea, powdered feverfew, and zinc tablets

19. You have tickets for a Broadway show. You most want to see:
    A. *The Sound of Music*
    B: *Phantom of the Opera*
    C: *Sweeney Todd*
    D: *Rent*

20. Your favorite character in *Gone with the Wind* is:
    A: Melanie
    B: Ashley
    C: Rhett
    D: Scarlett

Tally your answers. If you have a preponderance of A answers, then you are a "Janeite." If you have more B answers than any others, you are a member of the "Gentle Jane" school. If C answers dominate, then you believe in Jane Austen as cynic and satirist and belong to the "Ironic Jane" school of readers. If D is the prevailing letter, you are a person who loves Jane Austen for her contributions to feminism and can proudly consider yourself a member of the "Subversive Jane" school. Don't be concerned if you have a tie! It is eminently possible to belong to more than one school of Austen readership or to transport between them depending on your mood du jour.

ARE YOU A JANEITE?

The first school, the Janeites, proposes that Jane (and if you are a Janeite, you are on a comfortable first-name standing with your favorite author) provides an alternate, romantic reality more attractive than real life with its wars and deaths. This school, alternatively, can be regarded as Jane as comfort food, Jane as a pint of Ben & Jerry's ice cream or a Kraft macaroni and cheese dinner on a stormy night. Your Jane is a teller of fairy tales in which Cinderella always claims the prince in a sweetly satisfying, and never syrupy, idyll.

A JANEITE PAR EXCELLENCE

I am a Jane Austenite, and therefore slightly imbecile about Jane Austen. . . . She is my favourite author! I read and re-read, the mouth open and the mind closed. Shut up in measureless content, I greet her by the name of most kind hostess, while criticism slumbers. The Jane Austenite possesses little of the brightness he ascribes so freely to his idol. Like all regular churchgoers, he scarcely notices what is being said.

—E. M. FORSTER

DO YOU BELONG TO THE SCHOOL OF GENTLE JANE?

The second school consists of the students of Gentle Jane. These readers believe that Jane Austen depicts an ideal society in which goodness is always rewarded and a divine harmony shapes our ends. Jane Austen's novels can teach us how to become ladies and gentlemen, how to avoid vulgarity, how to conduct ourselves with civility. Jane Austen is not merely a beloved escape and consolation, but one who represents an attainable reality of a pleasantly well-ordered life. She is like a beloved aunt always providing the best and wisest counsel.

A MEMBER OF THE GENTLE JANE SCHOOL

*T*he great abstract nouns of the classical English moralists are unblushingly and uncompromisingly used: *good sense, courage, contentment, fortitude,* "some duty neglected, some failing indulged," *impropriety, indelicacy, generous candour, blameable distrust, just humiliation, vanity, folly, ignorance, reason.* These are the concepts by which Jane Austen grasps the world. In her we still breathe the air of the *Rambler* and *Idler.*

—C. S. LEWIS

DO YOU BELONG TO THE
IRONIC JANE SCHOOL?

The third school of Austen lover contends that Jane's muse is neither high romance nor the ideal of civility, but rather irony. This Jane Austen is brilliantly terrifying in her acerbic, quietly vitriolic observations about the human character. She is the one person whose insights about yourself you would most fear because you realize that her perceptions are penetrating, perspicacious, and piercingly accurate. This school loves Jane Austen because she has honed their intellectual judgments and intensified their irony quotients and, most of all, because she makes them chortle. If you laugh out loud or even chuckle softly to yourself when you hear the words "Maple Grove," "Mr. Suckling," "rears and vices," or "pollute the shades," you are probably already a thoroughgoing ironist who reads Jane Austen more for delight than for inspiration or instruction, although you would not be likely to deny that inspiration and instruction are abundant.

THE VOICE OF THE
IRONIC JANE SCHOOL

*H*er sharpness and refusal to suffer fools make you fearful of intruding, misinterpreting, crassly misreading the evidence.

—CLAIRE TOMALIN

DO YOU BELONG TO THE
SUBVERSIVE JANE SCHOOL?

Finally, the fourth major Austen Academy consists of those who see Jane Austen as a protofeminist whose prime interest was in ameliorating the lot of women. Her very real transgressive and subversive messages may be read between the lines of her parodic novels. Her novels are imbued with feminist commentary; she is the mother of upward mobility for women and the author of some of the first adventure stories for young ladies. Behind a veneer of civility lurks a deep anger that most women do not have the luxury of refusing to become chattel, and while England celebrates its navy and its clergymen, the wives, mothers, and sisters who are the backbone of the system are given only perfunctory public notice. Your Jane Austen exposes the injustice of this society. Furthermore, she made enormous strides in the art of narration of the novel. She was an innovator, ahead of her time in every way. You are intrigued by articles on covert lesbianism, or masturbation fantasy, or indirect critique of the Napoleonic Wars in Austen's novels and think that they explore a major layer of meaning.

Acutely conscious of other women's writing and of women's subordinate and marginal position within society, Austen began by writing burlesques that offer comic images of female power and possibility. Her unconventional portraits of women in the juvenilia reflect her scepticism about contemporary notions of what women were like—and what they should be like. . . . From picturing women who literally get away with murder in her burlesques, Austen went on to portray women who figuratively do so in her earliest realistic fiction—women who confront and reject conventional behavior. In her later novels, she managed to convey an increasing sense of women's insecure and even threatened position within their social worlds, without destroying a comic tone.

—JAN FERGUS, on the feminism inherent in Austen's works

There are obvious differences in these four slants on Austen, and Janeites will rarely see eye to eye with those who believe that the "real" Austen is a subversive "bad girl" full of ribaldry and revolution. Contemporary critics have unfolded new ways of looking at Austen, but the old ways have never diminished in popularity. Like Shakespeare and Dickens, Austen offers a world of possibilities for every kind of reader. She is both deep and accessible and appeals to "highbrow" and "middlebrow" readers. The worlds she created in her six finished novels are alluring to traditionalists, to radicals, and to those who like to stay in the middle of the literary road. She seems to have anticipated post-Freudian understanding of human character by layering her novels with substantial material to keep everyone happy.

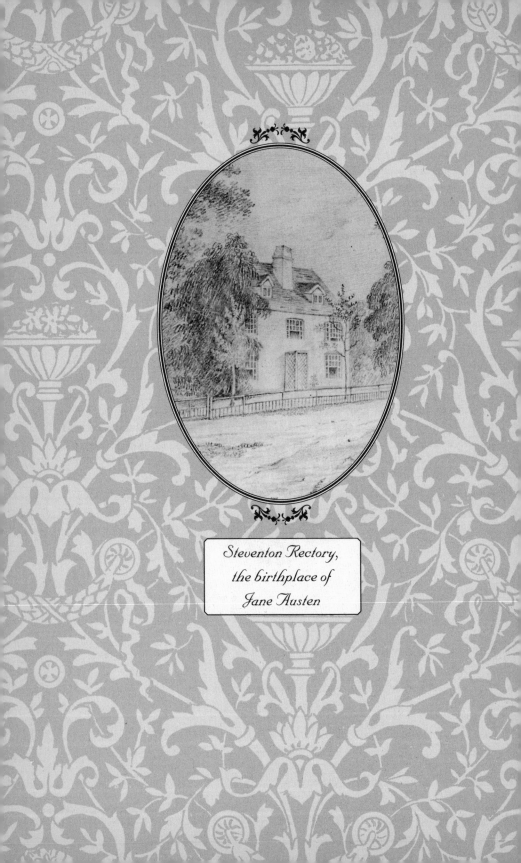

Steventon Rectory,
the birthplace of
Jane Austen

PART I

Early Life and Juvenilia

Early Life and Family

Steventon: The Austen Family

Jane Austen was born, the seventh of eight children, to the rector of Steventon George Austen, and his wife, Cassandra Leigh, on December 16, 1775. Steventon is in Hampshire, between Basingstoke and Whitchurch, and it is where Austen spent the first twenty-five years of her life aside from a period of almost two years at the Abbey School in Reading. Steventon Rectory had seven bedrooms, so it could not have been too cramped, but it perhaps lacked something in appearance. In later years Austen's nephew J. E. Austen-Leigh recalled it as "finished with less elegance than would be found in the most ordinary dwellings . . . the beams which supported the upper floors projected into the rooms below in all their naked simplicity."

Bringing Up Baby

Child psychologists have persuaded us that it is critical for infants to spend their early months closely "bonding" with their parents. If we don't pencil in

ON THE BIRTH OF JANE AUSTEN, BY HER FATHER

Y̶ou have doubtless been for some time in expectation of hearing from Hampshire, and perhaps wondered a little if we were in our old age grown such bad reckoners but so it was, for Cassey certainly expected to have been brought to bed a month ago: however last night the time came, and without a great deal of warning, everything was soon happily over. . . . Your sister thank God is pure well after it. . . .

—LETTER DATED DECEMBER 17, 1775,
FROM THE REVEREND GEORGE AUSTEN
TO HIS SISTER-IN-LAW, SUSANNA WALTER

The Reverend George Austen, Jane's father, as he appeared in 1801, the year he retired and moved to Bath with his wife and two daughters

"quality time" with our infants today, we are committing emotional abuse. In fact, there has never been any universally accepted method of infant care. When Jane Austen was young, infants of her class were shipped out to the home of a wet-nurse, who was paid a few shillings weekly to provide milk and basic care. Austen's mother chose to nurse her own infants for about three months and then to send them to a wet-nurse in the nearby village who returned the children as walking, talking toddlers, ready to engage, with at least a certain amount of sentience, in family life. Jane was an infant during a particularly cold winter and spent the first three months of her life in bed with her mother. But with the coming of spring she was evicted from the maternal bed and breast and sent out to a village wet-nurse, where she stayed for a year or eighteen months. In her biography of Jane Austen, Claire Tomalin points out the potential trauma in these major upheavals in an infant's life and suggests that Austen's lifelong sense of emotional distance from her mother may have had its genesis in this abrupt exile from home at such a tender age.

A Pruned Family Tree: Jane Austen's Immediate Family

Austen scholars have constructed elaborate family trees that detail all of Jane's family connections: Austen, Leigh, de Feuillide, Knight, Knatchbull, Hampson, Perrot, Cholmeley, Lloyd, Craven, Fowle, Lefroy. Their heroic efforts have proved that Austen is connected to King Edward III, Mary, Queen of Scots, Prince William of Wales through his late mother, Diana, Princess of Wales, and other luminaries. Yet more important to an appreciation of Jane Austen are her parents, her siblings, their spouses, and her nieces and nephews.

George Austen (1731–1805) married Cassandra Leigh (1739–1827) on April 26, 1764. Here is a brief account of their eight children.

REVEREND JAMES AUSTEN (1765–1819)

Jane's eldest brother had two wives; the first, Anne Mathew, who died in 1795, left him a daughter, Anna, who married the Reverend Benjamin Lefroy. With his second wife, Mary Lloyd, James had two children: James Edward Austen (Austen-Leigh after 1837) and Caroline. James's three children were particularly beloved by their aunt Jane, and all three contributed to the *Memoir of Jane Austen* (1870). Anna Lefroy wrote a continuation of *Sanditon,* and Caroline wrote *My Aunt Jane Austen.*

GEORGE AUSTEN (1776–1838)

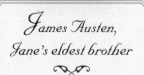

James Austen, Jane's eldest brother

The second son did not grow up with his family. He may have been deaf; he may have had cerebral palsy; he may have suffered from epilepsy; he may have been intellectually weak. In any event he was sent to board with another family.

Unlike his siblings, he did not return from the home of the village wet-nurse. Only recently has there been some lively debate

JANE AUSTEN'S GENERATION

*A*usten was born in the precise middle of the 1770s, a decade that produced many outstanding people. Many of her cocelebrants are noted for their fantastic imaginations and their contribution to Romanticism. Austen is clearly the comic genius of a fairly solemn bunch. Since comedy tends to wither under the test of time more so than grand canvases, majestic symphonies, philosophy, epic stories, lyrical poetry, and national anthems, Austen's accomplishments can be appreciated as monumental in their own right.

Ludwig van Beethoven
Georg Wilhelm Friedrich Hegel
William Wordsworth
Sir Walter Scott
Dorothy Wordsworth
Samuel Taylor Coleridge
William Henry Harrison
Friedrich von Schlegel
Charles Lamb
J. M. W. Turner
André Ampère
Henry Clay
E. T. A. Hoffmann
John Constable
William Hazlitt
Clement Clarke Moore
Francis Scott Key

about how his fate reflects the general treatment of "defective" children during the eighteenth century. When he was four years old, his father wrote, "We have this comfort, he cannot be a bad or a wicked child," and later that year his mother wrote, "My poor little George is come to see me to-day, he seems pretty well, tho' he had a fit lately." George spent his entire life being cared for by the Cullum family, who also cared for Mrs. Austen's younger brother Thomas Leigh, who, like George, had been separated from his family from an early age for similar unspecified "defects." Although the Leighs and the Austens supported these outcasts financially, they were no longer family members in any essential way. Both men lived with the Cullums until they died. Thomas Leigh lived to be seventy-four; George Austen died of dropsy at the age of seventy-two and was described on his death certificate as a "gentleman."

EDWARD AUSTEN (KNIGHT) (1768–1852)

Edward was evidently a charming lad. When he was twelve years old, Thomas Knight II, a distant cousin of the Austen family, and his bride, Catherine, requested his company on their honeymoon. Despite the seeming oddness of this plan, the Knights adored Edward. At the age of sixteen he was formally adopted by the wealthy, childless Knights and became their heir, although he retained the family name Austen until the death of Mrs. Knight in 1812, when he was a widower himself, at which point he was legally obligated to change his own surname and that of all of his children to Knight. This change of name is strikingly similar to that of Frank Churchill, the son of Mr. Weston in *Emma*.

Edward had married the multigravid Elizabeth Bridges, who produced eleven children between 1793 and 1808, when she shuffled off this mortal coil, evidently exhausted by her final confinement at age thirty-five. Fanny, her eldest daughter, then age fifteen wrote in her diary on October 10, 1808: "Oh! the miserable events of this day! My mother, my beloved mother torn from us! After eating a hearty dinner, she was taken *violently* ill and *expired* (may God have mercy upon us) in 1/2 an hour!!!!"

Cassandra Austen went to Godmersham to stay with the bereaved family. Although Jane Austen seems to have been sympathetic to the plight of the motherless children, she was not responsive to Cassandra's desire that she come to Godmersham to help the family, since the fifteen-year-old Fanny was too grief-stricken to be of much help. Jane wrote rather coldly that "soon we may hope that our dear Fanny's sense of duty to that beloved father will rouse her to exertion. For his sake, and as the most acceptable proof of love to the spirit of her departed mother, she will try to be tranquil and resigned." Of Edward's eleven children, Fanny was the most important to her aunt Jane Austen, who came to regard her as "almost another sister."

REVEREND HENRY THOMAS AUSTEN (1771–1850)

The fourth Austen son, wrote of his sister: "Her voice was extremely sweet. She delivered herself with fluency and precision. Indeed she was formed for elegant and rational society, excelling in conversation as much as in composition." Henry was Jane's favorite brother; this has surprised some biographers since he was clearly feckless and in frequent financial difficulty. Intellectual and optimistic (his niece Anna Lefroy said he created "a perpetual sunshine") he had a career in life that seems to parallel John Donne's inasmuch as he experienced a worldly youth and then was ordained at age forty-six. Unlike Donne, however, Henry was a bit of a slacker in that he returned home to live off his mother's largess when he was well into his fifties. Like his eldest brother, James, Henry was Oxford educated. He was the brother most directly responsible for handling the business transactions involved in publish-

The handsome Henry Austen, said to be Jane's favorite brother, after his midlife ordination

ing his sister's novels, and after her death he rushed *Northanger Abbey* and *Persuasion* to press.

His first wife, Eliza de Feuillide, was a first cousin, the widowed daughter of his aunt Philadelphia Hancock. Ten years older than Henry, Eliza commenced a flirtation with him when he was only sixteen. They were evidently a couple of startlingly attractive appearance. Glamorous and sociable, they moved easily in London's artistic circles. Eliza's first husband, Count Jean-François Capot de Feuillide, had been guillotined, and in 1802 Eliza and Henry traveled to France hoping to recover some of the de Feuillide assets. Considering the uneasy relationship between France and England at the time, this was a dangerous venture. Indeed, while they were in France, Napoleon gave orders for all English visitors to be detained. Their dramatic escape anticipates Dickens's *A Tale of Two Cities* in some senses: Eliza was able to use her fluent French while Henry bundled up and concealed himself as a comatose invalid.

A year after Eliza's death in 1813 Henry seems to have been out of mourning and flush enough to attend a ball at the ultrafashionable Burlington House in London sponsored by the ultraexclusive White's Club. In a letter to Cassandra, Jane proclaimed: "Henry at White's! Oh, what a Henry!" By 1816, however, Henry was bankrupt after several business losses and refashioned himself as a clergyman. In 1820 he married Eleanor Jackson. He wrote a biographical notice of his sister that was appended to the 1817 first publications of *Northanger Abbey* and *Persuasion*. Additionally he published several sermons of his own and a series of *Lectures upon Some Important Passages in the Book of Genesis*. Henry did not leave children.

CASSANDRA ELIZABETH AUSTEN (1772–1845)

The fifth child was the first daughter of the burgeoning Austen family. Cassandra was undoubtedly the most important person in Jane Austen's life. Whenever the sisters were separated, they wrote to each other, and virtually all of Austen's letters that we have were sent to Cassandra. One of the biggest tragedies, perhaps the defining tragedy of Cassandra's life was the death of her fiancé the Reverend Thomas Fowle in early 1797. Fowle, probably acting as private chaplain to one Lord Craven, had accompanied Craven as colonel of the Buffs to help put down a slave revolt in the West Indies in late 1795. He contracted yellow fever, died, and was buried at sea. Cassandra never again entertained the idea of marriage, perhaps because she could not bear the thought of another loss. In many respects she was "married" to her sister Jane. The sisters shared a bedroom for most of their lives and exchanged lengthy letters whenever they were separated. Cassandra's sense of humor was not as developed

as Jane's, but she was her sister's best and closest confidante and friend. Their relationship was undoubtedly similar to that of Jane and Lizzie Bennet in *Pride and Prejudice*.

SIR FRANCIS WILLIAM AUSTEN (1774–1865)

The first of Jane's two naval brothers eventually became an admiral of the fleet and died much honored at the age of ninety-one. As a young boy he was known as Fly, a tribute to his energy and his love of horse jumping. Just before his twelfth birthday, Frank, evidently the first member of his extended family to go to sea, was registered at the Royal Naval Academy of Portsmouth. Perhaps the fact that the academy offered free tuition and board was an inducement; two of the Austen sons had already gone to Oxford, incurring expense for the family. Frank must have influenced Austen's depiction of Fanny Price's adoration of her brother William, who also embarked on a naval career. Years after his sister's death he wrote: "I do not know whether in the character of Capt. Wentworth the authoress meant in any degree to delineate that of her Brother: perhaps she might—but I rather think parts of Capt. Harville's were drawn from myself. At least some of his domestic habits, tastes, and occupations bear a strong resemblance to mine."

In 1806 Frank married Mary Gibson, who bore him eleven children. After her death in 1823 he married Martha Lloyd, a dear family friend who had been living with Jane and Cassandra for many years. Frank was to be a great supporter of his sister, reading and commenting astutely on her novels. He also was very conscientious about preserving her anonymity, whereas Henry, a bit of a blabbermouth, revealed the name of the author of *Pride and Prejudice* to some members of the public.

In a letter to Eliza Quincy of Boston, Frank remembered his sister:

Of the liveliness of her imagination and playfulness of her fancy, as also of the truthfulness of her description of character and deep knowledge of the human mind, there are sufficient evidence in her works; and it has been a matter of surprise to those who knew her best how she could at a very early age and with apparently limited means of observation, have been capable of nicely discriminating and pourtraying such varieties of the human character as are introduced in her works. . . . [S]he was a most agreeable companion and by the lively sallies of her wit and good-humoured drollery seldom failed of exciting the mirth and hilarity of the party.

JANE AUSTEN (1775–1817)

CHARLES JOHN AUSTEN (1779–1852)

The baby of the family was an easygoing child and an affable man. Cassandra and Jane liked to call him "our own particular little brother." When Charles was twelve, he followed his brother Frank in enlisting in the Royal Naval Academy at Portsmouth. He spent much time overseas, including five years in North America. He was an enthusiastic supporter of Jane's novels and read *Emma* three times. In 1807 he married Frances Palmer, who died in childbirth along with the fourth of her daughters. In 1820 he married her older sister, Harriet, with whom he had two children, who lived to adulthood.

Charles had many adventures, close calls, and an actual shipwreck in his naval career, which certainly inspired his sister when she celebrated the navy and its officers with such high approbation in *Persuasion*. He died of cholera in 1852 while on active service in Burma.

Rear Admiral Charles Austen, Jane's youngest brother

Life at the Steventon Rectory

W as the Austen family really as wonderful as they seem and as they testify about one another? Actually it is refreshing to say yes. Even in this modern day of "dysfunctional" families, none of the Austens would have hastened to air any but the cleanest linen in public. Life was lively at the Steventon Rectory. Jane and Cassandra were surrounded by affectionate, animated brothers. To augment the family income, which was always more than a little strained, Reverend Austen took in boarders, whom he crammed for Oxford and Cambridge. These boarders added to the spirited witty and intellectual ambience. The Austens were not wealthy, but their financial resources were sufficient for a clerical family that enjoyed intellectual resources more than flashy materialism. A family member wrote: "The home conversation was rich in shrewd remarks, bright with playfulness and humour."

Steventon Rectory, Austen's birthplace, as drawn by her niece Anna Lefroy

Home theatricals were particularly popular at Steventon, and James, the eldest brother, was usually in charge of the productions, many of which were more ambitious than the *Lovers' Vows* production, aborted in *Mansfield Park* by the sudden return of Sir Thomas. Richard Brinsley Sheridan's *The Rivals* is only one of at least seven full-length plays that the Austens mounted in their dining room at the Steventon Rectory. During her adolescence Jane wrote three short plays designed to amuse her family, as the rest of her juvenilia seems to have been. Her mother, among several other family members, including Cassandra and brother James, was fond of dashing off poetry for all sorts of occasions. When James was at Oxford, he produced, along with the help of his brother Henry, a literary periodical called the *Loiterer*.

The Austens had about five hundred volumes in the family library, not at all inconsiderable for the times, and the family enjoyed discussing literature. No wonder Jane soaked up a decent education by listening and then contributing to the family colloquy. She was, by all reports, a happy child, and as a teenager she enjoyed entertaining her family with her satires and parodies. It must

have been a satisfyingly heady experience for the young Jane to develop her powers to engage and amuse her parents and older siblings. She early learned the re-

JANE AUSTEN'S MOTHER ON ANIMAL HUSBANDRY

I have got a nice dairy fitted up, and am now worth a bull and six cows, and you would laugh to see them, for they are not much bigger than jack-asses—and here I have got jackies and ducks and chickens. . . . In short, you must come, and, like Hezekiah I will show you all my riches.

—LETTER FROM JANE AUSTEN'S MOTHER TO HER SISTER-IN-LAW, MRS. WALTER

wards of an "antic disposition" and must have been Steventon's finest "stand-up comedian." Her early success as an entertainer may explain why she later was so guarded about her serious writing, concealing it whenever anyone approached her room. She may have felt diffident about her ambitions to find a larger audience.

Her siblings' support provided Austen with an atmosphere in which she could exercise her genius. That she was unvexed by boorish brothers or surly sisters certainly helped her focus on forwarding her career.

The Family Appearance

Unfortunately there is only one drawing of Jane Austen's face in existence. In that sketch, wrought by Cassandra, Jane looks thin-lipped, prissy, dour, impatient, almost defiant. But there is ample testimony that it does not do her justice; Jane's niece Anna Lefroy called it "hideously unlike." The Reverend Fowle said she was "Pretty—certainly pretty—bright and a good deal of colour in her face—like a doll—no, that would not give at all the idea, for she had so much expression—she was like a child—quite a child, very lively and full of humour—most amiable—most beloved." Mrs. Beckford, a friend and distant cousin via a convoluted chain, wrote: "I remember her as a tall thin *spare* person, with very high cheekbones, great colour, sparkling eyes not large but joyous and intelligent." Mary Russell Mitford noted that her mother said that Jane Austen was "the prettiest, silliest, most affected, husband-hunting butterfly." Jane's extravagant cousin Eliza de Feuillide asserted that Jane and Cassandra were "perfect Beauties & of course gain 'hearts by dozens.'"

In his *Memoir of Jane Austen,* James Edward Austen-Leigh, her nephew, describes her appearance: "In person she was very attractive; her figure was rather tall and slender, her step light and firm, and her whole appearance expressive of health and animation. In complexion she was a clear brunette with a rich colour; she had full round cheeks, with mouth and nose well formed, light hazel eyes, and brown hair forming natural curls close round her face."

Austen's niece Anna Lefroy was perhaps the most observant:

As to my Aunt's personal appearance, hers was the first face that I remember thinking pretty, not that I used that word to myself, but I know I looked at her with admiration— Her face was rather round than long— she had a bright, but not a pink colour—a clear brown complexion and very good hazle [sic] eyes—She was not, I beleive [sic], an absolute beauty, but before she left Steventon she was established as a very pretty girl. . . . I believe my two Aunts were not accounted very good dressers, and they were thought to have taken to the garb of middle age unnecessarily soon.

"CACOETHES SCRIBENDI": THE INCURABLE ITCH TO WRITE

Biographers of Austen have delighted in the evidence of her earliest childhood scrawls. Although not numerous, they are telling indeed. Jan Fergus, in her *Literary Life* of Jane Austen, reveals that what are apparently Austen's earliest written words to have survived appear in one of her childhood books, the French *Fables Choisis*. A firm adult hand has inscribed "Miss Jane Austen, 5th Dec. 1783" (eleven days before Austen's eighth birthday). Austen wrote her own name as well and two telling sentences. "I wish I had done" begins with a tidy, compact cursive, and each word gets larger, sloppier, as if to dramatize frustration and growing impatience. The second sentence—"Mothers angry fathers gone out"—is written in a small, elegant cursive. Fergus thinks that the latter sentence reveals that Austen, as a keen observer of the human panoply, wanted to note and preserve her "slyly humorous" observations quite early in life. Whether Father went out because Mother was angry or Mother was angry because Father had gone out is irrelevant; what matters, Fergus suggests, is that while most children would just scrawl their own names in books, Austen writes a miniature narrative; her five words tell a story.

At some point the young Jane boldly inscribed for herself not one but three imaginary marriages in the Steventon parish register. Still preserved in the Hampshire Record Office in her childish script is the record of Jane's hypothetical husbands:

the banns of marriage between *Henry Frederic Howard Fitzwilliam* of *London* and *Jane Austen* of *Steventon*

Edmund Arthur William Mortimer of *Liverpool* and *Jane Austen* of *Steventon* were married in this church

This marriage was solemnized between us, *Jack Smith & Jane Smith late Austen,* in the presence of *Jack Smith, Jane Smith*

Three husbands and three styles of announcing the marriages! The names are familiar. Fitzwilliam is, of course, the first name of Darcy, the elegant hero of *Pride and Prejudice* and Austen's grandest, wealthiest hero. The prefix "Fitz" often denotes that somewhere in the bloodline is an illegitimate offspring of a monarch. This cosmopolitan bridegroom is from London. From Liverpool, a city hardly as modish as London, comes Edmund Arthur William Mortimer. Although a self-avowed "partial, prejudiced and ignorant" historian, Austen would have been familiar with Edmund Mortimer, Earl of March and brother-in-law to Hotspur, from Shakespeare's *Henry IV, Part I*. Mortimer's planned share of England is "from Trent and Severn," and the Trent River does not run far from Liverpool. Edmund Mortimer would have appealed to Austen's romantic sensibility. Although he cannot speak Welsh, the only language of his wife, Glendower's daughter, he is sweetly uxorious. In a very pretty love scene he proclaims:

> *I understand thy kisses, and thou mine,*
> *And that's a feeling disputation.*
> *But I will never be a truant, love,*
> *Till I have learn'd thy language; for thy tongue*
> *Makes Welsh as sweet as ditties highly penn'd,*
> *Sung by a fair queen in a summer's bower,*
> *With ravishing division, to her lute. [III, i, 204–10]*

Finally there is Jack Smith, whose name anticipates Sir Walter's tirade against "one of the five thousand Mr Smiths whose names are to be met with every where." No guests, or witnesses, attend Austen's imagined marriage to Jack Smith. Austen's trio of potential husbands ranges from the very nearly royal to the ordinary Jack Smith, an indication of how wide-ranging her imagination was even as a child.

The Abbey School

Both Cassandra and Jane Austen preferred to study at home, but they also had about five years of formal schooling. In the spring of 1783 the girls, aged ten and seven, were first sent to be tutored by Mrs. Cawley at Oxford. James Austen was still at Oxford, and he acted as a tour guide, taking his sisters through "dismal chapels, dusty libraries, and greasy halls." Later in 1783 Mrs. Cawley took her charges to Southampton, where they all caught a "putrid fever." Jane Cooper, the girls' cousin, wrote to her parents, and her mother came to rescue the girls. Unfortunately Mrs. Cooper herself contracted the fever and died. This "putrid fever" was probably diphtheria, although it may have been typhoid fever. There is no more exact medical diagnosis in any of the Austen family memoirs. Several months after their daughters' brush with death, the Austens decided to send Cassandra to the Abbey School in Reading. Jane refused to be separated from her sister and insisted that she too wanted to attend this romantic-sounding academy in spite of her unfortunate memories of Mrs. Cawley's school. The Austens managed to pull together the money, and both girls were enrolled in the summer of 1785. They were now aged twelve and nine.

The Abbey School was well established and known throughout southern England as a place where the daughters of the gentry could obtain enough education—but not so much that they would become prodigies. The headmistress was Mrs. La Tournelle, née Sarah Hackitt, a woman in her sixties. She could not speak any French at all and was a corpulent woman who sported a cork leg (the mystery of when and how she lost her original fleshly leg must have fascinated Jane) who loved to gossip about theaters, actors, ghosts, and the supernatural. She was like a character out of Dickens. Studies were not exacting at the Abbey School, and Mrs. La Tournelle allowed the girls to spend the afternoons as they pleased. David Nokes writes: "Mrs. La Tournelle was entirely lacking in even the most rudimentary of learned qualifications . . . what she lacked in scholarly skills, she made up for by the cultivation of solemn mysteries. Her little wainscotted parlour was done out as a private shrine" with "chenille" weeping willows and tombs as the major decorative theme, very appropriate to her sense of high melodrama. Mrs. La Tournelle ordered dinner and made tea and regaled the

girls with anecdotes. The little formal instruction offered by the Abbey School consisted of a curriculum intended to reinforce the skills of young ladies. After morning prayers, led by Mrs. La Tournelle, the girls studied French, drawing, dancing, music, needlework, writing, and spelling, the last of which was given short shrift by Jane. Afternoons were free, given up to girlish hilarity. No doubt the young Jane Austen keenly observed the other girls at the Abbey School and found many more types of affectation, pretension, and sham than she would have in the Steventon neighborhood alone. After about eighteen months, when tuition became too high for the Austens to afford, Cassandra and Jane returned home to Steventon. Their formal education was now completed, and the Austen sisters only rarely refer to their months at school in their surviving letters.

Claire Tomalin points out that Jane did not enjoy school and as an adult "wrote both scathingly and pityingly of schoolmistresses." In 1805 Austen wrote to Cassandra: "To be rational in anything is great praise, especially in the ignorant class of school mistresses." And in *The Watsons*, Emma Watson says to *her* older sister, "I would rather be a teacher at a school (and I can think of nothing worse) than marry a man I did not like." Her sister agrees: "I would rather do anything than be a teacher at a school."

Dancing Days and Juvenilia

Highlights of the Juvenilia

Jane Austen speaks best for herself. The following quotations exemplify the bumptious spirit and the precocious wit of the brief novels composed during her adolescence. The slapstick and the exaggerations, the hints of surrealism, cannibalism, and murder show how much gusto (with an occasional sardonic understatement) Austen brought to her youthful writings.

On the other hand, it is evident that Austen is already concerned with the topics that inform her mature novels: courtship and romance, family relationships, and ironic observations on the excesses of feckless humanity. Austen's original spellings have been retained in the publication of her juvenilia, by the way, although the spelling has been corrected and standardized in her mature novels by all editors. She never really mastered the "*i* before *e* except after *c*" precept.

From this period the intimacy between the Families of Fitzroy, Drummond, and Falknor, daily increased till at length it grew to such a pitch, that they did not scruple to kick one another out of the window on the slightest provocation.

—FREDERIC AND ELFRIDA

The Johnsons were a family of Love, & though a little addicted to the Bottle & the Dice, had many good Qualities.

—JACK AND ALICE

She began to find herself rather hungry, & had reason to think, by biting off two of her fingers, that her Children were much in the same situation.

—HENRY AND ELIZA

Madam

An humble Admirer now addresses you—I saw you lovely Fair one as you passed on Monday last, before our House in your way to Bath. I saw you thro' a telescope, & was so struck by your Charms that from that time to this I have not tasted human food.

George Hervey

—AMELIA WEBSTER

Mr. Clifford lived at Bath; & having never seen London, set off one monday morning determined to feast his eyes with a sight of that great Metropolis. He travelled in his Coach & Four, for he was a very rich young Man & kept a great many Carriages of which I do not recollect half. I can only remember that he had a Coach, a Chariot, a Chaise, a Landeau, a Landeaulet, a Phaeton, a Gig, a Whisky, an Italian Chair, a Buggy, a Curricle & a wheelbarrow. He had likewise an amazing fine staff of Horses. To my knowledge he had six Grays, 4 Bays, eight Blacks & a poney.

—MEMOIRS OF MR. CLIFFORD

I murdered my father at a very early period of my Life, I have since murdered my Mother, and I am now going to murder my Sister. I have changed my religion so often that at present I have not an idea of any left. I have been a perjured witness in every public Tryal for these past twelve Years; and I have forged my own will.

—"A LETTER FROM A YOUNG LADY, WHOSE FEELINGS BEING TOO STRONG FOR HER JUDGEMENT LED HER INTO THE COMMISSION OF ERRORS WHICH HER HEART DISAPPROVED."

Sir Arthur never eats suet pudding Ma'am. It is too high a Dish for him.

—THE VISIT

Beware ye gentle Nymphs of Cupid's Thunderbolts, avoid the piercing Shafts of Jupiter—Look at the Grove of Firs—I see a Leg of Mutton— They told me Edward was not Dead; but they deceived me— they took him for a Cucumber.

—LOVE AND FREINDSHIP

Sophia shrieked and fainted on the ground—I screamed and instantly ran mad—. We remained thus mutually deprived of our senses some minutes, and on regaining them were deprived of them again.

For an hour and a quarter did we continue in this unfortunate situation.

—LOVE AND FREINDSHIP

His heart which . . . was as delicate as sweet and as tender as a Whipt-syllabub, could not resist her attractions.

—LESLEY CASTLE

Whether she [Lady Jane Grey] really understood that language [Greek] or whether such a study proceeded only from an excess of vanity for which I beleive she was always rather remarkable, is uncertain.

—THE HISTORY OF ENGLAND

[On Henry VI] This King married Margaret of Anjou, a Woman whose distresses & Misfortunes were so great as almost to make me who hate her, pity her. It was in this reign that Joan of Arc lived & made such a row among the English.

—THE HISTORY OF ENGLAND

"I begin to feel very chill already. I must have caught a dreadful cold by this time—I am sure of being lain-up all the winter after it—" Then reckoning with her fingers, "Let me see; This is July; the cold weather will soon be coming in—August—September—October—November— December—January—February—March—April—Very likely I may not be tolerable again before May."
—CATHERINE, OR THE BOWER

Authorial Apprenticeship and Ridiculous Novels

Austen's surviving juvenile authorial efforts date as early as 1787, her twelfth year, and include twenty-seven short works completed by her eighteenth year. She compiled them neatly into notebooks that she entitled *Volume the First, Volume the Second*, and *Volume the Third*. These apprentice writings consist mostly of fragments that ridicule the extravagant coincidences, lurid horrors, and saintly heroines of contemporary fiction. They are boisterous, rambunctious works that bespeak a vast imagination reveling in the ridiculous and satirizing the sentimental. These stories anticipate the mature noir work of Edward Gorey and Donald Barthelme, with a dash of Quentin Tarantino, a good sparkling of Salvador Dali, and a generous dollop of Eugene Ionesco. Her nephew James Edward Austen-Leigh wrote in his first edition (1870) of the *Memoir* of his aunt that there existed an old "copy-book, containing several tales, some of which seem to have been composed while she was quite a girl. . . . [T]he family have, rightly, I think, declined to let these early works be published." A. Walton Litz writes that because of public interest, the family reconsidered this embargo of the bumptious early works and decided to include the two-page "unfinished comedy" *The Mystery* in future editions of the *Memoir*. Litz notes that the language of the *Memoir* in describing the early works—"slight . . . flimsy . . . nonsensical"; "puerile . . . effusions . . . transitory"—must reflect "the family's uneasy response to the early writings (some members were said to oppose their publication as 'unfair' to Jane Austen's memory). Like Henry James's super-subtle children, a young lady under fifteen years old who could write knowingly of theft, deformity, drunkenness, and bastardy was subversive to the Victorian cult of the child"—and subversive to those of Austen's descendants who wanted to maintain the image of Aunt Jane as a

Mrs. Bennet (Hermione Gingold) cannot suppress her glee as Darcy (Farley Granger) dances with Elizabeth (Polly Bergen) in First Impressions, Alvin Theatre, New York, 1959. Note the body language: Darcy gazes sidelong at the floor while Elizabeth defiantly glowers at him.

devout Christian and a treacly spinster. The publication of the juvenilia was indeed slow. The first volume did not appear until 1933, *Volume the Second* was issued in 1922, and *Volume the Third* did not emerge until the second half of the twentieth century, in 1951!

THE *LOITERER*

The eighteenth century saw a proliferation of newspaper and magazines aimed at the general reader. Early in the century Joseph Addison and Sir Richard Steele collaborated on two publications, the *Tatler* and the *Spectator*. Both publications specialized in essays, often satirical. The *Gentleman's Magazine*, established in 1731 by Edward Cave, really defined the genre of magazine as we know it today. Its pages contained political commentary, poetry, general essays for the dilettante on subjects as diverse as "the Doctrine of Immortality," the duty of jurymen, antidotes for snakebites, worms, and whooping cough, and close studies of the development of the American colonies. Samuel Johnson was such a frequent contributor that his biographer, James Boswell, wrote that Cave thought of him as "a regular coadjutor in his magazine." The success of the *Gentleman's Magazine* launched numerous other periodicals. Johnson himself produced a periodical, the *Rambler,* and later the *Idler.*

James Austen was at St. John's College, Oxford, when he decided to issue a weekly periodical, the *Loiterer,* modeled on the great eighteenth-century literary journals for gentlemen. The first issue appeared in January 1789. Jane had just turned thirteen, and she took a lively interest in reading the *Loiterer* during its fourteen months of publication. Distributed not only at Oxford but in Bath, London, and Birmingham, the *Loiterer* was a success. One of its essays, written by James, was selected for the *Annual Register* in 1791. In the ninth issue of the *Loiterer* a letter from one "Sophia Sentiment" comments on the absence of love and women in its pages and suggests that "some nice, affecting stories" about lovers should be included. Some readers believe that this is a letter from Jane, but most Austen scholars do not find it consistent with her style. The possibility remains, however, that she wrote the letter and that it was heavily edited by her brothers before publication. She may have revered her older brothers, but she hardly feared them, and she loved to amuse them. Whether or not the thirteen-year-old Jane Austen was "Sophia Sentiment" seems less important than that she was receiving a model from her own family of the possibility of publication and of earning money from publication, in spite of her breezy assertion to Cassandra, when she was nineteen, that "I write only for Fame and without any view to pecuniary Emolument."

VOLUME THE FIRST: PULP FICTION

Volume the First now resides at the Bodleian Library at Oxford University. Beyond question, Austen would be genuinely delighted—and a little mirthful—to know that her earliest manuscripts had found a home in such elevated stomping grounds. Jan Fergus points out that Austen must have compiled the 184-page volume with the idea of preserving works that perhaps had hitherto been on separate scraps of paper. In copying them into a bound volume in her clear but still childish hand, she is asserting that she is a writer, that these stories are no mere ephemera to be cast aside and lost. She carefully numbered the pages, provided a table of contents, chapter divisions, dedications in many cases, and a clear "finis" to mark the end of each manuscript.

Volume the First contains ten pieces, which Austen has labeled variously "A Novel," "A Tale," or an "unfinished" work. It also boasts two comedies—*The Visit* and *The Mystery*—and a poem of sixteen lines, "Ode to Pity," which sounds like a parody of Wordsworth but was written at least five years before Wordsworth's first publications. "Ode to Pity" was dedicated to Cassandra "from a thorough knowledge of her pitiful Nature":

> *Gently brawling down the turnpike road,*
> *   Sweetly noisy falls the Silent Stream—*
> *The Moon emerges from behind a Cloud*
> *   And darts upon the Myrtle Grove her beam.*
> *Ah! then what Lovely Scenes appear,*
> *   The hut, the Cot, the Grot, & Chapel queer,*

And eke the Abbey too a mouldering heap,
*   Conceal'd by aged pines her head doth rear*
And quite invisible doth take a peep.

This rustic scene was undoubtedly conjured up to amuse Cassandra with its oxymorons: its stream, which is both silent and noisy, both brawling and gentle, and the abbey, which invisibly rears its head.

Volume the First contains but one effort at moral, didactic writing, a "fragment written to inculcate the practise of Virtue," which is sustained for only four sentences and then abandoned. This fragment is a part of a series of "Miscellanious [sic] Morsels" written for the edification of Austen's infant "neice" Anna. The other two sketches, considerably longer, feature a punning doctor and a seaman who sends "home a large Newfoundland Dog every Month to his family."

For the most part, the juvenilia is full of fun. Austen experiments with ludicrous place-names (Crankhumdunberry, Pammydiddle, Kilhoobery Park); moderate cursing (damme), and characters who are "gamesters," guzzlers, and gourmands (among the many foods consumed are cowheel and onion, tripe, suet pudding, Sir-loin, a curry with no seasoning, and a stinking partridge).

In *Jack and Alice* one character announces that a wife must have "Youth, Beauty, Birth, Wit, Merit, & Money." His claim is treated in burlesque fashion in the juvenilia, but it neatly sums up the themes that Austen's mature novels explore with considerably greater subtlety and nuance.

Frederic and Elfrida: *An Auspicious Debut*

Frederic and Elfrida is the first piece in the volume, and it celebrates identical cousins who are curiously similar yet different in every way. The work lovingly dwells on clothing and appearances and hats and muslins, always favorite topics of Jane's. One character, the "amiable Rebecca," is surrounded by "Patches, Powder, Pomatum & Paint," an alliterative arrangement that echoes that of Belinda and her "Puffs, powders, patches, Bibles, billet-doux" in Alexander Pope's *The Rape of the Lock*. In many respects *Frederic and Elfrida* touches on themes found in Jane's later works. For instance, it anticipates her steely stance on sensibility. In *Sense and Sensibility*, Jane shows the menaces of sensibility taken to an extreme when Marianne falls prey to hysteria. Elfrida too is a hysteric and "fainted & was in such a hurry to have a succession of fainting fits, that she had scarcely patience enough to recover from one before she fell into another." Another character, Charlotte, drowns by throwing herself "into a deep stream which ran thro' her Aunt's pleasure Grounds in Portland Place" because she is so agreeable that she has affianced herself to two men.

The Beautifull Cassandra

"A Novel in Twelve Chapters" fills barely three pages. While not precisely a bluestocking, the beautiful Cassandra certainly delights in flouting convention and in indulging her own impulses whatever the consequences might be. She falls in love with an "elegant Bonnet" that her mother, "a celebrated Millener," has completed for a countess. Cassandra steals the bonnet, puts it on her head, and pluckily steps forth to begin her picaresque adventures. She eats six ices at a pastry cook's, refuses to pay for them, and knocks down the pastry cook; she orders a hackney coach to take her to Hampstead and back and refuses to pay the coachman, although she does place the once-coveted bonnet on his head. Cassandra does not stop in her journey to talk to people although she encounters a viscount, a friend, and a widow. Having violated many rules of decorum, Cassandra returns home and whispers to herself, "This is a day well spent."

Cassandra so determinedly follows her own desires, her own appetites, her own caprices that many readers looking at the brief chapters out of context will conclude that she is a cow, a bull, or a horse rather than a willful young lady.

DECAPITATIONS ARE US: AUSTEN'S EARLY MOTIF OF BEHEADINGS

When Jane Austen was a child and begged to be allowed to go away to school with her older sister, Austen's mother said: "If Cassandra were going to have her head cut off, Jane would insist on sharing her fate." It was, perhaps not coincidentally, a time in which heads were in fact cut off, and with frequency, in France. Jane also knew about those historical figures in England who had been decapitated and lovingly retold their fates in her *History of England*: "It was in the reign of Henry the 7th that Perkin Warback . . . was set in the Stocks, took shelter in Beaulieu Abbey, & was beheaded with the Earl of Warwick . . ." and regarding the Earl of Essex: "he was beheaded on the 25th of Febry, after having been Lord Leuitenant [*sic*] of Ireland, after having clapped his hand on his sword, and after performing many other services to his Country." Her chapter on Henry VIII pays most attention to "Anna Bullen," who was "universally acquitted of the crimes for which she was beheaded."

Her fascination with decapitation might be ascribed to the melodramatic fancies of a child with a fantastic imagination. But as the revolutionary guillotine was busily chopping away across the English Channel, the Austens were kept quite up-to-date on its horrors by their frequent correspondence with Jane's cousin Eliza. Madame la Comtesse, as she was known, was married to the Frenchman Jean-François Capot de Feuillide, a rabid royalist and a landowner. Eliza was a great favorite among the Austen clan and reported to the family on her husband's fortunes and misfortunes during the twelve years of her marriage. An issue of the *Loiterer*, edited by Austen's brothers James and Henry, alludes to prisoners in the Bastille, if only to compare their tedious lives with those of an underpaid British curate's. This might seem hard-hearted, but the Austen family had a tendency to use satire to cope with unpleasantness. Eliza's husband was eventually guillotined in February 1794.

"MY HAT, ON WHICH MY PRINCIPAL HOPES OF HAPPINESS DEPEND"

In "Chapter the First" of Austen's first novel, *Frederic and Elfrida*, Elfrida writes a note to her friend Charlotte Drummond to request that Charlotte buy her a "new & fashionable Bonnet" to suit her complexion. Thus commences in earnest the "chapeau" motif that runs throughout Austen's novels. They abound with brief descriptions of hats and gowns. Her letters pullulate with references to hats and bonnets! In one of the first preserved letters from Jane to her sister Cassandra, she writes in the same sentence of having purchased some new ink and of a hat, "on which, You know, my principal hopes of happiness depend." Of course she is ironic; on the other hand, she knows that she feels better when she is wearing a hat she likes. In a later letter about a social gathering, she claims not to have been "so very stupid as I expected, which I attribute to my wearing my new bonnet & being in good looks."

Scoping out the fashionable hats was one of Jane's primary diversions in a trip to Bath in the summer of 1799. To Cassandra, back home at Steventon, she writes about the fad for decorating hats with fruit: "Flowers are very much worn, & Fruit is still more the thing. —Eliz: has a bunch of Strawberries & I have seen Grapes, Cherries, Plumbs & Apricots—There are likewise Almonds & raisins, french plumbs & Tamarinds at the Grocers, but I have never seen any of them in hats."

A week later, having investigated the cheaper stores, Jane concludes that flowers are a better bargain:

> We have been to the cheap Shop, & very cheap we found it, but there are only flowers made there, no fruit—& as I could get 4 or 5 very pretty springs of the former for the same money which would procure only one Orleans plumb. . . . I cannot decide on the fruit until I hear from you again. —Besides, I cannot help thinking that it is more natural to have flowers grow out of the head than fruit. —What do you think on that subject?

The Austen sisters did not have as much money for new gowns as they might have liked, but accessorizing their wardrobes with new hats and new ornaments for old hats was an elegant economy for them. Hats, silks, and muslins remain an abiding topic in Jane's letters to Cassandra throughout her life.

VOLUME THE SECOND: "SALLIES, BONMOTS & REPARTEES"

Volume the Second consists of four pieces longer than anything in *Volume the First*: *Love and Freindship*, *Lesley Castle*, *The History of England*, a *Collection of Letters* and some "scraps," dedicated to Austen's "neice" Fanny. The young author laments the fact that geographic distance prevents her from supervising Fanny's education and offers the scraps of "opinions and Admonitions" in lieu of "personal instruction."

Lesley Castle was written in early 1792, when Austen was sixteen. It is an epistolary novel in which the distinctive voices of the two primary letter writers, Miss Margaret Lesley and her friend Miss Charlotte Lutterell, show that Austen was taking pains to differentiate character. As the novel opens, Margaret Lesley is lamenting the fact that her sister-in-law has abandoned her family, "wantonly disgraced the Maternal character," and "openly violated the conjugal duties" to place herself in company with "Danvers and dishonour." Austen is still jesting about the trangressors of social laws, who will be more seriously treated in her mature novels. Charlotte Lutterell represents the kind of vacantly loquacious and annoying character that emerges later in the form of a Miss Bates or a Mary Musgrove. Charlotte's particular pride is her cooking. She asserts that no one can make a better "pye" than she can and that "few people understand the art of cutting a slice of cold Beef so well" as she does. She writes using metaphors of food and cooking and describes herself as being "as cool as a Cream-cheese," while planning revenge for a pigeon pye that was not sufficiently praised. *Lesley Castle* is a burlesque, but the young Jane Austen is getting closer and closer to capturing human foibles accurately.

Love and Freindship

At thirty-three pages, *Love and Freindship* became the longest sustained effort of the fourteen-year-old Jane Austen. It has the same sort of ludicrous plot and picaresque adventures as the earlier juvenilia. But it is more carefully structured, and more themes, especially that of female friendship, are delineated at length than in the earlier work. Laura, the main character, is now fifty-five years old and has "entirely forgot the *Minuet Dela Cour*," implying that she is well beyond the sensibility of youth, when she once was "too tremblingly alive to every affliction of my Freinds." Now she reports that she will "never feel for those of an other."

Her friend Isabel has reminded her that "if a woman may ever be said to be in safety from the determined Perseverance of disagreable Lovers and the cruel Persecutions of obstinate Fathers, surely it must be at such a time of Life." Isabel would like Laura to write the memoirs of her "Misfortunes and Adventures" to her own daughter, Marianne. Laura agrees since she thinks the "fortitude with which I have suffered the many Afflictions of my past Life" might be a "useful Lesson" for Marianne. The story of Laura's loves and friendships is told retrospectively, therefore, a fairly sophisticated literary strategy for a fourteen-year-old writer. From the start the reader knows that Laura will live to tell the tale. Even at this age, Austen seems unwilling to write conventional novels of suspense in which the intrigues of the plot leave the reader on tenterhooks. The epigraph of the novel, "Deceived in Freindship & Betrayed in Love," also implies that Laura's story will be an instructive one.

Laura is the "natural Daughter of a Scotch peer by an italian Opera-girl." She was "born in Spain" and received her education at a "Convent in France," and the family home is in Wales. Her adventures proceed to burlesque the novels of sensibility of the day with their excess of effusions. Laura spends much time "running mad," and frequent fainting is finally the end of her friend Sophia, whose final words to Laura are: "One fatal swoon has cost me my life. . . . Beware of swoons Dear Laura. . . . A frenzy fit is not one quarter so pernicious; it is an exercise to the Body & if not too violent, is I dare say conducive to Health in its consequences—Run mad as often as your chuse; but do not faint—" The young Sophia prefigures Marianne Dashwood of *Sense and Sensibility*, who almost kills herself for love of Willoughby. *Love and Freindship* also introduces a major theme that runs throughout Austen's work. Female friendships, she suggests, are essential to leaven the lump of mundane life. Indeed, those characters that are without them, such as Fanny Price in *Mansfield Park* and Anne Elliot in *Persuasion*, are the loneliest and most subdued of Austen's characters.

The History of England

Catherine Morland, in *Northanger Abbey*, Austen's first mature novel, complains that histories are written by men and that they depict "the quarrels of popes and kings, with wars or pestilences, in every page; the men all so good for nothing and hardly any women at all. . . ." Anne Elliot in *Persuasion*, Austen's last complete novel, repeats the lament: "Men have had every advantage of us [women] in telling their own story . . . the pen has been in their hands. I will not allow books to prove any thing."

The masculine ownership of history was evidently a sore point with Austen throughout her life. At age fifteen she devised an antidote to delight Cassandra. Entitled *The History of England from the Reign of Henry the 4th to the Death of Charles the 1st* and subtitled "By a partial, prejudiced, & ignorant Historian," Jane's history is full of women: not only the wives of each monarch, but Joan of Arc, Jane Shore, and Lady Jane Grey.

Fay Weldon remarks that "the young Miss Austen encompassed three hundred years of England's past in fifteen pages, in a kind of early *1066 and All That*. She shows herself as very clever, very funny, exhilarated and exhilarating

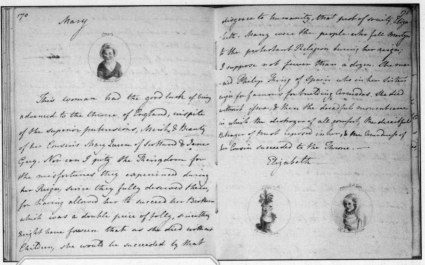

Cassandra's illustrations of Queen Mary, Queen Elizabeth I, and Mary, Queen of Scots. In accordance with Jane's profession of the "superior pretensions, merits, and beauty" of Mary, Queen of Scots, Cassandra has depicted her as a dazzler, compared with the straightforward Mary and the overdressed, shrewish appearance of Elizabeth.

and impatient." Austen revels in her partiality and her prejudices and cares not a fig for her ignorance. Her title page proclaims "N.B. There will be very few Dates in this History," and indeed, the only dates that appear are a seemingly obligatory one in the first sentence and the date of the execution of Mary, Queen of Scots. At the very end she inscribes "Finis Saturday Nov: 26th 1791," which reminds us that perhaps the most pertinent date is the date of her writing. Austen's work reverses history's typical verdict on Mary, Queen of Scots and Elizabeth I. Mary is clearly the heroine of the piece, and Elizabeth the villainess. Elizabeth I is "wicked," and her ministers are "vile & abandoned men" who encourage her "crimes." Mary is a "bewitching Princess" with a "noble mind" and "unshaken fortitude."

Austen is passionate in her defense of certain characters, but she is also willing to take a step back to laugh at them, to personalize them by adding references to her own family and to change the conventional appearance of histories by adding a "sharade." Cassandra supplied droll miniature portraits. In other words, they strove to amuse their readers.

Revolutions

What calm lives they had, those people! No worries about the French Revolution, or the Napoleonic Wars."
——WINSTON CHURCHILL, ON JANE AUSTEN'S NOVELS

Jane Austen's childhood was marked by a period of major revolutions that affected England. Her first years coincided with the successful revolt by the thirteen North American colonies against British rule. None of Austen's immediate family members was involved in the fight against the American colonists. The French Revolution, however, was much closer to home. The events that removed the French monarchy, established the First Republic, and completely transformed French society began in June 1789, when delegates of the States General met at Versailles to discuss a taxation crisis. The first two estates represented the nobility and the church and had advised the monarch since medieval times. The third estate, which represented the common people of France, had been established in 1484. Although it represented about 96 percent of the population, it had limited powers. The third estate, which had been joined by certain nobles and clergymen, demanded the formation of a National Assembly that would guarantee more equal representation. On July 14 a mob stormed the Bastille, supposedly crammed with political prisoners. The three estates were united, all church property was nationalized, and the aristocracy was abolished. Since the Austens' beloved cousin Eliza was a French countess, or at least had taken the title while her husband held lands awarded to his family by French royalty, there was probably reason for the family to worry about Eliza's fate. But for many years the band played on, and Eliza moved freely back and forth between France and England.

VOLUME THE THIRD:
EVELYN AND CATHERINE, OR THE BOWER

Volume the Third consists of two works. *Evelyn* is named for a village in Sussex, "perhaps one of the most beautiful Spots in the south of England," where "from the sweetness of the Situation, & the purity of the Air, in which neither Misery, Illhealth, or Vice are ever wafted" all the inhabitants are "remarkably amiable." The inhabitants of Evelyn have a cornucopia of happiness, gourmet food, the most exquisite of wine. Even the beer is frothy and better than nectar. The people are wealthy and fall in love with one glance. But the idyll is soon spoiled by death, madness, fainting fits, people returning from the dead. *Evelyn* was completed in just twelve pages, perhaps because it had become too fantastical to suit the taste of Jane, now sixteen, and rapidly advancing in her literary acumen. *Catherine, or The Bower* is the other work in *Volume the Third* and is more than fifty pages, Austen's longest work thus far. Catherine Percival is a wealthy orphan being reared by a strict maiden aunt. Catherine talks of the "mischief" of Elizabeth I, a familiar subject to the readers of Austen's *History of England*. Her source of imaginative relief from her cautious upbringing is a bower at the end of a walk in the garden, where she once spent much time with two friends, the Misses Wynne. Their father's death has forced them to leave the neighborhood. One of the Wynne daughters is sent to India to find a rich husband, in a parallel to what happened to Austen's own aunt Philadelphia Hancock. Catherine's, and Jane's, feelings on the matter of husband hunting are clear: "Do you call it lucky for a Girl of Genius & Feeling to be sent in quest of a Husband to Bengal, to be married there to a Man of whose disposition she has not opportunity of judging till her Judgement is of no use to her, who may be a Tyrant, or a Fool or both for what she knows to the Contrary. Do you call *that* fortunate?" Catherine ultimately falls in love with a a distant relative, Mr. Stanley, who does kiss her hand in her bower. He is suddenly sent abroad by snobbish parents who look down on the Percival branch of the family. Although the novel is not formally concluded, it appears as though Catherine's future will be a loveless one of solitude.

LADY SUSAN

*R*eader beware, You are about to encounter a glittering serpent, a wily dragon, a fabulous monster; a thoroughly bad human being.
—DOM NICHOLAS, ALTON ABBEY, ON LADY SUSAN VERNON

Most Austen scholars believe that *Lady Susan* was composed when Austen was eighteen or nineteen years old. The only manuscript copy in her hand, now in the Pierpont Morgan Library in New York, was probably transcribed about 1805.

Roger Gard writes:

Lady Susan has been an embarrassment to lovers of Jane Austen. Its chiselled brilliance and evident amorality . . . are unlikely to recommend it in any way to admirers of "gentle Jane" or "their dear, our dear, everybody's dear, Jane" (as

Henry James exasperatedly put it). . . . Like so many things in life, like the letters one has not sent or the Venetian shirt with scarlet piping, it would be better out of the way.

Indeed, Lady Susan is not a typical Austen heroine; she is even extraordinary among Austen's villains.

Lady Susan is in many senses a traditional eighteenth-century epistolary novel—that is, one in which the story is told through letters rather than by a straightforward narrator. The advantage of the epistolary form is that the reader gets to hear the points of view of sundry characters and is able to evaluate their honesty or hypocrisy as they represent themselves to one another.

Lady Susan Vernon, as a character, is highly reminiscent of the immoral, destructive Mme. de Merteuil of *Les Liaisons Dangereuses* (1782), a French epistolary novel by Pierre Choderlos de Laclos. Although it does not seem likely that Austen would have read such an amoral—really immoral—book, it remains possible that her worldly cousin Eliza might have told her about it.

> *T*hough you are surprised and repelled, you do not in the least feel that the tastes or tendencies of the writer are immoral. The very coldness and lifelessness of the story preclude any imputation of that kind.
> —GOLDWIN SMITH, 1890, on *Lady Susan*

Lady Susan, an unashamed adulteress and the self-proclaimed "most accomplished coquette in England," plans to undermine her daughter, Frederica, whom she describes as "a stupid girl," and force her into a marriage with a man she detests. In the end, she is outschemed and herself obliged to marry the fool she selected for her daughter. Lady Susan is a power broker, and men are the property she trades in. Only five of the forty-one letters that constitute the work are written by men, illustrating perhaps Austen's greater interest in the female point of view. Lady Susan is never overcome by emotion, as were so many of the young ladies of the juvenilia. Instead she coolly assesses situations: "My dear Alicia, of what a mistake were you guilty in marrying a man of his age!—just old enough to be formal, ungovernable and to have the gout—too old to be agreeable, and too young to die" and "There is exquisite pleasure in subduing an insolent spirit, in making a person pre-determined to dislike, acknowledge one's superiority."

How did the young Jane Austen have the knowledge to create such a Machiavellian character as the dishonest and cynical Lady Susan Vernon? "Artlessness will never do in Love matters," writes Lady Susan, who is artful enough to *appear* to be "pretty," "sweet" "clever and agreable," "generous, frank, and even affectionate" and who has a "happy command of Language" according to the perceptions of other characters. But she "aspires to the . . . delicious gratification of making a whole family miserable."

Lady Susan is a savory parody of the eighteenth-century female rake, such as Lady Booby in Fielding's *Joseph Andrews* or Lady Wishfort in Congreve's play *The Way of the World*, or Mme. de Merteuil.

Why would Austen never again create such a monstrously predatory and calculating character? Claire Tomalin suggests that "she decided to censor the part of her imagination that interested itself in women's wickedness, and particularly sexual wickedness." It is also possible that Austen preferred the greater artistic demands inherent in creating characters with more complex moral lives. She turned from malice and sarcasm to the delicate nuances of irony. With Lady Susan she bade adieu to the raucous and unruly characters of her juvenilia and went on to more subtle challenges.

Mrs. Leigh-Perrot: Austen's Brush with Incarceration and Other Scandals

In 1799, when Austen was twenty-three years old, her aunt, the wife of her mother's brother, Mrs. Leigh-Perrot, was involved in a bizarre scandal. Accused by a Bath shopkeeper of stealing some white lace from the store, she was remanded into custody for eight months before her acquittal at a trial. Her alleged offense, grand larceny, was serious enough that hanging or transportation to Botany Bay was a very real possibility.

Evidently Austen's parents offered to send either or both of their daughters Cassandra and Jane to provide female companionship to Mrs. Leigh-Perrot as she languished in the cramped quarters of the jail keeper's home. Mrs. Leigh-Perrot wrote that she could not "accept the Offer of my Nieces—to have two Young Creatures gazed at in a public Court would cut one to the very heart." There is some evidence that the charges were trumped up, but there is also evidence that Mrs. Leigh-Perrot was a kleptomaniac. Later she was involved in several more allegations of stealing, in one case "embezzling some green house plants" from a Bath gardener. Dr. Henry Harington, a magistrate and the mayor of Bath, allegedly penned the following lines:

To love of plants who has the greater claim,
Darwin the Bard or Perrot's wiley Dame?
Decide the cause Judge Botany, we pray,
Let him the Laurel take and her the Bay.

Some critics have speculated that Mrs. Leigh-Perrot, disliked by Jane Austen, provided a model for the despicable Aunt Norris of *Mansfield Park* (who is not above a little petty theft herself).

For a clergyman's daughter, Austen seems to have had more than a few brushes with notoriety in her family. There was Eliza, whose husband was guillotined when Jane was eighteen, and earlier, when Jane was only twelve, the husband of a second cousin used a razor and a sword to commit suicide in a particularly grisly and determined way by both cutting his throat and stabbing himself. Some relatives were involved in elopements, adultery, divorce, and various other intrigues. George Holbert Tucker, one of Austen's most astute biographers, has said that "she had a lively lifelong interest in scandal as well as other manifestations of human perversity." Indeed, most of her novels offer scandalous subplots that serve to reinforce the true virtues of her main heroines.

A Recipe for Syllabub

ℋer face as white as a Whipt syllabub
—LESLEY CASTLE FROM *VOLUME THE SECOND*

Austen's novels are punctuated by meals, but generally she is not distracted from her intense look at human foibles to describe menus at length. Austen was hardly indifferent to the pleasures of food, and in her letters to Cassandra she often mentions what delicacies she has eaten. During a repast of asparagus and lobster, for example, Jane generously longs for Cassandra's company. She was very fond of syllabub, a popular drink mixing milk and alcohol. Horace Walpole, the eighteenth-century wit, historian, and author of the Gothic novel *The Castle of Otranto,* liked to serve syllabub to visitors at his famous Strawberry Hill estate. He would lead them to his herd of cows and present them with a syllabub milked directly from the cow, although it was more common to bring the syllabub to the tippler than the tippler to the cow. Syllabubs were frequently served at balls and assemblys.

SYLLABUB

juice and grated rind of one lemon
1 cup sherry, white wine, or brandy
1 tablespoon sugar (or to taste)
1 cup whipping cream
freshly grated nutmeg

Allow the lemon rind to infuse in the liquor for several hours then remove it. Whip the cream until stiff and fold in other ingredients. Chill before serving.

Tom Lefroy, Harris Bigg-Wither, and Other Suitors

Perhaps Jane Austen's first "crush"—if one can use such a vulgar term—was on the darkly handsome Edward Taylor, whom she met when she visited Kent in 1794. Two years later she wrote, "We went by Bifrons & I contemplated with a melancholy pleasure re the abode of Him, on whom I once fondly doated." In a later letter she wrote: "I hope it is true that Edward Taylor is to marry. . . . Those beautiful dark Eyes will then adorn another Generation. . . ." Taylor did marry, and he became a member of Parliament.

Jane Austen's first serious flirtation that we *know* of was with Tom Lefroy, a handsome young man who had come to Hampshire from Ireland to visit his uncle. The twenty-year-old Austen wrote to Cassandra about Tom: "I am almost afraid to tell you how my Irish friend and I behaved. Imagine to yourself everything most profligate and shocking in the way of dancing and sitting down together. I *can* expose myself, however, only *once more*, because he leaves the country soon after next Friday, on which day we *are* to have a dance at Ashe after all. He is a very gentleman-like, good-looking, pleasant young man, I assure you." She goes on to say that he has only "*one* fault . . . it is that his morning coat is a great deal too light." In her next letter to her sister, Austen writes about the last ball that will be held before Tom Lefroy leaves the area: "I rather expect to receive an offer from my friend in the course of the evening. I shall refuse him, however, unless he promises to give away his white Coat." Her bantering tone hardly conceals what seems to have been a very sincere intention of accepting the offer. But there was no offer. Evidently Lefroy's family had stepped in to prevent a possible engagement to the penniless daughter of a clergyman. His large family was counting on him to marry well and to earn money. Jane never saw Lefroy after his return to Ireland following that last ball. When he was an old man and chief justice of Ireland, he wrote that he had indeed loved her, "but it was only a boy's love." Jane must have felt the sting of the separation deeply; three years later she wrote to Cassandra after Mrs. Lefroy had called. She did not mention her nephew, and "I was too proud to make any enquiries."

Harris Bigg-Wither, heir to a large estate, Manydown House, was the man who came closest to persuading Austen to marry and the only suitor who we know actually proposed to her. Bigg-Wither's three sisters were very friendly with Jane and Cassandra. Jane had known the family for quite a while. Two years earlier she had written to Cassandra: "Harris seems still in a poor way, from his bad habit of body; his hand bled again the other day," indicating a certain familiarity, if not exactly affection. In 1802, when Jane was twenty-seven, Cassandra and she went to Manydown to visit their friends. Bigg-Wither, five years her junior, proposed to her. She accepted his offer. She would become mistress of a large estate and could promise financial security for her family. After twelve hours of vacillation between the financial merits of Bigg-Wither and the fact that she did not love him, Jane Austen did *not* make the choice that Charlotte Lucas makes in *Pride and Prejudice*: to marry for financial security and thus liberate her family from caring for her financially. She rescinded her acceptance of Harris's offer, and that morning Jane and Cassandra left Manydown early, hastily. There must have been some unpleasantness or at the very least an uncomfortable feeling. She must have felt the impropriety of staying under the roof of the man whose offer she had accepted and then stunningly rejected, although the friendship of the families was soon repaired.

All thoughts about why Austen refused this offer are conjectural. If she wrote about it at all, those letters were destroyed. At the time of the offer Jane had completed three major novels and had offered one to a publisher. In spite of her lack of success, it is more than likely that she had already committed herself to a writing life. To be mistress of Manydown would have entailed an obligation to spend all her time in the domestic round, not to mention consorting with a husband who had scant appeal for her. Marriage and writing would have been an almost unimaginable combination. Austen might have been reduced to dashing off occasional verses, as her mother managed to do, but how could she have sustained a lengthy narrative, the form in which she was most interested? There is no evidence that Bigg-Wither was as unctuous and repulsive as Mr. Collins—how could he have been?—but he was evidently a bit of a social misfit with a stutter and could not possibly have matched Austen's wit and intellect.

Biographers traditionally have been at some pains to portray Bigg-Wither as an unsuitable, angry, reclusive young man, but the evidence suggests that there was nothing essentially wrong with him, aside from the "bad habit of body" that Jane mentioned in the earlier letter. Two years after she refused him, he married an heiress who bore him ten children and fulfilled all that was expected of a country squire's wife.

Family records rattle off a long list of probable suitors, ranging from an "unnamed gentleman" in Devonshire to Samuel Blackall (Jane called him "a piece of perfection, noisy perfection" and remarked that a wife for him should be "of a silent turn & rather ignorant"), Charles Powlett, and John Willing Warren. There is no record that anything serious happened between Jane and any of those men, some of whom were neighbors. Warren was one of her father's pupils, who did a sketch of Tom Lefroy for her. The Reverend Charles Powlett, grandson of the Duke of Bolton, attempted to kiss Jane at a Christmas party in

1796. His pass did not bother her, but despite his modicum of charm and wit, she did not like his extravagant ways. He soon married a wife whom Jane described as "silly & cross as well as extravagant ... at once expensively & nakedly dress'd." The Powletts spent well beyond their income and had to move to the Continent, where expenses were less stringent.

It is likely that in the summer of 1808 Jane Austen received a proposal of marriage from Edward Bridges, a clergyman four years younger than her and the brother of James's wife, Elizabeth. He then apparently tried his luck with Cassandra after Jane refused him. After her brief vacillation with the proposal of Harris Bigg-Wither, Austen made up her mind firmly: She would remain unmarried.

The "unnamed gentleman" in Devonshire is especially prominent in family reminiscences. Cassandra, long after Jane's death, told her nieces that Jane and this man had fallen in love with each other and that he had died suddenly. Caroline, Jane's niece, refers to him as "The Unknown." Although nobody seems to have seen him, many of Jane's nieces and nephews wrote that he was the true love of her life. While they may have been tempted to engage in some posthumous mythmaking about the thwarted romance of Aunt Jane, the fact that Cassandra verified the existence of this lover has been viewed as "unassailable evidence" by biographers. Austen's nephew James Edward Austen-Leigh in the *Memoir* of his aunt writes:

Many years after her [Jane's] death, some circumstances induced her sister Cassandra to break through her habitual reticence, and to speak of it. She said that while staying at some seaside place, they became acquainted with a gentleman, whose charm of person, mind, and manners was such that Cassandra thought him worthy to possess and likely to win her sister's love. When they parted, he expressed his intention of soon seeing them again; and Cassandra felt no doubt as to his motives. But they never again met. Within a short time they heard of his sudden death. I believe that, if Jane ever loved, it was this unnamed gentleman....

History is not content merely to regard Jane Austen as a genius but also wants her to have been a heartthrob. It is possible that her rational, lively, and satirical mind found no equal in a mate. However, the mysterious seaside man offers another explanation for her spinsterhood. Why compromise when she had felt true love and marry a lesser mortal? Why not devote her attentions to her writing and her family, for whom she had a genuine affection? Why not remain, like Cassandra, one who had known the sweetness of love and vowed to venerate the memory of the perfect, but dead, lover?

Leaving Steventon

In December 1800 Austen's father, George, decided to retire and remove to Bath, leaving his parishes to his eldest son, James. He was after all sixty-nine years old; his wife sixty-one. It is possible that they decided that Bath would provide a wider range of marital prospects for their two daughters, now ripened to the ages of twenty-six and twenty-four. Jane Austen evidently was shocked by having to leave her beloved home; traditionally biographers have said that she fainted when she heard the news. Until the Austen women moved to Chawton Cottage in July 1809, they had eight and a half unsettled years, during which they lived at several different residences in Bath and Southampton and traveled about southern England visiting friends, relatives, and seaside resorts. They never stayed in the same place for more than a few months at a time. The Steventon Rectory, Jane Austen's birthplace, was demolished in 1826.

Bath

Jane Austen spent much time in Bath, and two of her novels are set in part there. Bath remains a beautiful and fashionable city with crescents, squares, and terraces built of the local honey-colored stone. Legend tells us that the city was founded by Bladud, the father of King Lear. Bladud, a leper, had been expelled from court. He cured himself by rolling around in the muddy mineral waters found at the site of Bath. The Romans established a settlement there with baths and temples about A.D. 40 to 60. They called it Aquae Sulis. The Saxons captured Bath in 577. During the Middle Ages the city was a center for the cloth and wool industries, alluded to in Chaucer's depiction of the Wife of Bath in his *Canterbury Tales*. But not until the eighteenth century did Bath reach its height of popularity as a fashionable watering place. Beau Nash was master of the ceremonies, and he institutionalized the social order and the social activities that we see Austen's heroines engaging in, such as the evening promenades and the assemblies.

Jane's parents had met and married in Bath, and the town did have a reputation as a place to find husbands and wives: Catherine Morland met Henry Tilney there, Mrs. Elton of *Emma* met her Mr. E. there, and Anne Elliot and

Captain Wentworth finally arrive at a glorious understanding in Bath. Claire Tomalin conjectures that Jane might have felt a little diffident, perhaps even humiliated, for fear that her parents wanted her to be on the Bath marriage market. Certainly the display of great crowds of fashionable people trying to impress one another would have been of scant interest to Austen. How could excellent conversation flourish under such conditions?

Bath was essentially Jane's home from the spring of 1801 until the summer of 1806, when Southampton became the main home of the sisters and their mother for about two years before their move to Chawton. It was an unsettled life in many ways, and Jane never really felt at home. Both Jane and Cassandra got away from Bath at times in order to visit friends and family elsewhere, and several of Jane's letters to Cassandra depict a certain ennui with Bath, with yet another "stupid party" and nonsense chatter. She wrote: "I cannot anyhow continue to find people agreable." The view from her residence consisted of "putrifying Houses." Anne Elliot too disliked the "white glare of Bath." Mr. Austen was delighted with enjoying some travel in his retirement, so the family visited several resort towns, including Sidmouth, Dawlish, Teignmouth, and Lyme Regis. Jane did enjoy the sea and delighted in the bathing machines, contraptions designed to preserve the privacy of female swimmers.

Thomas Rowlandson's The Comforts of Bath: "The Concert." Note the feathers in the singers' hair, an expensive and coveted tonsorial accoutrement for the ladies of Bath.

I am proud to say that I have a very good eye at an adultress, for tho' repeatedly assured that another in the party was the *She*, I fixed upon the right one from the first. . . . Mrs. Badcock and two young women were of the same party, except when Mrs. Badcock thought herself obliged to leave them to run around the room after her drunken husband. His avoidance, and her pursuit, with the probable intoxication of both, was an amusing scene.

—LETTER TO CASSANDRA, MAY 1801, DESCRIBING ONE OF THE "STUPID" PARTIES

Mr. Austen Exits Life's Pulpit

In January 1805 the Reverend George Austen, aged seventy-three, was suddenly taken ill and died at Bath. Jane wrote to her brother Frank: "Our dear Father has closed his virtuous & happy life, in a death almost as free from suffering as his Children could have wished . . . being quite insensible of his own state, he was spared all the pain of separation, & he went off almost in his Sleep," adding in a second letter that "The Serenity of the Corpse is most delightful!—It preserves the sweet benevolent smile which always distinguished him."

An immediate concern following the death of the paterfamilias was how to support Mrs. Austen, Cassandra, and Jane. Like Mr. Bennet of *Pride and Prejudice,* he had not left his female dependents with any provision or wherewithal. Claire Tomalin reminds us that "The Church did nothing for widows and orphans of clergymen." The Austen sons immediately started planning support for their mother and sisters. Frank offered a hundred pounds a year; James and Henry offered fifty, and Edward and Charles certainly would be able to add some more. Cassandra had a very small amount of capital, left to her from Tom Fowle's legacy. Jane had absolutely nothing. Without this quintet of generous brothers, Jane and Cassandra would have been in a precarious situation. As it was, their position was now contingent on the continuing life, success, and munificence of their brothers.

Regina Barreca:
Jane Austen as "Bad Girl"

Regina Barreca is a professor of English and feminist theory at the University of Connecticut. She is the author of Sweet Revenge: The Wicked Delights of Getting Even; Untamed and Unabashed: Essays on Women and Humor in Literature; Perfect Husband (and Other Fairy Tales); and They Used to Call Me Snow White, but I Drifted. She is also the editor of numerous books, including The Penguin Book of Women's Humor.

NT: *I love the way that you characterize Jane Austen as a "bad girl" in your book on women's humor* They Used To Call Me Snow White . . . But I Drifted. *What is a bad girl?*

RB: The bad girl is somebody who breaks apart the idea of silent and humorless women. Certainly many of Austen's characters do exactly that. They disrupt the social order designed to keep them in place. Even though they stay within the structure, they mess it up, and that is what is great. By doing this, Austen gives the readers an interesting double reading of her books. We see some of her characters just throwing off the straitjackets that would be put on them even as they would seem to be accepting them. When Elizabeth marries Darcy at the end of *Pride and Prejudice*, one of the last lines is that he has not yet learned to joke about himself. There's definitely a happy ending to the book, but that line is there for a reason. In all the happy endings at the end of all the novels there is a slight caveat that says, "You need a happy ending, so here it is. But remember I am not telling you that everything is going to go smoothly from now on." And I think that is a great thing. Certainly at the end of *Mansfield Park*. You've just had three hundred and fifty pages of a guy who is in love with another woman and suddenly turns to Fanny, and basically the author leaves the room. Jane Austen says, "Well, however long it took for these two people to fall in love in your opinion, well, that's exactly how long it took." She walks out. She says, "You want it, you make it. Let other pens dwell on guilt and misery; I'm out of here. You write your own ending." Her endings are the equivalent of shotgun marriages.

At the beginning of *Sense and Sensibility* we hear that maybe sixteen and thirty-six should not keep company together, and then at the end Colonel Brandon's still wearing flannel waistcoats. It seems to me that she is dangerous in all sorts of ways and that the humor extends to a very subtle, deeply encoded, but nevertheless very significant refusal to make the happy ending a promise that now everything is going to be okay. I think it is fun that she is playing with these ideas.

And the fact that Jane Austen makes a dead baby joke! There is a kind of wickedness in her letters, an ability to use the sharper edge of humor that she does not allow herself much of in her novels. Clearly she was incredibly irreverent, and I think that she laid down a lot of paths that other irreverent writers have followed. In the letters there is another side of her that comes out. When she tells the secretary to the Prince Regent that she won't write a historical novel about the Saxe-Coburgs, she says, "I could not write that under any motive but to save my life and I would be hanged before I had finished the first chapter."

NT: *Yes, she wrote that to the representative of the monarch-in-waiting. How ballsy!*

RB: Exactly. Her refusal to accept good advice is something that we see in our favorite heroines of hers. She would say, "Of course your advice is wonderful." But only as a way of making people shut up faster. That is the usefulness of that sort of compliance.

CONFINEMENTS: THE PERILS OF "LYING IN"

Some readers of Austen's letters have been taken aback by her references to pregnancy and childbirth and find a lack of sympathy in such comments as "That Mrs Deedes is to have another Child I suppose I may lament" and "Mrs Hall of Sherbourne was brought to bed yesterday of a dead child, some weeks before she expected, owing to a fright. I suppose she happened unawares to look at her husband." Later, concerned that her niece Anna was having children at too brisk a pace, Austen wrote: "Poor Animal, she will be worn out before she is thirty.—I am very sorry for her."

Austen did not dislike children; indeed, her nephews and nieces provided her with great delight. Her ambivalence about childbirth is natural considering that of her four brothers who had children, three of them had wives who died in childbirth. Appreciating, even adoring the wit, intelligence, and literary bent of her nieces—especially Anna, Caroline, and Fanny—Austen knew that the inevitable childbearing after their marriages might be fatal.

Austen loved her nieces and nephews, but she may have reacted generally against the "baby worship" that much of contemporary literature was indulging in. There is no evidence that she agreed with the Wordsworthian idea of the baby as a tiny "seer," a "prophet blessed."

NT: *What are some of your favorite funny passages in the novels?*

RB: I think the funniest is when, in *Pride and Prejudice*, Mr. Collins is giving his proposal to Elizabeth and she keeps saying no and he won't listen. He keeps saying, "But I know that elegant young women are always supposed to say no." And she asks him, "Please do grant me the ability to formulate a rational response." He can't hear what she is saying, and she is looking at him, going, "Read my lips; I'm telling you no. I don't like you. This is not going to happen." And he can't hear her. In her novels we have a perpetual undercutting of masculine authority when masculine authority is based on ignorance.

She does not choose scapegoats to make fun of. The people she makes fun of are people in positions of authority who misuse their positions.

I think she is anything but gentle. I think there is something really savage about her, and that is what I like. One of my favorite scenes is when Lydia comes back married with this big ring on her finger and she is waving it out of the coach so people will see her. Lydia does not come to an awful end. Lydia gets what she wants: She gets a ring; she gets married; she gets to come back and flaunt herself. Lydia returns untamed and unashamed. She is not subdued and ashamed of herself. Austen refuses to condemn her. Sanctimonious readers of Austen would no doubt want Lydia to come back ashamed. I like Lydia. The more I read Lydia, the more I think she is hysterical. She is a complete narcissist. Like the bull in the china shop, she just goes in and everything is changed in her wake, like a volcano or a tornado. She is like an act of nature.

NT: *Who are some of the other bad girls in Austen that you like?*

RB: I love Mary Crawford. I really think she is a riot. She is just absolutely shameless. And such a contrast to Fanny. In a lot of ways Emma is a bad girl. She really does "excess," which I mean is one of the hallmarks of the bad girls, the sense of excess. She overdoes everything.

Catherine Morland is also defiant. General Tilney is not a grand man. She is not coming up with the same kind of Gothic stories that she thought that she would, but she is also discovering things that other people have left unexamined. And if those books she has read have taught her not to accept conventional values, then they have done good as opposed to evil for her. Catherine has to come to some sort of synthesis of her imaginative world and the world that is actually out there, but they are not as far apart as some people would have us make them.

Marianne is my favorite. I feel sorriest for Marianne and am probably most like Marianne, somebody who has all of that adolescent vision of how the world is supposed to look. She is the one that is so completely punished for her defiance. The others get off lightly, and Marianne really takes a wallop for having an imagination and for having desire.

As one ages, one becomes increasingly sympathetic to various characters. Mrs. Bennet no longer seems to be such a ditzy character. I get really pissed off at Mr. Bennet. Can't he get off his butt and do something? If he's the ideal man for his daughters, then they are all going to be in trouble.

If Jane Austen were around now, I don't think she would be doing stand-up comedy, but I do think that she would prefer that people call her Miss Austen rather than Jane or Austen. It always astonishes me when students come in and they talk about Jane as though they knew her.

NT: *I wonder if the whole cult of the Janeites started as a way to domesticate or to tame her?*

RB: Oh, absolutely to domesticate her; she is just a perky little sister or something as opposed to this terrifying grown woman. I prefer the terrifying grown woman.

The Watsons

Of all of Jane Austen's adult works, *The Watsons* seems the orphan, the least loved child of a writer who spoke of her other works in maternal terms. Probably started sometime in 1803 and abandoned before 1805, *The Watsons* came in the center of a period in which Austen did not write much. The death of Austen's father in January 1805 followed fast upon the unexpected death of her dear friend Anna Lefroy, who had been thrown by a temperamental horse on Austen's twenty-ninth birthday, December 16, 1804. These two traumatic events may explain the abandonment of *The Watsons*, which Austen never finished.

Most biographers point out the melancholy similarities between the plight of Emma Watson and that which Jane Austen may have felt herself to be in: an unmarried encumbrance upon a financially strained family.

THE ISOLATED HEROINE

Emma Watson is the first of Austen's three heroines who is isolated by having no close, congenial female friends. The other two are Fanny Price of *Mansfield Park* and Anne Elliot of *Persuasion*. These three heroines seem to bring out Austen's compassion more than any others. For them, she absents herself from irony *almost* entirely. Emma Watson's family is full of "rivalry" and "treachery between sisters." Fanny Price, also removed from her childhood home, is snubbed by her cousins Maria and Julia. Anne Elliot's sisters are too overwhelmingly narcissistic to pay heed to her. The lonely lives of these three heroines underscore the very real, essential closeness that Elinor and Marianne feel in *Sense and Sensibility* and that Jane and Elizabeth share in *Pride and Prejudice*. Although Emma Woodhouse is not particularly close to her sister, she has a dear friend in Mrs. Weston, who functions very much in that role.

Emma Watson is nineteen and has been brought up, since the age of five, by a rich aunt and uncle. Her uncle unexpectedly has failed to provide for her in his will. Her widowed aunt remarries, and Emma goes back to join her original family in their shabby gentility, knowing that "an absence of fourteen years had made all her brothers and sisters strangers" to her. Her brother sums up her position: "to find yourself, instead of heiress of eight or nine thousand pounds, sent back a weight upon your family, without a sixpence. . . . After keeping you at a distance from your family for such a length of time as must do away all natural affection among us and breeding you up (I suppose) in a superior style, you are returned upon their hands without a sixpence."

Emma indeed finds no sympathy within her own family. Her sisters are calculating husband hunters (but what else could they be?), and her brothers are not sympathetic. The upper classes, depicted at a ball, are not congenial in *The Watsons*. Lord Osborne and Tom Musgrove have all the graces of John Thorpe in *Northanger Abbey* without all the chatter. Musgrove is sullen, and Osborne is rakish and cold. One of the most successful and endearing scenes in *The Watsons*, however, takes place at this ball. Ten-year-old Charlie Blake has been promised the first two dances by Miss Osborne, but she dismisses him, and Emma offers to dance with him, to his delight. Claire Tomalin remarks of Charlie that "his delight and gratitude at having such a pretty partner, and staying up so late, and being able to tell her about his life—Latin lessons, his first horse and his first hunt, the stuffed Fox and Badger he would like to show her at the castle—is tenderly realistic. He is proof of how carefully Austen listened to children talking; and he is the most attractive child in her work." Douglas Bush remarks that *The Watsons* is more "modern" than anything else Austen was to write, with the exception of *Sanditon*, because of its "drably realistic strain."

Austen told her sister Cassandra her plan for the novel: that Emma Watson would reject Lord Osborne's offer of marriage and instead marry Mr. Howard, a clergyman. Readers therefore may be frustrated by the truncation of the rich writing but need not be in suspense about the story's outcome.

The Marriage Plot

E ach of Jane Austen's novels pivots about the same primary plot: A young woman loves a man of superior social standing and waits nervously, anxiously for him to make a declaration of love and an offer of marriage. In every case the novel ends happily as eventually the declaration and offer are made and accepted. This core plot would seem to suggest that Austen works within narrow limits, especially since an experienced reader will recognize early in

SILENCES: YEARS OF MYSTERY

*P*erhaps the biggest mystery of Jane Austen's life, at least for her contemporary readers, is why she fell silent, as a writer, for such a long time. In her teenage years she had filled three volumes with promising work, and she had gone on to complete *Lady Susan* and three full-length novels before she was twenty-five. The three novels were the first incarnations of *Northanger Abbey* (then called *Susan*), the epistolary novel *Elinor and Marianne*, which became *Sense and Sensibility*, and *First Impressions*, which was revised as *Pride and Prejudice*. This is a prodigious output for a young woman. But for almost ten years she wrote virtually nothing. Between twenty-five and thirty-five, Austen for all practical purposes was silent.

Only one letter survives from the spring of 1801 until January 1805, and very few letters exist from 1805 until the summer of 1808, so any discussion of Austen's life must necessarily be conjectural. She may have been depressed, jaded, bitter, or just too unsettled to write much. It is more likely that she continued her lifelong habit of writing to Cassandra and that the letters were all destroyed because they expressed too much bitterness, or too much passion, or too much of *something* that Cassandra did not want revealed to posterity. At Steventon Jane had had a routine worked out that included considerable time for writing. She did not return to a regular writing pattern until she moved to Chawton Cottage in the summer of 1809. There once again she could develop a reliable routine for writing.

Claire Tomalin, along with other biographers, believes that the move from Steventon left Austen too depressed to write. David Nokes suggests that the years of silence may have been years of happiness, happiness with an "abundance of amusements" that left no time for writing. Jan Fergus reminds us that Austen was on the move so much during those years that time would have been precious and that Austen did not entirely forget her writing. She sold *Susan* to the hapless publisher Richard Crosby in 1803. She also made a fair copy of *Lady Susan* during those years. Perhaps Crosby's failure to publish *Susan* deterred her for some time. It is indeed maddening for the lover of Austen to calculate the number of novels that might have appeared had those years not been fallow.

each novel how it will end, but in fact the marriage plot enables her to take on the largest of themes, the complexity of human behavior, the difficulty of discerning the motives underlying human behavior, and the difficulty of judging character in a world of deceptive appearances.

The marriage plot compels Austen's heroines to learn how to read human character, because a poor reading of character could lead to a disastrous marriage, and considering the husband's absolute power over his wife in Austen's time, a disastrous marriage meant a ruined life. Hence it is also an education plot. The difficulties for the heroine are compounded in Austen's world by the rigid roles of social deportment that prevented any candid discussion between marriageable women and available men. Any hint of love on the woman's part would be interpreted as husband hunting, and any on the man's would be tantamount to an offer of marriage. Within these constraints, hero and heroine must study each other's character and in so doing must also study their own.

In *Pride and Prejudice*, Elizabeth Bennet is more candid than she should be with Wickham, because she misreads his character and because she is reacting to her initial poor impression of Mr. Darcy. By showing an apparent preference for Wickham, she alienates Darcy's affections for a time. Meanwhile Jane Bennet is falling in love with Bingley and agonizing over the implications of his every action; her absolute decorum, however, prevents her from giving him any encouragement, so he is easily persuaded of her indifference and abandons his courtship.

Jane's behavior is above reproach, and she is eventually rewarded by Bingley's love, but Elizabeth must suffer for her mistakes in judgment and in fact is forced to reassess her opinion of herself as she comes to terms with her errors about Wickham and Darcy. Finally coming to understand Darcy and Wickham accurately, she comes to know herself correctly for the first time.

Within the simple lines of the marriage plot, Jane Austen plays endless variations. In *Northanger Abbey*, Catherine Morland's susceptibility to imaginative literature, and her consequent errors in judgment, enable Austen to develop the theme of *Don Quixote* and to anticipate that of *Madame Bovary*. That theme of course is the danger of mistaking romance for reality. In *Sense and Sensibility* the marriage plots of the two Dashwood sisters explore the dangers of the eighteenth-century cultivation of "sensibility," which is exposed as wallowing in the indulgence of dangerous emotions.

All the novels, especially *Emma*, examine the dangers of class pride and of too much self-reliance, though in *Persuasion* Austen also considers the dangers of too little self-reliance. The novels, especially the rigorous *Mansfield Park,* are also concerned with fundamental questions of right and wrong, about the ways in which even the most seemingly trivial of moral lapses may have dire consequences.

Austen understood how serious marriage was to women's lives, and she demonstrated how much the idea of women as property (or, conversely, as economic liability) was ingrained in society. She also recognized the link between property and propriety. Since female adultery could result in a false heir and undermine the economic basis of British society, transgressors such as Maria in *Mansfield Park* must face banishment. Female desire had to be absolutely suppressed in order to avoid such calamities. Falling prey to desire or a "guilty connection" leads to ruined lives for Colonel Brandon's sister-in-law Eliza and her illegitimate daughter, also named Eliza, who has been seduced and left with child by Willoughby.

It is only thanks to swift intervention by Darcy that Lydia Bennet is not permanently ruined after she has eloped with Wickham. Marianne Dashwood's passion for Willoughby proves nearly fatal. On the other hand, Austen was not as conservative as many in her day. The writer and evangelist Hannah More warned Austen's peers that some women had an unfortunate propensity to think for themselves and even to move about as though they were not the property of their husbands:

> If a man selects a picture for himself from all its exhib-
> ited competitors, and brings it to his own house, the
> picture being passive, he is able to *fix* it there: while
> the wife, picked up at a public place and acus-
> tomed [*sic*] to incessant display, will not, it is
> probable, when brought home stick so quietly to
> the spot where he fixes her; but will escape to the
> exhibition room again, and continue to be dis-
> played at every subsequent exhibition, just as if she
> were not become private property, and had never been
> definitively disposed of.

More's chilling quotation makes us think of Robert Browning's dangerously demented Duke of Ferrara, who has his charming wife executed but continues to admire her portrait on the wall. If a woman proved to be too liquid an asset, she might not have been liquidated, like Browning's Duchess, but divorce, exile, and expulsion from society were very real consequences for women who submitted to desire outside wedlock.

Jane Austen's heroes, however, are prepared to respect their wives. Not one of them will treat his wife as a decorative accessory. Their marriages are love matches, affairs of the heart, not merely of the pocketbook. None of Austen's heroines will be passive wives, like Hannah More's portrait on the wall, and none will be "exhibiting" herself in any public marketplace because they are endowed with the probity and discernment that would make such wanton display repulsive to them. Moreover, if they are not innately endowed with this acute discernment, they learn it before their mistakes become disastrous. In some cases Austen's heroines must endure the vulnerabilities of the men that they love and wait for *them* to be the ones to learn and grow. Elinor Dashwood, who perfectly well knows how to "govern her emotions" from the start, must wait helplessly while Edward Ferrars deals with the consequences of his earlier mistakes. Edmund Bertram must undergo the trial of temptation as represented by the alluring Mary Crawford. He is much weaker than Fanny Price, who tenaciously resists the magnetic Crawfords who have galvanized the rest of the neighborhood with their blandishments.

In all of Austen's novels the lovers face a challenge and in every case the lessons of maturity, correct conduct, and rational thought are mastered.

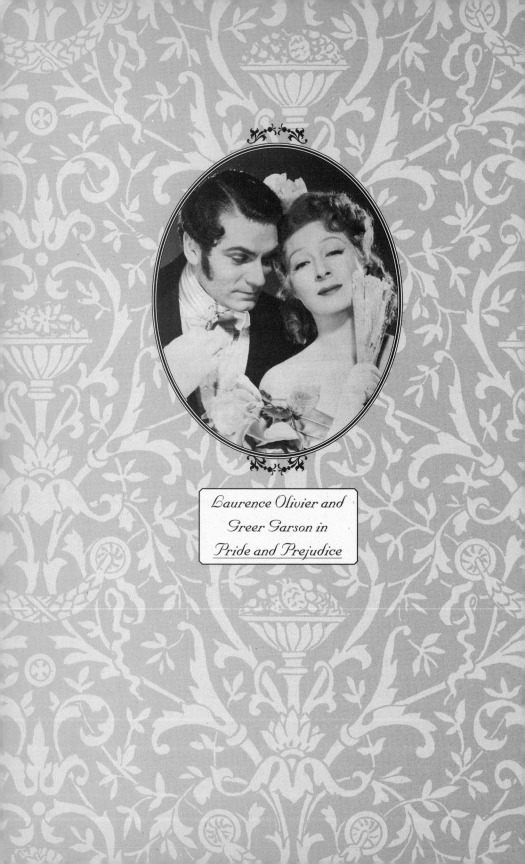

Laurence Olivier and
Greer Garson in
Pride and Prejudice

PART II

Major Works

Northanger Abbey

I cannot speak well enough to be unintelligible.
—CATHERINE MORLAND

M ost specialists consider *Northanger Abbey* Austen's first "mature" novel, although it was not published until after her death in 1817. It retains the bustling burlesque of the juvenilia but also has the more acerbic tendencies of the older Austen. It manages both to parody and to defend novels, novelists, and novel writing.

Northanger Abbey begins by introducing us to its heroine, seventeen-year-old Catherine Morland, who lives in a small village. Austen satirizes the popular novels of the time from the very first sentence: "No one who had ever seen Catherine Morland in her infancy, would have supposed her born to be a heroine." The typical Gothic novel foreshadowed its heroine's significance by claiming all kinds of ominous portents evident from the moment of her birth. A Gothic heroine is always remarkably beautiful, but Austen tells us that the entire Morland family is "very plain" and that Catherine is "as plain as any." Even her mother only allows that Catherine is "almost pretty" sometimes. Austen continues with a series of deadpan facts about Catherine, all of which prove that she is completely unexceptional.

Anticipating Flaubert's Emma Bovary, a woman who reads too much, young Catherine is a heroine whose imagination has been fed by literature. Catherine sets out on an adventure. Leaving her small village, she goes to explore the excitements of Bath with good-natured guardians, Mr. and Mrs. Allen. The first half of the novel follows Catherine's adventures in Bath, where she rapidly gains experience in learning how to read people. Her texts in this exercise are two sets of siblings: Isabella and John Thorpe and Eleanor and Henry Tilney. The Thorpes and the Tilneys serve as counterpoints. Catherine is initially pleased by the attentions that John and Isabella Thorpe lavish on her, but she soon becomes painfully aware of how vulgar, stupid, and insincere they seem compared with the other pair of siblings she has met. Eleanor and Henry Tilney charm Catherine with their good manners, wit, and intelligence. They are not vainglorious and boastful like the Thorpes. They teach Catherine about the picturesque aspects of Bath as opposed to the purely social delights of balls, dancing, and romancing that preoccupy the Thorpes. Catherine is delighted, however, when Isabella Thorpe agrees to marry her brother and when the Tilneys invite her to spend some time at their country home, Northanger Abbey.

Catherine is in ecstasy envisioning Gothic ruins and hidden mysteries. She suspects that General Tilney, the father of Eleanor and Henry, might be a blackguard who has killed his wife. With the determined zeal of a Nancy Drew, she wants to explore the abbey and detect proof of a murder. At the same time, her love for Henry grows and her friendship with Isabella deepens. She receives a letter from James announcing that Isabella has jilted him for a potentially richer match with Frederick Tilney, the older brother of Henry and Eleanor, a rake who does not share the refined sensibilities of his siblings. A letter follows from Isabella asking her to smooth the way for her to get back together with James since "Tilney has left." Catherine is now shocked by Isabella's "shallow artifice . . . inconsistencies, contradictions, and falsehood."

At the same time she is unceremoniously evicted from the abbey by her host, General Tilney, who has instructed Eleanor to send Catherine packing. Making the trip home alone, Catherine is crestfallen to have been so summarily dismissed. Henry Tilney, shocked by his father's rudeness and lack of gallantry, let alone common good manners, pursues Catherine and asks to marry her.

While Catherine had hoped to have the kinds of adventures that heroines in novels encounter, she instead realizes that the horrific Gothic potpourri of misfortune, disguise, falseness, madness, and murder is matched by the less dramatic, but no less inscrutable reality of the range of human conduct and morality. She learns a lesson seen in virtually all of Austen's novels: that the ability to know oneself and to read the people in one's life is essential to becoming a discerning adult. Catherine develops the ability to distinguish between true friends and those who toy with and trivialize friendship, just as she learns to tell the difference between genuine feeling and overblown and meretricious affectations.

She also finds that families are not all neat packages. General Tilney and his elder son, Frederick, are as materialistic, insolent, and self-righteous, as are the Thorpes. Austen's novels are full of similarly inconsistent families. In fact, the main horror that Catherine faces is that in a society bound by rigid conventions, money is held more important than character; virtue is unrelated to one's position at birth.

Publication: A Fraught Road

The story of how *Northanger Abbey* came finally to be published is as full of peril and vicissitude as the plot of a Gothic novel. According to Cassandra, Austen wrote the novel, initially entitled *Susan,* in 1798 and 1799, and in 1803 she made her first literary sale in a circuitous way. An employee of Austen's brother Henry sold the *Susan* manuscript to the London publishers Richard Crosby and Co. for ten pounds. Crosby actually advertised the book for publication, but it never appeared, for reasons that are not clear. After a more than generous waiting period of six years, Austen wrote a letter of inquiry to Crosby and Co. using the pseudonym of Mrs. Ashton Dennis (and signing her letter M.A.D.). She demanded an explanation, proffered another copy of the manuscript in the event that the first one had suffered some misadventure, and finally said that she would approach another publisher if nothing were to happen. Crosby's only response seems to have been a suggestion that he would take up legal proceedings against any publisher who might usher *Susan* into the world, but that he *would* return the manuscript "for the same price as we paid for it." Not surprisingly Austen did not return the ten pounds, which represented a goodly portion of her income at the time but apparently decided to concentrate her efforts on *Sense and Sensibility* (1811) and *Pride and Prejudice* (1813).

After the publication of *Emma* in 1815, Austen decided to buy back the manuscript of *Susan* from Crosby. In 1816 she composed an "Advertisement" to the novel, then known as *Catherine,* which diffidently but also with a sense of hardly suppressed anger and puzzlement, apologizes for the delay in publication, during which time "places, manners, books, and opinions have undergone considerable changes." Austen's wording acknowledges that the novel was written as a satire on contemporary fiction and that she feared something might have been lost in the delay. Her frustration with Crosby and Co. is made clear in the advertisement: "This little work was finished in the year 1803, and intended for immediate publication. It was disposed of to a bookseller, it was even advertised, and why the business proceeded no farther, the author has never been able to learn. That any bookseller should think it worth while to purchase what he did not think it worth while to publish seems extraordinary." Even then all was not smooth. There was a further postponement, and in March 1817 Austen wrote that "Miss Catherine is put upon the Shelve for the present, and I do not know that she will ever come out."

Poetic justice prevailed: After *Emma* was published, Austen finally had the funds to repurchase the manuscript of *Susan* from Crosby. Henry Austen took great pleasure afterward in revealing to Crosby the true identity of the author, the famous lady who had written the successful moneymaker *Pride and Prejudice*.

Ultimately *Northanger Abbey* was published along with *Persuasion* in December 1817, five months after Austen's death.

Rakes and Rattles

In *Northanger Abbey* the young Jane Austen continued to perfect her delineations of the rake and the rattle, two of the least appealing types of men who bedevil Austen's heroines. Rakes and rattles pervade her juvenilia, perhaps because they are easier and perhaps more entertaining to create than serious heroes. The Regency society in which Austen lived—the age of Lord Byron, Beau Brummel, and a dissolute Prince Regent's court—offered numerous examples of cads and blackguards and of those would-be rogues who never could do much more than talk about imagined exploits.

Austen's novels lack the sinister villains and mad monks popular in the Gothic novels of her time, but they are not short of dangerous men. For Austen, danger appears in the form of a threat to a young lady's reputation for propriety and chastity. These threats come primarily from young men characterized by high spirits and carelessness for the consequences of their actions.

The rattle, a considerably lesser threat than the rake, is unlikely to have designs on a lady's chastity, but he may compromise her reputation by involving her in his jokes or his general vulgarity of manner. Best represented by John Thorpe in *Northanger Abbey,* the rattle is likely to be an aspiring rake, a lout who represents himself as moving in a "fast set" in fashionable society. He is too obviously a fool to succeed in seducing any woman of sense, but his foolish prattle may compromise a woman's reputation, and his show of intimacy with any sensible woman inevitably makes her appear less judicious to others; just to be seen with a rattle shows a lack of taste and judgment. Thorpe's teasing, presumptuousness, and loose tongue are typical of the rattle and are more the marks of a fool than a knave, but he still manages to ape the part of the more sinister villains of the Gothic novel. Driving Catherine Morland away from her friends, in both senses of the word, is embarrassing for the aspiring heroine, but it is a far cry from the kidnappings that abound in the novels of Ann Radcliffe. One staple of the Gothic novel is the tendency of young men to trick young ladies into their carriages and drive them to perdition. The rattle, a comically diminished type of the Gothic villain, is nevertheless a realistic social threat in eighteenth-century England, where young ladies are judged by the company they keep.

"LEARNING TO LOVE A HYACINTH"

*C*atherine Morland learns just this lesson as a part of a larger moral and aesthetic training under the guidance of the Tilney family. The Tilney siblings, Henry and Eleanor, are well educated and have a mature appreciation of the eighteenth-century ideal of the "picturesque." Austen does not seem to believe that "natural" human instinct is innately good, as did her contemporaries the Romantic poets. Instead, she seems to have believed that most behaviors are learned and not innate. Although Fanny Price of *Mansfield Park* is endowed with infallibly correct taste, most of Austen's heroines need to improve what Fanny calls our "inner guide." Taste—in flowers, in books, and in men—is supremely important in Austen's world, so it is important to know how correct taste is formed. Austen reserves some of her most scathing characterizations for the preposterous vulgarities of those characters who rely on what they regard as their "natural" proclivities. That Catherine is willing, and eager, to learn must explain much of her appeal to Henry Tilney, as in the following exchange:

> "What beautiful hyacinths!—I have just learnt to love a hyacinth."
> "And how might you learn?—By accident or argument?"
> "Your sister taught me: I cannot tell how. Mrs. Allen used to take pains, year after year, to make me like them; but I never could, till I saw them the other day in Milsom-street; I am naturally indifferent about flowers."
> "But now you love a hyacinth. So much the better. You have gained a new source of enjoyment, and it is well to have as many holds upon happiness as possible. Besides, a taste for flowers is always desirable in your sex, as a means of getting you out of doors, and tempting you to more frequent exercise than you would otherwise take: and though the love of a hyacinth may be rather domestic, who can tell, the sentiment once raised, but you may in time come to love a rose?.....I am pleased that you have learned to love a hyacinth. The mere habit of learning to love is the thing; and a teachableness of disposition in a young lady is a great blessing."

HYACINTHS.

Henry clearly approves of Catherine's ductility and her eagerness to learn. The love of the young Tilneys for sublime and picturesque landscapes, for walking and for nature in general, contrasts with their father's mercantile and faddish love of his highly cultivated gardens, hothouses, succession houses (forcing houses with graded temperatures into which plants are moved in rotations), and his pinery, where pineapples are grown. That General Tilney takes the "utmost care" to secure the "most valuable fruits" may seem like an ironic commentary on the care he is taking to procure suitable marriages for his children that will be as financially "showy" as his exotic fruits.

A salient part of Catherine's education in *Northanger Abbey* is to learn that people do not live above concealed dungeons but that mundane boorishness and crapulous egos are more the stuff of reality. John Thorpe has "told her of horses which he had bought for a trifle and sold for incredible sums; of racing matches, in which his judgment had infallibly foretold the winner; of shooting parties, in which he had killed more birds (though without having one good shot) than all his companions together." To interpret the inflated fustian of the bombastic rattler is no simple lesson for a trusting girl of seventeen, "for she had not been brought up to understand the propensities of a rattle, nor to know to how many idle assertions and impudent falsehoods the excess of vanity will lead." In *Sense and Sensibility* Elinor and Marianne promptly identify Robert Ferrars as a rattle when they meet him at a Piccadilly jeweler's. Robert Ferrars is ordering a toothpick case for himself and must examine and debate at great length the "size, shape, and ornaments." Later he treats Elinor to a long rattle about his love for cottages and his taste in cottages:

> I advise everyone who is going to build to build a cottage. My friend Lord Courtland came to me the other day on purpose to ask my advice, and laid before me three different plans of Bonomi's. I was to decide on the best of them. "My dear Courtland," said I, immediately throwing them all into the fire, "do not adopt either of them, but by all means build a cottage." And that, I fancy, will be the end of it.

Elinor knows how to handle a rattle: She "agreed to it all, for she did not think he deserved the compliment of rational opposition." In *Pride and Prejudice,* Mrs. Reynolds, the housekeeper at Pemberley who gives such a glowing report of Darcy as master of the estate, adds that if some people call him proud, it is only because "he does not rattle away like other young men."

The rake, however, is a decidedly more dangerous type than the rattle and can be encountered in the private balls and public assemblies frequented by even the most demure and naive maidens. The rake, often an officer, prides himself on his gallant appearance and seductive powers and is always ready to lead the unwary maiden into the infamy of sin and then to abandon her. Austen's first rake appears in the juvenilia: The callous Charles of *Jack and Alice* "wounds the hearts & legs of all the fair." He is not content with merely breaking hearts but has steel traps on his estate that seize the legs of Lucy, who has been so importunate as to seek him out even after his rejection of her. Captain Frederick Tilney, Wickham, Willoughby, and Henry Crawford are examples of the type, and all exhibit considerable powers to captivate even the best of society—and to ruin the most unsuspecting of maidens. Even Henry Crawford, whose worst tendency is a fairly harmless propensity to have seemingly innocent fun in private theatricals, and who has power to charm even the morally hyperconscious Fanny Price, eventually reveals himself as a rake and an unmitigated cad. Like all rakes, Henry has a general power to please, but he reveals his rakish propensities by a willingness to step beyond the bounds of strict propriety. The rattle and the rake invariably remind Austen's readers of the dangers of high-spirited behavior.

We are quick, too quick, to understand that Northanger Abbey *invites us into a snug conspiracy to disabuse the little heroine of the errors of her corrupted fancy—Catherine Morland, having become addicted to novels of terror, has accepted their inadmissible premise, she believes that life is violent and unpredictable. And that is exactly what life is shown to be by the events of the story: it is we who must be disabused of our belief that life is sane and orderly. . . . Little Catherine Morland is silly and even vulgar in her prying into the fancied secrets of Northanger Abbey, yet she is proved right, essentially if not circumstantially, in the ridiculous certitude, induced in her by a sudden immersion in "culture," the impassioned surrender of her mind to sensational novels, that the ethos of the great house is not in fact what it appears to be, that its noble candour masks the base and shameful.*
—LIONEL TRILLING, on Catherine Morland

The posters . . . are advertising "Jane Austen's Northanger Abbey*" as if to distinguish what's inside from Aeschylus, Tertullian or St. John Chrysostom's* Northanger Abbey. *But the reason is not hard to see, given the public's dipsomaniac craving for adaptations of this lady's work. If things go on like this, we will have to set up drying-out or aversion-therapy clinics, where demure maidens in period crinoline biff addicts over the head with cudgels while American academics read them interminable essays on the semiotics of Jane Austen.*
— BENEDICT NIGHTINGALE, on the Plethora of Theatrical Productions of Austen's Novels in the 1990s

Joan Vredenburgh on Bath and General Tilney

Professor Joan R. Vredenburgh has taught at Roger Williams University. She is the author of articles on Jane Austen and is an active member of the Jane Austen Society of North America.

NT: *You wrote your dissertation on* Northanger Abbey. *Why did you decide to focus on this novel?*

JRV: When I finished my M.A., I went to Bath, England, for six weeks. I absolutely fell in love with the city. It is called a living museum, and it truly is. Much of the architecture is Georgian, many of the buildings mentioned in Austen are still there: the abbey, the Assembly Rooms, the Circus, etc. You can do what Catherine does: take the water at the Pump Room, shop on Milsom Street, visit the Circus, even take in the view on Beecham Cliff! When I was there, I could imagine being in an Austen novel. Later, when I was trying to decide what I was going to do my dissertation on, I thought about how Bath was central to two of Jane Austen's novels, about the significance of the English country house in Jane Austen, and about how I had visited Lacock Abbey, which some consider a model for Northanger Abbey. In doing the research for my dissertation, I gained a better appreciation for the novel. Before, I had ranked it number five or number six; now it is right up there with *Pride and Prejudice* and *Persuasion*.

NT: *How is* Northanger Abbey *different from the other novels?*

JRV: Many critics focus on what they perceive as flaws in the novel. Since it was an early novel, they suggest that it is not as polished or mature as her others. They point also to what is perceived as an abrupt shift in tone and style from the Bath section to the Northanger Abbey section and that the shift in Catherine's character in the Northanger Abbey section (where she imagines all sorts of Gothic horrors) is somewhat unbelievable. It may not be as polished, but Jane Austen's subtlety, humorous social criticism, characterization, and use of place are as sophisticated as in any of her later novels.

As for what makes this novel unique, there is a freshness, a genuine playfulness of youthful exuberance in this novel that are not as apparent in some of the others. Catherine is a thoroughly believable seventeen-year-old girl, with all the naiveté and awkwardness any seventeen-year-old would have. She is not as witty as Elizabeth Bennet or as mature as Elinor Dashwood. Yet this lack of maturity and sophistication is what makes her so real. In some ways Catherine is a more believable character than other of Jane Austen's heroines. She is real; her stumbles are more apparent. She worries about what dress she is going to wear to the ball, worries when she thinks Henry is cold to her in the theater, et cetera. Again, the typical seventeen-year-old.

NT: *Can you tell me more about your article on General Tilney as a meretriciously materialistic salesman?*

JRV: Given his character, he is probably spitting nails seeing himself characterized as a salesman. He is such an interesting character! His appearance is striking. He is a general with a capital *G*. That title alone may inspire awe and deference. He is so polite to Catherine. Yet that title is a facade. He is such a rat underneath. There are clues to this in the first half of the novel. His speeches to Catherine when he thinks she is an heiress are so-o-o-o flattering.

In the second half of the novel his character becomes clear. He is a selfish man, more concerned about appearance and his own convenience than anyone else's feelings, rushing everyone to dinner after a tiring journey from Bath just to dine at the fashionable hour, showing off his many possessions to impress Catherine.

One telling scene is where Catherine, at the breakfast table with the Tilneys, receives the letter from her brother telling her his engagement with Isabella is over. Catherine understandably is upset and crying. Yet the general does not even notice! He is too caught up with his mail and his food. Talk about self-absorbed. And don't for-

> ## WILLIAM DEAN HOWELLS ON CATHERINE MORLAND
>
> *C*atherine Morland is a goose, but a very engaging goose, and a goose you must respect for her sincerity, her high principles, her generous trust of others, and her patience under trials that would be great for much stronger heads.
>
>

get, the only reason he even invited Catherine was pure greed: He wants a rich wife for his son. Of course at the end his behavior is inexcusable. He turns Catherine out of the house with no warning and no money. He is the Gothic villain that Catherine took him for because such actions do place her in danger. And why does he do this? Simply because he made a mistake about Catherine's fortune.

I think it is important for first-time readers to realize that Austen is enjoyable, subtle, and humorous. Austen is wickedly funny. Some of her characters *are* ridiculous. Go ahead and laugh; you're supposed to. Austen is also subtle. Think about what she is writing. Don't simply dismiss her "stories about marriage."

The Nature of Gothic Novels

The intellectual tenor of the late eighteenth century was characterized by a strong faith in the power of rational thought to comprehend and explain the natural world and by skepticism about the supernatural (except in the case of orthodox Anglican Christianity). But perhaps because of the emotional and imaginative sterility of merely rational thought, a strong countercurrent in the arts established a fashion for literature that would excite the emotions of fear and wonder. Among the first of such exercises in supernaturalism was Horace

Walpole's "gothick" novel *The Castle of Otranto* (1764), which features a labyrinth of hidden tunnels, ghosts, bizarre portraits of doom, and Catholicism (for the eighteenth-century British reader, a still-surviving body of medieval superstition). Walpole's Gothic novel was followed over the subsequent decades by hosts of others. One of the most famous is Matthew Gregory "Monk" Lewis's *The Monk* (1796), a Faustian tale of rape, murder, incest, and the supernatural. A late example of the genre is Charles Robert Maturin's *Melmoth the Wanderer* (1820), the story of Melmoth, who sold his soul to the devil in the seventeenth century and is still alive and suffering eternal life. (Oscar Wilde, after his conviction, assumed the pen name of Melmoth, and Nabokov's Humbert Humbert takes Lolita on their cross-country odyssey in a Melmoth automobile.)

Ann Radcliffe wrote five Gothic novels, including *The Mysteries of Udolpho* (1794) and *The Italian, or, The Confessional of the Black Penitents* (1797), whose villainous monk Schedoni is a prototype of the Byronic hero. Usually set in Spain or Italy, Radcliffe's novels involve conniving southern European archvillains, heroines struggling to maintain not only their lives but their virtue, and the increasingly familiar props of Gothic castles with labyrinthine passages and supernatural portraits. Radcliffe's novels, however, bow to the rationality of the age, and as in the contemporary children's cartoon *Scooby-Doo,* the seemingly supernatural is always shown to have a rational explanation and to have been caused only by the connivance of the wily villains.

Jane Austen shared Radcliffe's faith in rational explanation, but she was wary of the emotional excesses provoked in readers as heroines underwent harrowing dangers and profound fear during the leisurely development of Radcliffe's plots. The danger of indulging in literary fantasy is exposed conspicuously in the sufferings of Marianne Dashwood in *Sense and Sensibility* and even more conspicuously in *Northanger Abbey,* in which Catherine Morland is brought to a comically high pitch of fear and wonder by Radcliffe's novels and becomes absurdly suspicious about her surroundings even in the Tilneys' modernized Gothic abbey. The climax of Austen's satire of Gothic fiction occurs when Catherine has convinced herself that her host, General Tilney, is a stereotyped Gothic villain who has either killed or imprisoned his wife. Eventually Henry sets Catherine straight, but in doing so he presents a picture of English life that might well make one long for the imaginative scope of another time and place. Austen gives us Catherine's new and educated point of view on the topic after she has soaked up some of the Tilney wisdom:

Charming as were all Mrs Radcliffe's works, and charming even as were the works of all her imitators, it was not in them perhaps that human nature, at least in the midland countries of England were to be looked for. Of the Alps and Pyrenees, with their pine forests and their vices, they might give a faithful delineation; and Italy, Switzerland, and the South of France, might be as fruitful in horrors as they were there represented. . . . But in the central part of England there was surely some security for the existence even of a wife not beloved, in the laws of the land, and the manners of the age. Murder was not tolerated, servants were not slaves, and neither poison nor sleeping potions to be procured, like rhubarb, from every druggist. Among the Alps and Pyrenees, perhaps, there were no mixed characters. There, such as were not as spotless as an angel, might have the dispositions of a fiend. But in England it was not so; among the English, she believed, in their hearts and habits, there was a general though unequal mixture of good and bad.

Catherine's thoughts reflect Jane Austen's preference for the subtlety of psychological realism to the excesses of the Gothic. But in their wistfulness they also hint at the limitations of imaginative scope within a civilized community and at the reasons why eighteenth-century readers were attracted to Gothic literature, as people in our time are attracted to horror films and science fiction. Nevertheless, just as the less serious genres of literature are deplored today by some intellectuals, so too in the time when the Gothic novel prevailed did the poet Coleridge write that "where the reading of novels prevails as a habit, it occasions in time the entire destruction of the powers of mind."

David Riede on Jane Austen and Romanticism

David G. Riede *is a specialist on Victorian and Romantic poetry and poetics and a professor at the Ohio State University. He is the author of books on Algernon Charles Swinburne, Matthew Arnold, and Dante Gabriel Rossetti and of* Oracles and Hierophants: Construction of Romantic Authority. *His current research interests include the cultural impact of Tarzan, the relation of Romantic imagination to nineteenth-century imperialism, and Victorian melancholy. His teaching interests include the eighteenth- and nineteenth-century Gothic novel, the novel of sensation, and aestheticism.*

NT: *Why isn't Jane Austen considered a Romantic when she wrote in the midst of the Romantic movement in England?*

DGR: That question is difficult to answer only because there are so many definitions of Romanticism to consider. But I think it is safe to say that Austen was not a Romantic writer, that in fact, her emphasis on reason, propriety, and decorum makes her closer in spirit to the late-eighteenth-century Age of Reason than to the Romanticism that generally rebelled against eighteenth-century values. Possibly the best indication of Austen's non-Romanticism is seen in Charlotte Brontë's objection that Austen's novels are remarkably accurate transcriptions of real life, but for that very reason, they are "more real than true."

Generally most definitions of Romanticism involve some notion of inspiration, or imaginative visionary power to see beyond mere realities to some realm of transcendent and abiding truth, but Jane Austen never aspires to such a realm in her novels. She remains fundamentally concerned with the social reality of her day.

NT: *What do you think is Jane Austen's distinctive contribution to the novel?*

DGR: This is also a difficult question because, as Virginia Woolf once said, of all great novelists, Jane Austen is the most difficult to catch in the act of greatness. The reason is that Austen's innovations were so effective and influential that they became incorporated in the novels of the next two hundred years, so that her contributions to the art of novel writing have almost come to look "natural" to later generations—not innovative in art but simply the way novels just are. But in the late eighteenth century the novels Austen could look to as models were generally divisible into two main types of narrative: first-person narrative, as in the imitation autobiographies of Defoe's *Robinson Crusoe* and *Moll Flanders* and in the shifting first-person narration of epistolary novels like Richardson's *Clarissa* and *Pamela* or Fanny Burney's *Evelina,* or omniscient narration, in which the author takes on the role of a detached showman, exhibiting his characters for an audience, as in Fielding's *Tom Jones.*

Jane Austen's most important innovation, I think, was to develop a style of narration that could shift seamlessly from the authorial point of view to the points of views of the different characters, enabling her to control and interpret the action from a detached, ironic perspective and to enter directly into the consciousness of her characters.

NT: *What about Austen's striking lack of metaphor in her novels? Is that an artistic failure in any sense?*

DGR: Austen's infrequent use of metaphor sets her apart from her Romantic contemporaries, for whom metaphors were fundamental to imaginative creativity in language and even, as Shelley saw it, to the necessarily continual revitalization of language. But no, I would not view it as in any sense an artistic failure. Austen's genius is in her supple prose and subtle irony, and she does not need metaphors for her purposes. Also, as an author aiming more at the real then the "true," she not surprisingly shied away from the transformative powers of metaphor.

NT: *Who are some of your favorite characters from Austen's novels?*

DGR: Most of my choices are the obvious ones. I like Elizabeth Bennet for her wit and courage and Catherine Morland for her naive vision and her willingness and ability to be educated. In general I confess to liking all the major protagonists for their ability to see through pretentiousness and sham. In this sense I suppose my favorite character is the narrator of the novels. Of course

I also enjoy the outrageously silly characters, such as Mr. Collins, Lady Catherine de Bourgh, and John Thorpe.

NT: *Which character would you most like to have as your own daughter?*

DGR: I am sorry to be so predictable, but I'd choose Elizabeth Bennet. Jane Bennet and Fanny Price would be easier to "manage" perhaps, but Elizabeth Bennet combines rigorously high principles with a more playful and amusing disposition than the other heroines have. Emma Woodhouse of course is abundantly playful, but without a Knightley around to manage her, she might be difficult to handle.

NT: *Leaving aside all questions of money, entailment, and primogeniture, which character would you most enjoy as a son-in-law?*

DGR: This is more difficult, but perhaps Mr. Bingley. Darcy is a bit stiff, and most of the other men are disqualified by being in professions I'd be uncomfortable with: the clergy, in the cases of Henry Tilney, Edward Ferrars, and Edmund Bertram, and the military, in the cases of Captain Wentworth and Colonel Brandon.

"A Neighborhood of Voluntary Spies"

In *Northanger Abbey,* when Henry Tilney discovers Catherine Morland's "surmise of such horror" about his father, he reacts with a series of astonished questions:

> Dear Miss Morland, consider the dreadful nature of the suspicions you have entertained. What have you been judging from? remember the country and the age in which we live. Remember that we are English, that we are Christians. Consult your own understanding, your own sense of the probable, your own observation of what is passing around you—Does our education prepare us for such atrocities? Do our laws connive at them? Could they be perpetrated without being known, in a country like this, where social and literary intercourse is on such a footing; where every man is surrounded by a neighborhood of voluntary spies, and where roads and newspapers lay everything open? Dearest Miss Morland, what ideas have you been admitting?

Henry of course means to represent the dearth of Gothic horrors in civilized England as entirely positive, yet it is difficult not to hear something sinister in

MARRIAGE AS A COUNTRY DANCE

*H*enry Tilney tells Catherine Morland:
"I consider a country-dance as an emblem of marriage. Fidelity and complaisance are the principal duties of both; and those men who do not chuse to dance or marry themselves have no business with the partners or wives of their neighbors. . . . You will allow that in both, man has the advantage of choice, woman only the power of refusal; that in both, it is an engagement between man and woman, formed for the advantage of each; and that when once entered into, they belong exclusively to each other till the moment of its dissolution; that it is their duty, each to endeavor to give the other no cause for wishing that he or she had bestowed themselves elsewhere, and their best interest to keep their own imaginations from wandering towards the perfections of their neighbors, or fancying that they should have been better off with anyone else."

George Cruikshank's concept of a dance party, circa 1800

the phrase "a neighborhood of voluntary spies." This was a time, it must be remembered, of general paranoia following the American Revolution and then, even closer to home, the French Revolution and the Reign of Terror. Foreign plots might be abounding. Anyone might be not merely a voluntary neighborhood spy but a Jacobin sympathizer determined to bring down the social structure in England.

Austen anticipates later-nineteenth-century concerns about the loss of privacy entailed in closely knit communities. By the mid-nineteenth century John Stuart Mill was arguing that surveillance by the community, even if only in the form of gossip, constitutes an almost tyrannical suppression of even mildly nonconformist behavior. As England became increasingly civilized and urbane, the individual became increasingly secure, but partially at the cost of privacy and even of individualism itself.

By the mid-Victorian period, as the circumstances outlined by Henry Tilney were increasingly realized, the Gothic format became less and less plausible and consequently less and less exciting. Eventually the thrills that had been provided by Gothic novels were provided by a new type of novel, the so-called sensation novel, which featured villains who were masters of disguises and deceit, villains who could disrupt the tranquillity of English life precisely by avoiding or misleading the "voluntary spies." Similarly, the heroes of many novels, culminating in Sherlock Holmes, were fashioned from unusually adept "voluntary spies"—usually gentlemen detectives.

A Very Respectable Man, Though His Name Was Richard

In the first paragraph of *Northanger Abbey* Austen tells us that Catherine Morland's father, a clergyman, was "a very respectable man, though his name was Richard," an echo of her treatment in *The History of England* of Richard III, who is also "a very respectable man." Here we catch Austen in the interstice between her rollicking juvenilia, which was designed to amuse her family with jokes and hyperbole, and her mature works. The name Richard is never given to a hero of Austen's later works, although Richard, along with Robert, Ralph, David, Jem, Will, Ned, and Rodolphus, is one of the numerous scions of Mr. and Mrs. Willmot of the three-chapter tale *Edgar and Emma,* which was probably composed before Austen was fourteen. At twenty she wrote to Cassandra that "Mr. Richard Harvey's match is put off till he has got a Better Christian Name, of which he has great Hopes."

One is tempted to think that Austen may have included the seeming non sequitur about the name Richard as a small stiletto jab at Richard Crosby, who retained the manuscript for thirteen years without publishing it. He was hardly a worthy foster father for the precocious, antic child he had purchased for ten pounds. Austen's description of another Richard, the unfortunate Richard Musgrove in *Persuasion,* has occasioned shudders in some readers who think that it betrays a callousness:

> . . . The Musgroves had had the ill fortune of a very troublesome, hopeless son; and the good fortune to lose him before he reached his twentieth year; that he had been sent to sea, because he was stupid and unmanageable on shore; that he had been very little cared for at any time by his family, though quite as much as he deserved; seldom heard of, and scarcely at all regretted, when the intelligence of his death abroad had worked its way to Uppercross. . . . [H]e had, in fact, though his sisters were now doing all they could for him by calling him "poor Richard," been

nothing better than a thick-headed, unfeeling, unprofitable Dick Musgrove. . . .

Perhaps this unfeeling, unprofitable character is none other than the spirit of Richard Crosby, properly chastised and killed off for his stupid mis-evaluation of Austen's talents.

John Thorpe's Horse and Gig

*J*ohn Thorpe, no matter how much he may not wish it so, finds that his horse refuses to take a slow gait. He defies "any man in England to make [his] horse go less than ten miles an hour" and proudly points out his equipage to Catherine: ". . . look at his loins; only see how he moves; that horse *cannot* go less than ten miles an hour; tie his legs and he will get on. What do you think of my gig, Miss Morland? a neat one, is not it? Well hung; town built." This is John Thorpe's first meeting with Catherine, and one cannot but speculate that he is extolling the celerity of his horse and his "well hung" gig as a not very subtle form of self-advertisement. Contemporary men are often chided for projecting their sexuality onto their automobiles, and John Thorpe, who promises to take Catherine out riding every day, also implies that he will take her prodigious distances: "forty! aye fifty miles a day." Thorpe uses his speedy horse and gig to compete with Henry Tilney, who prefers to walk with Catherine and who, according to Thorpe, has a horse that is merely "some very pretty cattle."

Henry Tilney's Knowledge of Muslin

In a sharp contrast with John Thorpe's gambit of impressing Catherine with his "equipage," Henry Tilney, in his first meeting with Catherine, delivers pronouncements on muslin and displays a frankly unmasculine interest in textiles. He boasts to Catherine and Mrs. Allen that he is "allowed to be an excellent judge" of muslins and that he purchases muslin for his sister, Eleanor. He even ventures to assert his opinion that Catherine's "sprigged muslin robe with blue trimmings" will not "wash well" and "will fray." He has the immediate instinct to console her, however, by reminding her that "muslin can never be said to be wasted" since she can use it for a cap or a cloak. Henry Tilney's ideas of domestic economy delight Catherine, who keeps "him on the subject of muslins till the dancing recommenced."

ON THE POPULARITY OF MUSLIN

According to Lucy Huntzinger, "Muslin and cotton were essential for Regency outfits. Muslin takes embroidery very well, and comes in many different weights. Because the ladies were emulating the light robes of the classic Greek look they wanted a fabric that was sheer and that clung to the outline of the figure. So it was both a covering and a revealing fabric. The ideal look was very columnar: flowing robes imitating the classical Greek look. The popularity of muslin is also related to the French Revolution. Everyone had been wearing a great deal of silk, a very expensive material, and nobody wanted to look aristocratic anymore. Even prior to the French Revolution, Marie Antoinette dressed up in her little shepherdess outfit, attempting to look like one of the simple people. And that kind of mentality filtered over to England, where they had not had a revolution but were very concerned about the possibility. Jane Austen made all her own clothing."

❧ Quiz: Letter Writing in the Novels ❧

Your task is to identify which characters wrote the following passages from letters in Jane Austen's novels and to whom the words were directed.

1. I have burnt all your letters, and will return your picture the first opportunity. Please to destroy my scrawls—the ring with my hair you are very welcome to keep.

2. The death of your daughter would have been a blessing in comparison of this.

3. Be not alarmed, Madam, on receiving this letter, by the apprehension of its containing any repetition of those sentiments, or renewal of those offers, which were last night so disgusting to you. I write without any intention of paining you, or humbling myself, by dwelling on wishes, which, for the happiness of both cannot be too soon forgotten.

4. You pierce my soul. I am half agony, half hope. Tell me not that I am too late, that such precious feelings are gone for ever. I offer myself to you again with a heart even more your own. . . .

5. My esteem for your whole family is very sincere; but if I have been so unfortunate as to give rise to a belief of more than I felt, or meant to express, I shall reproach myself for not having been more guarded in my professions of that esteem. That I should ever have meant more you will allow to be impossible, when you understand that my affections have been long engaged elsewhere, and it will not be many weeks, I believe, before this engagement is fulfilled.

6. I wear nothing but purple now: I know I look hideous in it, but no matter—it is your dear brother's favourite colour.

7. You will laugh when you know where I am gone, and I cannot help laughing myself at your surprise to-morrow morning, as soon as I am missed. I am going to Gretna Green, and if you cannot guess with who, I shall think you a simpleton.

8. What dreadful weather we have had! It may not be felt in Bath, with your nice pavements; but in the country it is of some consequence . . . but I have my usual luck, I am always out of the way when any thing desirable is going on; always the last of my family to be noticed. . . .

9. Though we cannot contribute to your Beau Monde in person, we are doing our utmost to send you company worth having; and think we may safely reckon on securing you two large families, one a rich West Indian from Surrey, the other a most respectable girls' boarding

QUIZ: AN URBAN LEGEND?

*J*ohn Thorpe most graciously greets his mother with a "Ah, mother! how do you do? Where did you get that quiz of a hat, it makes you look like an old witch." Catherine and Isabella talk about "dress, balls, flirtations, and quizzes." John Thorpe also quizzes his sisters. "Quiz" is both a noun and a verb, associated with the Thorpes more than with any other characters in Jane Austen's works. According to both the 1894 edition of *Brewer's Dictionary of Phrase and Fable* and the 1913 edition of *Webster's Dictionary*, the word "quiz" derives from one Mr. Daly, manager of a Dublin playhouse. He had a bet that he could create a word of no meaning and have it be the talk of the city within twenty-four hours. He chalked the letters *q u i z* up on walls all over Dublin and won the wager. The venerable *Oxford English Dictionary*, however, is dubious about the veracity of the Daly story but admits that the origin of "quiz" is obscure and may well be fanciful. The first citation in literature was in Mme. d'Arblay's diary of June 1782: "He's a droll quiz, and I rather like him." Webster's 1813 dictionary notes that "quiz" means "to puzzle" and is "a popular, but not an elegant word." The use of slang phrases is a sure sign of vulgarity in Jane Austen's characters and is another hint of the risibility of John Thorpe. And would any gentleman compare his mother with an old witch? James Edward Austen-Leigh, vicar of Bray, in his *Memoir* of his aunt Jane, wrote that she never "abused" or "quizzed" her neighbors and adds that quiz was "the word of the day; an ugly word, now obsolete."

school, or academy, from Camberwell—I will not tell you how many people I have employed in the business—Wheel within wheel—But success more than repays.

10. A poor honourable is no catch, and I cannot imagine any liking in the case, for, take away his rants, and the poor Baron has nothing. What a difference a vowel makes!—if his rents were but equal to his rants!

11. I have the honour, my dear madam, of being your husband's son, and the advantage of inheriting a disposition to hope for good, which no inheritance of houses or lands can ever equal the value of.

John Thorpe and Henry Tilney on Mrs. Radcliffe

The reader might expect that John Thorpe, the vulgarian, would be a fan of Gothic novels and that Henry Tilney, the intellectual clergyman and graduate of Oxford, would eschew novels for the classics. However, in one of *Northanger Abbey*'s many reversals, we find out that John Thorpe does not know who wrote *The Mysteries of Udolpho*. Catherine suggests that he "must like *Udolpho,* if you were to read it; it is so very interesting." Thorpe replies:

> "Not I, faith! No, if I read any, it shall be Mrs Radcliffe's; her novels are amusing enough; they are worth reading, some fun and nature in *them*."
>
> "Udolpho was written by Mrs Radcliffe," said Catherine, with some hesitation, from the fear of mortifying him.
>
> "No sure; was it? Aye, I remember, so it was. I was thinking of that other stupid book, written by that woman they make such a fuss about; she who married the French emigrant."
>
> "I suppose you mean Camilla?"
>
> "Yes, that's the book; such unnatural stuff!— An old man playing at see-saw! . . . I assure you it is the horridest nonsense you can imagine; There is nothing in the world in it but an old man's playing at see-saw and learning Latin."

Contrast Thorpe's diction and attitude with those of Henry Tilney, who responds to Catherine's diffident query "You never read novels, I dare say?" with his assertion that "The person, be it gentleman or lady, who has not pleasure in a good novel, must be intolerably stupid. I have read all of Mrs Radcliffe's works, and most of them with great pleasure. *The Mysteries of Udolpho,* when I had once begun it, I could not lay down again;—I remember finishing it in two days—my hair standing on end the whole time."

Henry Tilney is the epitome of reasonableness, and can enjoy even a Gothic novel in the spirit of pure entertainment in which it is intended.

Jim Buckley on General Tilney's Rumford Fireplace

Jim Buckley is an expert fireplace builder. He specializes in Rumford fireplaces. He has published articles on Count Rumford and on the fireplaces. His Web page at www.rumford.com includes pictures of Rumford fireplaces and directions on how to have one put into your own home.

NT: *Can you tell me something about the Rumford fireplace?*

JB: Rumford fireplaces are tall and shallow to reflect more heat, and they have streamlined throats to eliminate turbulence and carry away the smoke with little loss of heated room air.

Rumford fireplaces were common from 1796, when Count Rumford first wrote about them, until about 1850. Jefferson had them built at Monticello, and Thoreau listed them among the modern conveniences that everyone took for granted, along with venetian blinds and plaster walls.

NT: *Who was Count Rumford?*

JB: Count Rumford was born Benjamin Thompson in Woburn, Massachusetts, in 1753. He was a precocious American kid, playing with disappearing ink. Because he was a loyalist and ingratiated himself with the English governor John Wentworth, he was able to leave with the British in 1776. He spent much of his life as an employee of the Bavarian government, which gave him the title Count of the Holy Roman Empire, and he took the name Rumford in honor of his wife's hometown, Rumford (now Concord), New Hampshire. In his long and productive life Rumford improved our knowledge about heat transfer, coffeepots, ovens, boats, and, of course, the improvement of fireplaces. He made tham smaller and shallower with widely angled covings so that they would radiate better. He also streamlined the throat, or in his words, "rounded off the breast," so as to "remove those local hindrances which forcibly prevent the smoke from following its natural tendency to go up the chimney." Almost immediately in the 1790s his Rumford fireplace became state-of-the-art worldwide.

NT: *So why do you think General Tilney had a Rumford installed?*

JB: People switched to Rumfords because they were more efficient, cleaner-burning fireplaces. Rumford was something of an environmentalist and hoped to clean up the air in London as well as curb the appalling waste of fuel wood. A Rumford could substantially cut the amount of wood (and work) needed during a heating season. The servants especially appreciated that.

NT: *Can I get a fireplace like General Tilney's?*

JB: Yes. We've made it easier by making the directions available and by manufacturing clay components that save work and result in a better fireplace. Masons can still build Rumford fireplaces from scratch exactly as they did in Rumford's day.

Money

In each of Jane Austen's novels, with the exception of *Emma,* her heroines have significant economic problems. While Emma is immune from economic worries, her neighbors Mrs. Bates, Miss Bates, and Jane Fairfax are shown struggling financially. Austen usually tells her readers the precise annual incomes of her main characters. The historian Edward Copeland has described the approximate value of income in Austen's novels. One hundred pounds a year is a very low income, typical of very poor curates. Two hundred a year is an uncomfortable income for a family. When Austen's parents tried to live on this amount with their growing number of children, they were very hard pressed and had to devise ways to augment the family income. Three hundred pounds a year: Colonel Brandon, in *Sense and Sensibility,* claims that this is "comfortable" for a bachelor, though he does not have to live on it himself. Four hundred a year is an income that does not go very far if there is a family to care for. Fanny Price's mother has this much. Five hundred a year was the amount that Jane, Cassandra, and Mrs. Austen had to live on after the death of Mr. Austen. It is also what the four Dashwood women are going to be left with, much to their anxiety. Seven hundred to one thousand a year is a comfortable living. Elinor Dashwood says that it would make her happy to live on a thousand pounds a year, although Marianne wants about eighteen hundred to two thousand pounds to fulfill her needs. Copeland points out that this was the minimum income that would have perhaps supported a carriage. Austen's father found a carriage too expensive to maintain when he reached the peak of his income at seven hundred pounds a year. Two thousand pounds a year is the amount that Colonel Brandon has in *Sense and Sensibility.* It is also the income of the Bennet family in *Pride and Prejudice.* But with it they have to provide dowries for five daughters, which would have made domestic economy essential. Four thousand a year is the amount that marks real wealth. Mr. Bingley has  four or five thousand a year, and Darcy, the best catch of them all, has ten thousand pounds a year. With such a yearly livelihood comes an enormous amount of discretionary income. No wonder Mrs. Bennet is so giddy when such wealth comes into the neighborhood!

Heiresses usually have incomes that are reported as bulk sums. The annual yield would be approximately 5 percent. In the case of Elizabeth Bennet, however, she has one thousand pounds invested at 4 percent. Mr. Collins, in his elegant marriage proposal, reminds her that she can never hope to have more than forty pounds a year on her own, but he reassures her that "no ungenerous reproach shall ever pass my lips when we are married." When Darcy writes to Elizabeth he reveals that his sister has a fortune of thirty thousand pounds, which would have yielded fifteen hundred pounds yearly—enough to make even the covetous Wickham happy. Emma Woodhouse also has a fortune of thirty thousand pounds.

Mansfield Park commences with a financial report: Miss Maria Ward with *only* seven thousand pounds "had the good luck to captivate Sir Thomas Bertram." Yet her fortune is considerably greater than that of any of Austen's heroines aside from Emma. Jane Austen herself had a personal annual income of little more than fifty pounds for most of her life. She wished to be above the frugality of "Vulgar Economy," as she wrote to Cassandra, and enjoyed her visits to her prosperous brothers, who could afford to provide good wine and exquisite desserts.

Average Income, England and Wales, 1803

S o how did the Austen family compare with other families?
The following table breaks down the population of England and Wales into numbers of families and their estimated average annual income for 1803:

CATEGORY	NUMBERS OF FAMILIES	ESTIMATED AVERAGE FAMILY INCOME
The King	1	£200,000
Peers	287	8,000
Bishops	26	4,000
Baronets	540	3,000
Knights	350	1,500
Esquires	6,000	1,500

CATEGORY	NUMBERS OF FAMILIES	ESTIMATED AVERAGE FAMILY INCOME
Gentlemen	20,000	700
Clergy (higher)	1,000	500
Clergy (lower)	10,000	120
Education (higher)	500	600
Education (lower)	20,000	150
Naval Officers	3,000	149
Army Officers	5,000	139
Theatre People	500	200
Lunatic Keepers	40	500
Farmers	160,000	120
Merchants (higher)	2,000	2,600
Merchants (lower)	13,000	800
Tailors	25,000	150
Shopkeepers	74,500	150
Innkeepers	50,000	100
Clerks	30,000	75
Artisans	445,726	55
Pedlars	800	40
Seamen	38,175	38
Soldiers	50,000	29
Labourers	340,000	31
Lunatics	2,500	30
Pensioners	30,500	20
Paupers	260,179	16.4
Vagrants	220,000	10

Although there were only forty of them, it is surprising to see how much better lunatic keepers, at five hundred pounds' average annual income fared than innkeepers, who averaged one hundred. It is also interesting to see the high numbers of farmers, artisans, laborers, and vagrants compared with the upper classes. For every peer and his family there were almost two thousand paupers and vagrants.

Information derived from Patrick Colquhoun's *A Treatise on Indigence* (1806), reported in Harold Perkins's *The Origins of Modern English Society 1780–1880* (1969).

"The Tell-Tale Compression of the Pages"

The anxiety, which in this state of their attachment must be the portion of Henry and Catherine, and of all who loved either, as to its final event, can hardly extend, I fear, to the bosom of my readers, who will see in the tell-tale compression of the pages before then, that we are all hastening together to perfect felicity.
—NORTHANGER ABBEY

Jane Austen's awareness that the novelist cannot conceal the impending completion of her work displays a metafictional concern worthy of the true satirist. Metafiction is fiction that calls attention to itself as fiction. Perhaps the best-known example from the eighteenth century is *The Life and Opinions of Tristram Shandy, Gentleman* (1760) by Laurence Sterne. "Shandyesque" and "Shandean" are words that have entered the language to mean a sort of playful literary chaos; all sorts of digressions, diversions, eccentricities, and even blank pages and a profusion of typographical oddities are included in the book. Austen read and enjoyed *Tristram Shandy*. The comic melodrama of Austen's juvenilia can be quite Shandyesque, but in general, as her career progressed, she increasingly eschewed the touches that we might describe as metafictional. That so much of *Northanger Abbey* comments on novels, novel writing, and the reader's expectations of a novel (not to mention the expectations of the characters within the novel) makes it startlingly innovative. Austen knows that the reader *knows,* by "the tell-tale compression of the pages," that the novel must soon end, and happily.

Sense and Sensibility

"*It is not everyone,*" *said Elinor,* "*who has your passion for dead leaves.*"
—SENSE AND SENSIBILITY

Many readers regard *Sense and Sensibility* as the darkest of Austen's novels, treating, as it does, not merely sense and sensibility but sickness, secrecy, stymied sexuality, sadness, shame, scoundrels, stealth, seduction, selfishness, sighing, solitude, snobbishness, status, stoicism, stress, suffering, and the Steele sisters.

"*Sense and Sensibility: A Novel.* In three volumes. By a Lady" was published in November 1811 by Thomas Egerton. Although he published the novel at his own expense, it remained a calculated risk since any losses he might incur would have to be reimbursed to him by the author. Austen's brother Henry wrote that Jane actually "made a reserve from her very moderate income to meet the expected loss." Happily, she made 140 pounds on the first edition, which sold out within twenty months. Austen used the familiar maternal metaphor to describe the book in response to Cassandra's question whether she was too busy to think of her forthcoming book. Jane wrote: "No indeed, I am never too busy to think of S & S. I can no more forget it than a mother can forget her sucking child."

Sense and Sensibility contrasts two sisters who embody two of the prevailing emotional tenors of the time: rationalism and Romanticism. Elinor, the older, exemplifies sense; she is rational, reliable, self-contained, and polite. Marianne, the younger, is full of the emotional outpourings that represent some of the worst stereotypes of the Romantic. She relies on her spontaneous feelings as a guide for her behavior, whereas Elinor values tact, compromise, and conciliation as no less sincere motivations for maintaining emotional involvement with society. The unanticipated death of their father forces Elinor, Marianne, their mother, and their younger sister, Margaret, to live with a greatly reduced income. They are forced to leave Norland, the Sussex home they love, to move to more affordable lodgings. Luckily a cousin, Sir John Middleton, invites them to rent a cottage on his estate in Devonshire, Barton Park. Elinor's prudence welcomes this move, even though it will give her fewer opportunities to see Edward Ferrars, the amiable brother of her virago sister-in-law, Fanny Dashwood. Elinor feels a deep attachment to Edward, although no words of love have been exchanged between them.

After moving to Barton, Marianne meets John Willoughby in a dramatic encounter. Walking out on a rainy day, Marianne has fallen and twisted her ankle. A handsome stranger appears from the mists and sweeps her into his arms and carries her home. From that moment Marianne is captivated by the dashing, romantic Willoughby and falls deeply in love. Their intimate behavior leads everyone to assume that they are engaged. Elinor, in the meantime, learns that Edward Ferrars has long been engaged to the vulgar, ambitious Lucy Steele. His sense of honor will never permit him to break his engagement.

Then, shockingly, Willoughby disappears. Marianne, distraught, pursues him. When she finds out that he has married a wealthy heiress, she becomes dangerously ill. Colonel Brandon, a neighbor from Barton, does everything in his power to bring assistance to Marianne. Meanwhile Edward loses his inheritance, and Lucy Steele suddenly elopes with Robert, his brother. Now free, Edward proposes to Elinor, the woman he has always really loved. Marianne recovers from her near-fatal illness and eventually recognizes her love for the steady, dependable, and devoted Colonel Brandon.

Each sister has been troubled with a love the consummation of which appears to be impossible. Marianne's reaction to the loss of Willoughby anticipates that of Heathcliff and Catherine in *Wuthering Heights:* She becomes gravely ill; she gnashes her teeth and writhes about in despair. Elinor suffers quietly, but the reader is aware that her feelings are as strong as Marianne's. She does not allow herself to act out her emotions, proving that a breaking heart need not be accompanied by high dramatics, that sincere suffering need not, should not, be nakedly displayed. The culmination of *Sense and Sensibility* reinforces Elinor's values, and Marianne learns that the heart's affections are not always manifest in a rugged appearance. In learning the true excellence of Colonel Brandon's character, she realizes that a nearly middle-aged man in a flannel waistcoat is at least as capable of tenacious love as a youthful one who skulks about like a supercilious and disaffected Byronic hero.

The Novels of Sensibility

Sense and Sensibility is the first of Austen's novels in which two abstract qualities are weighed against one another. The novel of "sensibility," being that of sensitive feeling and emotion, arose early in the eighteenth century and was a counterpoint to the neoclassicism of the Augustan Age (1700–1750) and the age of Johnson (1750–1798). Sensibility denoted a rejection of the neoclassical values of correct judgment and restraint, and an emphasis on instinct, feelings, and intuition. The literature of sensibility reacted against the view, propounded most notably by Thomas Hobbes, the seventeenth-century philosopher, that people are motivated by inherent selfishness, offering instead a view of humans as innately benevolent and sympathetic to the sufferings of others. One English novel, *The Man of Feeling* by Henry MacKenzie (1771), describes a man who is so moved by his own emotions that he eventually dies from the extreme sentiment of describing his feelings to his lady love. An anecdote from Laurence Sterne's *Sentimental Journey Through France and Italy* also exemplifies sensibility. In the story a person has a caged sparrow and everyone who sees it declares how much he is moved to deep sentiment by its plight. It is passed from hand to hand all over Europe, but nobody thinks to release it because of the great depth of sensibility it evokes. Like Sterne, Austen demonstrates the self-indulgence of sensibility.

The Dangers of Sensibility

The eighteenth-century cult of sensibility rose in opposition to the rationalism and neoclassicism of the Augustan Age and held the deepest feelings of the individual to be a surer moral guide than reason. This frequently led people into absurd excesses and moral carelessness. For devotees of sensibility, proud of their emotional depths, even reading poetry may be a dangerous spur to emotions best left undisturbed.

Some of Austen's characters who fall victim to those "unerring guides, the feelings" include Captain Benwick in *Persuasion* and Marianne Dashwood in *Sense and Sensibility*. The cult of sensibility involved the belief that since people are made in the image of God and corrupted by worldliness, the deepest emotions, those leading to the innermost recesses of our being, are necessarily morally good because they are in touch with the uncorrupted depths of our godlike natures. Such a notion can be seen clearly, for example, in James Boswell's diary entry recording his devotion at religious services along with his deep desire to arrange an assignation with a prostitute. Instead of pondering the incompatibility of these feelings, Boswell simply accepted them both as morally admissible and even perhaps laudable sides of his complex nature.

Austen ridicules excessive sensibility, from the false, pretended sensibility of Isabella Thorpe to the more genuine and consequently more dangerous sensibility of Marianne Dashwood. Encouraging her feelings and never restraining them with reason, Marianne is easily led into intense emotional attachment to the worthless Willoughby, who reads poetry with such feeling. She is just as easily led into nearly fatal despair when his true nature is revealed.

Perhaps the clearest brief account of the dangers of sensibility is provided early in *Sense and Sensibility* when Elinor Dashwood doubts the propriety of one of her sister's actions. In response to Marianne's "defense" that she "never spent a pleasanter morning in her life," Elinor remarks: "I am afraid that the pleasantness of an employment does not always evince its propriety." Marianne's response sums up the dangers of the cult of sensibility: "On the contrary, nothing can be stronger proof of it, Elinor; for if there had been any real impropriety in what I did, I should have been sensible of it at the time, for we always know when we are acting wrong, and with such a conviction I could have had no pleasure." It falls to Elinor to maintain propriety because her sister, in indulging her belief that the only rules of conduct should come from her unerring and inherently moral feelings, is dangerously self-centered.

Sense and Sensibility: A Checklist

Who has sense? Who has sensibility? And how can you tell? Here's a handy guide. The two words imply a completely contrasting *Weltanschauung*. Elinor, who represents "sense," is a preserver of society and civilization. She believes that "the pleasantness of an employment does not always evince its propriety." Marianne, by contrast, has the Rousseauvian idea that scientific progress can corrupt human happiness and that emotional impulses should be glorified above pure rational thought. The dichotomy that the Dashwood sisters display is not limited to themselves alone:

SENSE	SENSIBILITY
Elinor	Marianne
Wagner	Mahler
Renata Tebaldi	Maria Callas
Switzerland	Italy
Trollope	Dickens
Atlanta	New Orleans
Caroline Kennedy Schlossburg	John F. Kennedy, Jr.
Lord Byron	Percy B. Shelley
Elizabeth Barrett	Robert Browning
Agatha Christie	Ngaio Marsh
Herbert von Karajan	Leonard Bernstein
Andrew Lloyd Webber	Stephen Sondheim
Susan Powter	Richard Simmons
Arthur Rubenstein	Glenn Gould
Placido Domingo	Luciano Pavarotti
Han Solo	Luke Skywalker
George Eliot	George Sand
Hamlet	Othello
Katharine Hepburn	Greta Garbo
Ethel Mertz	Lucy Ricardo
The Marriage of Figaro	*The Magic Flute*
cats	dogs
Matthew Arnold	Algernon Charles Swinburne
Queen Elizabeth II	Princess Margaret Rose

James Battersby on Jane Austen and the Eighteenth Century

James Battersby is a celebrated Johnsonian and eighteenth-century critic. He is the author of, among other books, Rational Praise and Natural Lamentation: Johnson, "Lycidas" and Principles of Criticism; Paradigms Regained: Pluralism and the Practice of Criticism; *and* Reason and the Nature of Texts.

NT: *Jane Austen is often incorrectly described as a Victorian novelist, but of course she was a product of the eighteenth century. What eighteenth-century contexts might help us understand her work?*

JB: Like most of the rivers of England, the range of Austen's interests was narrow and deep rather than broad and shallow. Also, I think it is useful to remember that the eighteenth century, like all centuries before and after it, is a highly fractionalized and factionalized period of history, comprised of many disparate and even conflicting ideas, tendencies, values, and commitments, and that Jane Austen's allegiances and affiliations, her preferences and prejudices place her squarely in but one section—arguably the most prominent and distinctive one—of the variegated carpet.

Socially and culturally, in her life and in her novels, Jane Austen takes up residence in the middle world of life, the world of small towns, rural hamlets, country homes, occupied by landed gentry and their relations, Anglican clergymen with modest livings and large families, the daughters and second and third sons of noble families, relatives of military and especially naval officers—the sorts of people who pay visits, go to balls and parties with one another, and spend part of each year at Brighton and especially Bath, where families of more and less distinction can intermingle, romances can be kindled, hopes formed and dashed, and hearts joined or broken.

This is not the world of tradesmen and laborers, of Industrial Revolution and exploitation, of Quakers, Anabaptists, and Methodists, of farmers (except an occasional tenant farmer like Robert Martin in *Emma*), of religious controversy and philosophical debate, of political wrangling, social reform, and military engagements, of terror, fear, and other manifestations of the sublime, and so on.

In short, it is the familiar world of eighteenth-century fiction and of the values and emphases of what used to be called the Augustan Age or of the Tory squirearchy, the world of reason, restraint, opposition to sentimentality, enthusiasm, and affectation

NT: *Do Austen's novels follow any particular eighteenth-century novel tradition?*

JB: The uninformatively brief, quite uncontroversial, utterly conventional, *and*, to my mind, indisputably correct answer to this question is yes, and that tradition is the mainline tradition, originating with Richardson and sustained by such successors as Fielding, Burney, Smollett, and Edgeworth.

The tradition in which Austen works might best be called the novel of moral action, in which the focus is on the initiation, development, complication, and resolution of situations of moral seriousness and perplexity. These are works in which complexity and resolution are based on moral character and psychological motivation, and in which the whole is covertly shaped and directed by an underlying authorial purpose. More immediately, Austen works in the part of this broad field that concerns the entanglements in intricacies of love, courtship, marriage, and the conditions of personal and domestic happiness, a field staked out by Richardson, Burney, and others and brought to a state of rich and productive cultivation by Austen.

NT: *The eighteenth century was a great age of satire. Are Austen's novels in this tradition?*

JB: Yes, most emphatically. Satire in Austen's works is various and pervasive, extending from burlesque to character evisceration to passing shots at local tics, gestures, practices of incidental and main characters.

Like Fielding, Austen is always alert to the ridiculous in action or sentiment, and like him, she knows that the true source of the ridiculous is affectation, which proceeds from either vanity (the relatively benign assumption of traits of which one is conspicuously deficient) or hypocrisy (the generally wicked concealment of one's true beliefs and motives). But it seems to me that Austen's satire owes as much to Swift, Johnson, Crabbe, and Cowper as to Fielding (of course, as far as satire is concerned, she seems to be to the manner born; there is an unmistakable strain of satire in her work that undoubtedly has progeny but no ancestors—that is, has imitators but no models).

NT: *Was Austen influenced by the great dramatists of the eighteenth century?*

JB: The Austen family had an abiding and durable interest in the theater, often entertaining one another with staged readings of favorite eighteenth-century plays, and among the most popular and, not so incidentally, the most congenial to Austen's own artistic spirit were those by Richard Brinsley Sheridan (principally, *The Rivals* and *The School for Scandal*) and Oliver Goldsmith (particularly *She Stoops to Conquer*). The authors who most interested and influenced her were also specialists in the depiction of character and motive.

NT: *As a student of Samuel Johnson's works, do you see any Johnsonian elements or attitudes in Jane Austen's work?*

JB: Definitely. Unfortunately nothing short of a book-length study would do justice to this question. But for brevity's sake, let me make a couple of remarks. As many readers know, Austen greatly admired Johnson, referring to him in her letters on several occasions as "dear Dr. Johnson." Also, some critics have seen in Mr. Knightley an exemplar of the principal values that she associated with Johnson: strength of mind, a capacity to make sharp distinctions, probity of character, refined sensibility, the sort of deep wisdom that comes from experience, and freedom from cant, superstition, and illusion. Everywhere in Austen's work it is apparent that she has drunk deep from the wells of Johnson's writings.

In sum, socially, culturally, artistically, Jane Austen is very much a product of the eighteenth century.

Georgian London

I n the course of the eighteenth century, as reformed agricultural practices drove much of the rural population from the land and into urban factories, England was transformed from an agrarian to an urban industrial society. The major cities swelled in population, and London, the national center in every respect, be-

London's Royal Academy of Art, 1787. Dogs were evidently welcome visitors to the academy in the late eighteenth century.

A. A. GILL ON THE GEORGIANS

*H*ow did they make all the furniture, all those tables and chairs and sideboards and stuff? When they were bored with ordinary furniture, they made gear that had no known or conceivable use: davenports, pembrokes, break-fronted side cabinets, secretaries, folding commodes, reading stands with concealed card tables and whatnots. "What you making, Jude?" "Dunno, it's just a sort of what not." They ran out of names before they ran out of furniture."

came increasingly central to the national identity. During the period of rapid growth from the mid-eighteenth century, the London Improvement Act of 1762 and later the metropolitan improvement undertaken by George IV transformed the West End of London (the seat of government) into a national showcase. Gas lighting, widened streets, and improved sewers, the redesign of Regent's Park and St. James's Park, and the construction of Regent Street and Trafalgar Square combined to make London a model city and a magnificent spectacle.

Nevertheless, the hordes of London poor were only hidden by the new Georgian facade, and the city remained what William Cobbett called the "great wen," a vast and bewildering accumulation of buildings and of people, pullulating in both prosperity and poverty. Both views of London are evident, if only in passing, in Austen's novels. In *Sense and Sensibility* it is the glittering, spectacular London, the manners and amusements that attract Mrs. Jennings to invite the Dashwood sisters to town. Elinor and Marianne unfortunately cannot enjoy the pleasures of London because of the latter's obsession with her lost love, Willoughby, and the former's concern for her sister. They later learn the harrowing story of Colonel Brandon's charge Eliza; the city can be a fierce and dangerous place for an unprotected girl. In *Pride and Prejudice* it is to the great mass of people, the anonymity of the crowd, that Wickham and Lydia flee in order to hide, for "where else," as Mr. Bennet asks, "can they be so well concealed?"

Jane Austen seemed to believe that country life is more wholesome than city life, in spite of the ample evidence that she savored her visits to London, where she stayed with her brother. Henry and his wife, Eliza, lived in fashionable neighborhoods, such as Sloane Square. Writing to Cassandra in 1796, she says: "I am once more in this scene of dissipation and vice, and I already begin to find my morals corrupted." Her jaunty tone does not, however, mean that she feels that London is not a dangerous place. She probably would have agreed with William Blake's idea that industrial London, with "each charter'd street" by the "charter'd Thames" had the "dark Satanic Mills" that pollute "England's green and pleasant Land." Austen admired Oliver Goldsmith's poem *The Deserted Village* (1770) and George Crabbe's *The Village* (1783) and *The Borough* (1810), all of which lament the rural poverty resulting from the industrialization of British society. The characters she most approves of, such as Fanny Price and Edmund Bertram, are "attached to country pleasures."

Harriet Walter on Fanny Dashwood

Harriet Walter played the role of Fanny Dashwood in the film Sense and Sensibility, directed by Ang Lee. She has delighted theater, film, television, and radio audiences with her versatility in roles as diverse as Ophelia, Hedda Gabler, and Harriet Vane in Lord Peter Wimsey. Recently she played Jane Austen's Lady Susan for BBC Radio. She is the author of Other People's Shoes: Thoughts on Acting.

Harriet Walter

NT: *Tell me something about how you prepared to play Fanny Dashwood?*

HW: Ang Lee, the director, circulated questionnaires to the actors. We had to determine some biographical facts about our characters. They could be invented or based on historical research. I think that helped enormously.

Ang Lee, being from Taiwan, was quite happy to confess his own ignorance of the English way of life in the nineteenth century. Some of his biographical questions for each character were "What time do you eat?"; "What time do you get up?"; "What is the first thing you do every day?"; "Compose a sort of autobiography based on where you were born, when you married," those sorts of things. It was great for the actors to do detailed homework about the period and to imagine themselves living in that period and to imagine a typical day in their lives. Then he asked things such as "What are your biggest fears?"; "Which other characters do you like, which don't you like?"; "What do you most dread, what do you most hope for?" Quite philosophical questions! He asked another question that was quite interesting: "If you were living in 1995, what do you think your character would be?" I decided that Fanny Dashwood would be a pushy theatrical agent.

NT: *What ideas did you have about Fanny's daily life and background?*

HW: It is very hard for a late-twentieth-century woman to imagine a life of such apparent leisure where you don't have much to think about except what you are going to wear, what ball you are going to go to, who has got more money than you have. They had such preoccupations because they had so little to take up their intelligence. Fanny was probably intelligent, but I don't know quite how intelligent. She would not have been particularly educated. I invented a whole story around her having to look after her father, who had been dying through most of her late teens, when she should have been out looking for a husband. Her mother, Mrs. Ferrars, was quite a gadabout and had left it to her daughter to have the responsibility of caring for the father. She was also older than her brothers, so the burden would have fallen on her. Her brothers would have been guaranteed a way of life and an income. Fanny needed to get married for that. So there was a source of bitterness for her. And if she was not happy, she wanted to make sure no one else was happy. That was really the foundation of the Fanny I played in the film.

For me the telling moment was when she's speaking to Mrs. Dashwood, looking out the window and watching Edward and Elinor walking down the path together, and she sees that their friendship is budding, so she puts Mrs. Dashwood in the picture as to how Edward would be cut off if he married someone like Elinor. Ang Lee helped me; he gave me a little reflective moment where I was watching them before the dialogue started, and you could see that Fanny had had a certain amount of pain, a certain amount of yearning that she had not had an affair like that.

Her need to control others is her compensation for what she has missed out of in life. Money becomes a big compensation for her for lust, emotional starvation, love really.

I think she was quite like her mother. She followed in those footsteps. I sense that Jane Austen is not compassionate toward those people. She wrote them when she was quite young, and she probably had very little sympathy for that type of attitude. I feel a certain amount of sympathy for someone whose only status is derived from how rich her father, her husband, her brother, or some male in her family is. Fanny focuses all kinds of attention on the males in her life because it is through them that she gets self-respect. She does not get love, so the next best thing is dressing beautifully and waltzing around being grand because she thinks that way she will be somebody.

I read the book two or three times. I read Emma Thompson's script several times to see where they differed. The main difference with Fanny Dashwood is that she does not have a child in the film.

If I were playing the character straight from the book, I would have justified, if that is the right word, a lot of Fanny's behavior on the grounds that she herself justified it in terms of doing things for the good of her child. I did not have that excuse in the movie, so it appeared as though I was a terrible character basically. But there are such people, and you don't have to explain them if the story does not need it.

NT: *I loved the moment of hysteria you depicted when Fanny realizes that Lucy Steele thinks she can marry one of her brothers.*

HW: Yes. We worked on that scene. Emma had simply said to me that Fanny is doing some embroidery or some equally useless task. When I went for the costume fitting for that scene, we looked at all these costumes. At the time the film was set there was a big fashion for hats with feathers. You could pay eight pounds for an ostrich feather, which is quite a bit of money. I thought it would be good if instead of just doing embroidery, Fanny is trying to make a fan out of feathers. The costume and props department provided a wonderful sack of feathers. Of course, when we broke into a fight and I pinched and twisted Lucy Steele's nose, the feathers spontaneously flew into the air. It was like the proverbial hen fight, which was a happy coincidence.

I was really grateful that Ang Lee did not overdo Fanny and put her on camera too much because then it would not have been funny. It was delicate, his handling of the character. She came in just at the right moments for just the right length of time. The director can make or break your performance this way.

Fanny Dashwood and King Lear's Daughters

Some readers think that Elinor and Marianne are more interesting than their eventual spouses, that they have, to use the phrase of William Congreve's witty heroine Mrs. Millamant of *The Way of the World,* "dwindled into a wife." *Sense and Sensibility* does in fact have a strong feeling of dwindling, a decrease of youthful joy and spirits, that contrasts with the sense of an expanding world in Austen's other novels.

The novel opens with the death of Mr. Dashwood and the removal of his wife and three daughters from their large Sussex estate, Norland, to the small Barton cottage in Devonshire. In Chapter 1 Mr. Dashwood's heir, John Dashwood, his son from a previous marriage, promises his dying father that he will do "everything in his power" to make the female Dashwoods comfortable. Austen introduces him with lukewarm praise couched in terms of negativity and ambiguity: "He was not an ill-disposed young man, unless to be rather cold hearted and rather selfish, is to be ill-disposed." John Dashwood, at the beginning of Chapter 2, has resolved to give his sisters a thousand pounds apiece. His wife, Fanny, argues him down with brilliantly comic rationales: First she proposes giving five hundred pounds to each sister, next a "present of fifty pounds now and then," followed by the idea that "presents of fish and game," might suffice until finally she concludes: "They will live so cheap! Their housekeeping will be nothing at all. They will have no carriage, no horses and hardly any servants; they will keep no company, and can have no expences of any kind. . . . They will be much more able to give *you* something." Her chipping away at any legacy for the Dashwood sisters resembles the mathematical reduction and cold ratiocination that Goneril and Regan apply to King Lear's knights. Roger Gard points out that the *logic* of John and Fanny is "nearly identical" to that of Goneril and Regan:

> REGAN: I look'd not for you yet, nor am provided
>   For your fit welcome. . . .
>   fifty followers?
> Is it not well? What should you need of more? . . .
>   I entreat you
> To bring but five-and-twenty: to no more
> Will I give place or notice. . . .
>
> LEAR: (to Goneril) . . . I'll go with thee:
> Thy fifty yet doth double five-and-twenty,
> And thou art twice her love.
>
> GONERIL: Hear me, my lord.
> What need you five and twenty, ten, or five?
> To follow in a house where twice so many
> Have a command to tend you?
>
> REGAN: What need one?
>   [II, iv, 236–269]

Like King Lear, the Dashwood sisters lose place and possessions. Later in the book they lose, temporarily, their hopes for love. Of course Barton Cottage is not the tempestuous heath of prehistoric Britain, and the Dashwood women are not left cold and homeless like King Lear. But it is as expedient for John and Fanny Dashwood to get rid of them as it is for Lear's wicked daughters to dispose of him. In deepest Devon the Dashwood sisters will not be thrown into company with Fanny's brothers, for whom she entertains hopes of elegant, rich wives, and they will leave the Norland plate and china and linen for Fanny and John to keep.

❧ QUIZ: WHO SAID THAT? ❧
❧ GREAT LINES FROM JANE AUSTEN'S NOVELS ❧

Name the speaker and the novel from which each quotation is culled.

1. "A woman of seven and twenty can never hope to inspire affection again."

2. "A whole day's tête-à-tête between two women can never end without a quarrel."

3. "We all have a better guide in ourselves, if we would attend to it, than any other person can be."

4. "Songs and proverbs all talk of woman's fickleness. But perhaps you will say, these were all written by men."

5. "I have the greatest dislike to the idea of being overtrimmed—quite a horror of finery. I must put on a few ornaments *now,* because it is expected of me. A bride, you know, must appear like a bride, but my natural taste is all for simplicity."

6. "A sick chamber may often furnish the worth of volumes."

7. "Every savage can dance."

8. "My comfort is, I am sure Jane will die of a broken heart, and then he will be sorry for what he has done."

9. "It is better to know as little as possible of the defects of the person with whom you are to pass your life."

10. "An egg boiled very soft is not unwholesome."

11. "I was therefore entered at Oxford and have been properly idle ever since."

12. "The yeomanry are precisely the order of people with whom I feel I can have nothing to do. A degree or two lower, and a creditable appearance might interest me."

13. "One has not great hopes from Birmingham. I always say there is something direful in the sound."

14. "A man is in greater danger in the navy of being insulted by the rise of one whose father, his father might have disdained to speak to."

15. "I sometimes amuse myself with suggesting and arranging such little elegant compliments as may be adapted to ordinary occasions; I always wish to give them as unstudied an air as possible."

16. "The sooner every party breaks up, the better."

17. "To be mistress of French, Italian, German, Music, Singing, Drawing, etc., will gain a woman some applause, but will not add one lover to her list."

18. "Only give me a carte-blanche.—I am Lady Patroness, you know."

19. "Oh! dear! one never thinks of married men's being beaux—they have something else to do."

20. "You need not tell her so, but I thought her dress hideous the other night. I used to think she had some taste in dress, but I was ashamed

of her at the concert. Something so formal and arrangé in her air! and she sits so upright! My best love, of course."

21. "There is not one in a hundred of either sex, who is not taken in when they marry."

22. "There is not the hundredth part of the wine consumed in this kingdom, that there ought to be. Our foggy climate wants help."

23. "I am something like the famous Doge at the court of Lewis XIV; and may declare that I see no wonder in the shrubbery equal to seeing myself in it."

Elinor Dashwood: Governor of Her Own Feelings

Jane Austen introduces Elinor Dashwood in the first chapter of *Sense and Sensibility* with the highest accolades. None of Austen's other heroines is given the author's full approbation so early in the novel:

> Elinor, this eldest daughter whose advice was so effectual, possessed a strength of understanding, and coolness of judgment, which qualified her, though only nineteen, to be the counsellor of her mother, and enabled her frequently to counteract, to the advantage of them all, that eagerness of mind in Mrs. Dashwood which must generally have led to imprudence. She had an excellent heart;—her disposition was affectionate, and her feelings were strong; *but she knew how to govern them* [author's italics].

Throughout the novel Elinor suffers as much as anyone; she hardly has a stress-free moment. But she does not parade her suffering. When her father dies, Elinor sees that Mrs. Dashwood and Marianne are overpowered by agonies of grief and that they are "seeking increase of wretchedness." In spite of her own "affliction," Elinor is a model of patience, perseverance, and fortitude, and she spends the novel politely suffering through weary social obligations and telling the necessary "white lies" that good manners enforce on her. She graciously tolerates company that Marianne considers very inferior: Mrs. Jennings, Lady Middleton, Mr. and Mrs. Palmer, the Steele sisters.

When Lucy Steele with her "little sharp eyes" reveals her secret engagement to Edward, Elinor speaks to her with "a composure of voice, under which was concealed an emotion and distress beyond anything she had ever felt before. She was mortified, shocked, confounded." Elinor is not subject to hysterical effusions, but she feels quite as deeply as Marianne, although her sister often accuses her of being cold-hearted. Marianne tweaks Elinor by saying: "I thought our judgments were given us merely to be subservient to those of our neighbours. This has always been your doctrine, I am sure." Elinor responds accurately: "No, Marianne, never. My doctrine has never aimed at the subjection of the understanding. . . . I am guilty, I confess, of having often wished you to treat our acquaintance in general with greater attention; but when have I advised you to adopt their sentiments or conform to their judgment in serious matters?" Marianne, significantly, does not answer her.

Emma Thompson, as Elinor Dashwood in her own screen adaptation of Sense and Sensibility

Rebecca Dickson, who teaches at the University of Colorado, asserts unconditionally that "Elinor is one of my role models." Dickson respects the way that Elinor "understands [that] her mother and sisters need a respite from emotional scenes, so she keeps her troubles to herself." Dickson cites the passage where Austen describes Elinor's relief at Marianne's recovery:

> Elinor could not be cheerful. Her joy was of a different kind, and led to anything rather than to gaiety. Marianne restored to life, health, friends, and to her doting mother, was an idea to fill her heart with sensations of exquisite comfort, and expand it in fervent gratitude;—but it led to no outward demonstrations of joy, nor words, no smiles. All within Elinor's breast was satisfaction, silent and strong. . . .

Dickson further comments: "Elinor does not allow her emotions to bounce between despair and cheerfulness in a matter of moments. . . . [S]he handles her emotions carefully. . . . [T]his is a mature, capable woman."

When Thomas, the Dashwoods' "man-servant," reports that Mr. Ferrars is married, Marianne is the one who gave "a violent start . . . and fell back in her chair in hysterics." Elinor's very real suffering must be subordinate to Marianne's more dramatic response. The greatest emotional relief to Elinor of course is the discovery that Edward is not married to Lucy. She bursts into "tears of joy" but only after leaving the room so that her emotions will be private.

Elinor is a wonderful model of a strong, capable woman. Her emotions are not repressed or suppressed. They are "governed," and that control gives her the kind of power and autonomy that Marianne comes to respect.

The Madness of Marianne

Marianne Dashwood is the only major character in Austen's novels who goes nearly mad for the sake of love. She comes dangerously close to succumbing to the fate of Sophia in *Love and Freindship,* who dies from too much fainting on wet grass, which results in a "galloping Consumption." Marianne Dashwood too is attracted to wet grass (as well as dry leaves). In contrast, when Elinor learns the devastating news that her beloved Edward is apparently engaged to Lucy Steele, she feels in "no danger of an hysterical fit, or a swoon." Elinor never cries publicly, whereas Marianne has a tendency to rush from the room in tears. After Willoughby has deserted her, she has trouble eating, sleeping, talking. She tells Elinor that "misery such as mine has no pride. . . . I must feel—I must be wretched." The repetition must suggest that Marianne is in some ways acting the part of the heroine of sensibility. She cannot govern her emotions as her sister can, because the novels and poetry of sentimentality and sensibility have told her that in her circumstances, she must succumb: "Marianne would have thought herself very inexcusable had she been able to sleep at all the first night after parting from Willoughby. She would have been ashamed to look her family in the face the next morning, had she not risen from her bed in more need of repose than when she lay down in it." These sentences reflect Marianne's self-consciousness of her role as abandoned heroine. The following sentences, however, tell the reader that Marianne is in fact sincere in her distress: "But the feelings which made such composure a disgrace, left her in no danger of incurring it. She was awake the whole night, and she wept the greatest part of it. She got up with an headache, was unable to talk, and unwilling to take any nourishment; giving pain every moment to her mother and sisters, and forbidding all attempt at consolation from either. Her sensibility was potent enough!"

Marianne's favorite writers have taught her that unrequited love leads to madness and death. William Cowper's character Crazy Kate, from *The Task* (1785),

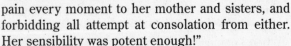

was a servant girl obsessed with a lover who had abandoned her. Crazy Kate inspired imitations in poetry and prose, and she was depicted in well-known paintings of the period, much as Tennyson's cursed Lady of Shalott inspired several nineteenth-century painters. The quintessential novel of sensibility, Henry Mackenzie's *The Man of Feeling* (1771), features a madwoman who has been driven insane by the intensity of her melancholy about a lost love. Her plight inspires tears in those who see her.

Austen, however, does not sentimentalize Marianne's plunge toward death. Instead she shows us what hardship and anxiety Marianne's illness incurs in her family and in all who know her. Marianne herself "knew not that she had been the means of sending the owners of Cleveland away, in about seven days from the time of their arrival. It gave her no surprise that she saw nothing of Mrs. Palmer; and as it gave her likewise no concern, she never mentioned her name." There is no romance and glamour in the nights that a devastated Elinor sits up with her apparently dying sister. Ultimately "reflection" with "calm and sober judgment" forces Marianne to acknowledge the danger of her behavior. She believes that her own conduct has been abhorrent. Elinor checks her, however, by asking: "Do you compare your conduct with [Willoughby's]?" Marianne replies: "No. I compare it with what it ought to have been; I compare it with yours." Marianne has learned that she must emulate Elinor, that "my feelings shall be governed."

Anne Stevenson, the British poet, has described Austen's novels as "Six little circles of hell with attendant humours," in response to those who would dismiss them as "novels of manners" or "hymenal theology."

Austen goes on to comment: "Marianne Dashwood was born to an extraordinary fate. She was born to discover the falsehood of her own opinions, and to counteract, by her conduct, her most favourite maxims. She was born to overcome an affliction formed so late in life as at seventeen, and with no sentiment superior to strong esteem and lively friendship, voluntarily to give her hand to another!" This rhetoric is a mix of slyness and sincerity, very typical of Austen's commentary. By saying that Marianne was born to an "extraordinary fate," she mocks the hyperbole of the language of sentiment. On the other hand, to discover the falsehood of one's opinions is indeed an extraordinary fate in a world in which this level of self-knowledge is rare.

Many readers suggest that Austen is punishing Marianne by putting her into a marriage that is based on "strong esteem" and "lively friendship," not on romance and passion. Esteem and lively friendship, however, are so frequently Austen's basis for love that readers might also consider that Marianne and Colonel Brandon will follow the path to love of Emma and Mr. Knightley or Fanny Price and Edmund Bertram.

Cowper and Crabbe

William Cowper (1731–1800) was Jane Austen's favorite "moral writer" in verse, according to the "Biographical Notice" that Henry Austen prepared as a preface to *Northanger Abbey*. His poetry is alluded to in *Sense and Sensibility, Mansfield Park, Emma,* and *Sanditon* and in several of Austen's letters. Cowper was afflicted with suicidal depressions and religious mania. He moved to Olney to be near a spiritual adviser, a powerful evangelical divine, the Reverend John Newton, who had once been a blasphemous, alcoholic sailor. Cowper's most famous works include the evangelical *Olney Hymns* ("God moves in a mysterious way" and "Oh! For a closer walk with God!") and *The Task,* which begins in the mock-epic mode with "I sing the Sofa." The purpose of *The Task,* according to Cowper, was to "discountenance the modern enthusiasm after a London life, and to recommend rural ease and leisure as friendly to the cause of piety and virtue." He believed that "God made the country and man made the town." His belief in the redeeming nature of country life is echoed by Marianne Dashwood in *Sense and Sensibility* and by Jane Austen's settings in general. In all of Austen's novels, only two families live more or less permanently in town, the Gardiners in *Pride and Prejudice* and Isabella and John Knightley in *Emma*.

One of the Austen family jokes was that Jane wanted to marry the poet George Crabbe (1754–1832). She told her nieces that if she ever "married at all, she could fancy being Mrs. Crabbe," and she looked for him when she went to the theater in London. When the actual Mrs. Crabbe died, she joked to Cassandra that "I will comfort *him* as well as I can, but I do not undertake to be good to her children. She had better not leave any." Austen's choice of George Crabbe as a favorite may be a reflection of her lack of sympathy for the Romantic poets, who were different in spirit and tone from the clergyman Crabbe, although he shared their fondness for opium. Crabbe, however, did not have high flights of fanciful poetry or romantic effusions. Most of his work is grimly realistic, but disillusioned and witty at the same time, a clue to why he appealed so much to Austen. Francis Jeffrey, editor of the important *Edinburgh Review,* wrote that Crabbe was one of "the most original, nervous, and pathetic poets of the present century." His best-known works include *The Village, The Parish Register,* and *The Borough,* which includes the poem about Peter Grimes that inspired Benjamin Britten to write his opera of the same name. Fanny Price and Edmund Bertram share a fondness for Crabbe in *Mansfield Park*. Indeed, Austen borrowed the name Fanny Price from the works of George Crabbe.

Lucy Steele

L ucy knows that the art of flattery will get her far in society. Indeed, it gets her married to an heir. Readers of *Sense and Sensibility* are treated to her shameless blandishments to Lady Middleton and her obnoxious children. Lucy knows when to be a toady and to court and fawn on the Ferrars family. All the time affecting that she is a simple girl deeply in love, Lucy is calculating her best chances for advancement. She has an instinctive knowledge that the Dashwood sisters will despise her for groveling before Lady Middleton, so she has to modify her fulsomeness in front of them. She has an inbuilt barometer that tells her how far she can go with her manipulative flatterings. Lucy would never have prematurely told Fanny Dashwood the truth about her engagement with Edward, but her older sister, Nancy, who is, according to Mrs. Jennings, "a well-meaning creature, but no conjurer," ruins the plot to win over Edward's sister by spilling the beans. Lucy herself, who is quite a conjurer, manages to snare the affections of Robert "The Rattle" Ferrars, once he has received Edward's portion of the family money.

Throughout most of the novel Lucy knowingly plays a cunning mental game of chess with Elinor, trying to see if she can checkmate Elinor into any important revelations. Elinor, despite her misery, guards herself carefully and does not openly concede any points to Lucy.

Austen depicts Lucy as being clever in the worldly sense of finding a wealthy husband and in her ability to judge the extent to which she can flatter and manipulate people. She has not, however, used her brain to acquire some of the basic principles of English grammar, indicating that she does little reading and has not pursued her own education at all. Lucy Steele has bigger quarries to hunt than the pages of English grammar books!

Sexy Men

T he fact that John Willoughby is the only sexy man in *Sense and Sensibility* has dismayed some readers. Most of the heroes in the novels are described succulently. But here is our first glimpse of Elinor's mate: "Edward Ferrars was not recommended to their good opinions by any peculiar graces of person or address. He was not handsome, and his manners required intimacy to make them pleasing." Edward himself speaks of his own "natural awkwardness." He thinks: "I must have been intended by nature to be fond of low company, I am so little at my ease among strangers of gentility." Perhaps that is his rueful reflection on his engagement to Lucy Steele. He goes on to admit to having an inferiority complex and is often "silent and dull." Elinor's love for Edward testifies to her ability to see beneath the surface of a dull and diffident man. Austen has perhaps made Edward so very unglamorous in order to accentuate Elinor's fine qualities of discernment.

Marianne's future husband is first introduced to us as "silent and grave. His appearance however was not unpleasing, in spite of his being in the opinion of Marianne and Margaret an absolute old bachelor, for he was on the wrong side of five and thirty; but though his face was not handsome his countenance was sensible, and his address was particularly gentlemanlike." Willoughby, the cad, however, causes immediate "wonder" and "admiration" in the eyes of Elinor and Mrs. Dashwood and not merely because he is carrying Marianne, who has twisted her ankle. His manners are "so frank and so graceful"; his person is "uncommonly handsome" and receives "additional charms from his voice and expression." After he leaves, his "manly beauty and more than common gracefulness were instantly the theme of general admiration" among the Dashwood women. Marianne's emotions are rapidly enslaved by this paragon of beauty, and Mrs. Dashwood too seems more than a little titillated by his charms.

Even the circumspect Elinor responds almost erotically to Willoughby when he comes, drunk, to Cleveland after hearing of Marianne's serious illness. His expostulations engage her sympathy, and their conversation is the longest and the most emotionally laden in the entire novel. During his interview with Elinor, she blushes, she softens, and she has to invoke her own pools of prudence: "Elinor's heart, which had undergone many changes in the course of this extraordinary conversation, was now softened again;—yet she felt it her duty to check such ideas in her companion." Elinor finally, after hearing out Willoughby's lengthy (and self-centered) apologia, feels "compassionate emotion." Her rational side blames "the world" and a too early "independence" for making Willoughby "extravagant and vain." She largely acquits him of the responsibility for his own villainous behavior and tells him that "she forgave, pitied, wished him well—was even interested in his happiness."

Willoughby's extravagant good looks and his verbal effusions are another indication of the dangers of excess sensibility. He is a prototype of the Byronic hero who

Colin Keith-Johnston, 1935, plays a haughty, albeit overdressed, Darcy.

flaunts his sexuality and can influence even so canny a character as Elinor. He is mad, bad, and dangerous to know. After we know his history and see how he can influence even the careful Elinor, the modesty and reserve of Edward Ferrars and Colonel Brandon seem not merely safe but desirable.

Not all of Austen's lovers are as diffident as the heroes of *Sense and Sensibility*. Darcy's love for Elizabeth Bennet is described as bitter, warm, and violent, and Frederick Wentworth has to overcome much anger before he will renew his addresses to Anne Elliot in *Persuasion*. The endings of most of the novels explicitly or implicitly speak of marriage as the perfect felicity of the couple. Though we cannot sincerely doubt the felicity of the Dashwood girls' matches, the ending of *Sense and Sensibility* refers to the great happiness that Elinor and Marianne have in "living almost within sight of each other."

EMMA THOMPSON ON THE MEN OF *SENSE AND SENSIBILITY*

Brandon is, I suppose, the real hero of this piece but he has to grow on the audience as he grows on Marianne. Making the male characters effective was one of the biggest problems. In the novel, Edward and Brandon are quite shadowy and absent for long periods. We had to work hard to keep them present even when they're offscreen. Willoughby is really the only male who springs out in three dimensions (a precursor to her other charm merchants, Frank Churchill in *Emma,* Wickham in *Pride and Prejudice,* and Henry Crawford in *Mansfield Park*).

Weddings

Weddings were generally much simpler two hundred years ago. Long engagements usually occurred only when there was a financial difficulty to be worked out; the four-year secret engagement between Lucy Steele and Edward Ferrars is not at all typical. In *Emma,* for example, Mr. Elton leaves Highbury right after Christmas and meets, marries, honeymoons, and ensconces his bride at the vicarage by mid-March. Most weddings were small, and only members of the immediate family were in attendance. Mrs. Elton, always a voice of vulgarity, laments that Emma Woodhouse's wedding boasted "very little white satin, very few lace veils; a most pitiful business."

Caroline Austen, one of the author's nieces, described the wedding of her half sister Anna:

The wedding of Anna . . . to Benjamin Lefroy [was] between nine and ten on a cold November morning, the bridal party consisting of the couples' immediate families departed from the bride's home for the church—the ladies in carriages, and the gentlemen on foot. The groom's father, a clergyman, read the service to the small congregation, and James Austen gave his daughter away. The party then returned to the bride's home for breakfast. The breakfast was such as best breakfasts then were: some variety of bread, hot rolls, buttered toast, tongue or ham and eggs. The addition of chocolate at one end of the table, and the wedding cake in the middle, marked the speciality of the day. Soon after breakfast the bride and groom departed for their home in Hendon. . . . In the evening the servants had punch and cake.

There are several letters from Jane to Cassandra at the time of Anna's wedding, and it is clear from their contents that the wedding itself was not important to Anna's aunts, uncles, and grandmother. In one letter Jane jokingly fantasizes about meeting Lefroy's aunt and saying, "I am afraid the young Man has some of your Family Madness—& though there often appears to be something of Madness in Anna too, I think she inherits more of it from her Mother's family than from ours—"

Austen's novels go into little detail about weddings. Perhaps she thought that weddings were ostentatious and vulgar. After all, the tasteless Lydia Ben-

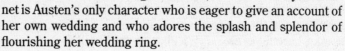

net is Austen's only character who is eager to give an account of her own wedding and who adores the splash and splendor of flourishing her wedding ring.

Pride and Prejudice

*For what do we live, but to make sport for our neighbors,
and laugh at them in our turn?*
—Mr. Bennet

Pride and Prejudice is a sparkling gem, an effervescent glass of Moët et Chandon champagne, a gourmet's banquet of savories, succulents, sweetmeats, and some julienned crudités to add a salubrious touch to the bill of fare. The bare bones of the material may not promise scintillation—a country family must find husbands for five daughters—but Austen's remarkable gift for characterization beguiles the reader. Elizabeth Bennet, the second of the pentarchy of daughters, is arguably the most beloved character in any English novel. Her wit and intelligence, as well as her ability to admit her mistakes and to stand up to the forces of tyranny, make her irresistible. Although never smug, she prides herself on her ability to sniff out hypocrisy. Much of the plot is devoted to Elizabeth's realization that she has in fact made mistakes and her consequent determination to know herself clearly and truly. But Elizabeth is not the only memorable character. Her unforgettable mother, determined to find husbands for the five Bennet daughters, is vulgar, pushy, and ultimately, successful. By the end of the novel only two of the girls remain unwed.

As the novel begins, Jane, the eldest daughter, soon falls in love with Mr. Bingley, a delightful and delightfully wealthy young man. Elizabeth is drawn to

PRIDE &
PREJUDICE

JANE AUSTEN'S CELEBRATED NOVEL
Dramatized by HELEN JEROME
Directed by ROBERT SINCLAIR
Scenery and Costumes designed by JO MIELZINER
AS PLAYED ENTIRE SEASON IN NEW YORK

A highly stylized image of Elizabeth Bennet and Mr. Darcy from the Playbill cover of the 1935 production of Pride and Prejudice

the proud Darcy, in spite of a most unpropitious meeting where he snubs her at a ball. Darcy in turn resists his attraction to Elizabeth and tries to prevent his friend Bingley from associating with Jane. He thinks that the Bennet family is too common. Elizabeth is further disgusted with Darcy because she believes that he has abused Wickham. When Elizabeth discovers that Darcy has interfered with Jane's happiness, she roundly rejects his offer of marriage. Darcy writes her a long letter in which he reveals his qualms about the Bennet family and the truth about Wickham's dastardly behavior. Elizabeth begins to respond to the sexiness of Darcy's aloof posture. Darcy has the traditional appeal of the Gothic hero: He is tall, dark, and handsome, traits that in the Gothic novel signify that tormented emotions roil underneath a haughty facade. Darcy's emotions, however, are not tormented; he just needs to overcome a certain prejudice that is neither preternatural nor supernatural. He is exactly the type to inflame a young woman, but happily he is not harboring grave secrets or blood-drinking propensities. When Wickham runs away with the young Lydia, Darcy tracks down the errant couple and pays all of Wickham's debts in order to secure a marriage that will save Lydia from disgrace. This good deed, along with Elizabeth's visit to Darcy's home, Pemberley, where she learns only good of him, persuades her that she does indeed love Darcy. When Darcy and Bingley return to the vicinity, they propose to the two older Bennet sisters and are accepted with joy.

The Famous First Sentence

The opening sentence of *Pride and Prejudice* is second only to "Call me Ishmael," among the best-known openings in all literature: "It is a truth universally acknowledged, that a single man in possession of a good fortune, must be in want of a wife." Are any truths universally acknowledged? Jane Austen almost certainly agreed with William Blake that "to generalize is to be an idiot." When she speaks of the "truth universally acknowledged," what she is doing is making a compact with her reader. It is evident to the discerning reader by the end of the first brief chapter that the only "truth" established is that Mrs. Bennet believes single women need wealthy husbands and that it suits her to believe the reverse. Her "truth" is "wishful thinking," and the truth that the narrator and the reader soon establish between themselves is that we can articulate Mrs. Bennet's desires more honestly than she can.

The Publication History of *Pride and Prejudice*

When Austen was twenty-one and had completed *First Impressions*, the original title of *Pride and Prejudice,* her supportive father was delighted, as he had been by her juvenilia. He wrote a letter to Cadell & Davies, a major publishing company in London:

> SIRS
>
> I have in my possession a Manuscript Novel, comprised in three Vols. about the length of Miss Burney's Evelina. As I am well aware of what consequence it is that a work of this sort should make its first appearance under a respectable name I apply to you. Shall be much obliged therefore if you will inform me whether you chuse to be concerned in it; what will be the expense of publishing at the Author's risk; & what you will advance for the Property of it, if on a perusal it is approved of?

Should your answer give me encouragement I will send you the work.

I am, Sirs, Yr. obt. hble. Sevt:

GEO AUSTEN

Steventon near Overton
Hants
1st Novr. 1797

Inscribed on the letter is the legend "declined by Return of Post," which must have been a great disappointment to Jane and her family. However, after the success of *Sense and Sensibility* in 1811, Austen was able to sell *Pride and Prejudice*, revised from its earlier form as *First Impressions*, to Egerton for 110 pounds. The success of the novel was considerable enough that Egerton published a second edition along with a second edition of *Sense and Sensibility*, and Austen was able to write to her brother Frank that she had earned 250 pounds—"which only makes me long for more."

When the book was published, Jane wrote to Cassandra on January 29, 1813:

I want to tell you that I have got my own darling child from London. . . . Miss Benn dined with us on the very day of the books coming & in the evening we set fairly at it, and read half the first vol. to her, prefacing that having intelligence from Henry that such a work would soon appear, we had desired him to send it whenever it came out, and I believe it passed with her unsuspected. She was amused, poor soul! *That* she could not help, you know, with two people to lead the way, but she really does seem to admire Elizabeth. I must confess that I think her as delightful a creature as ever appeared in print, and how I shall be able to tolerate those who do not like *her* at least I do not know. There are a few typical errors; and a "said he," or a "said she," would sometimes make the dialogue more immediately clear, but

> *I do not write for such dull elves*
> *As have not a great deal of ingenuity themselves.*
> [Scott, *Marmion* (1808) 6.38]

The second volume is shorter than I could wish, but the difference is not so much in reality as in look, there being a larger proportion of narrative in that part. I have lop't and crop't so successfully, however, that I imagine it must be rather shorter than S & S. altogether. . . . .

Certainly *Pride and Prejudice* was Austen's first immediately successful novel, and she lived to see it go into more than one edition and to be translated into French.

Primogeniture and Entailment

Laws and custom protected landed estates by prohibiting landowners from dividing their holdings among their children. Primogeniture designated the eldest son as heir to the entire estate, including the land. Subsequent sons were lucky to inherit some money, if the estate had been well maintained. Most younger sons had to find a profession, and the ranks of the clergy were swollen with them. Entailment, along with primogeniture, was the legal way the British aristocracy could maintain its great estates through the generations. An entailed estate was an estate tied up so that its inhabitants, such as the Bennets at Longbourn, would not have rights to sell, mortgage, or dispose of it in any other way than the entailment dictated. Because these laws with few exceptions did not permit female children or their children of either sex to inherit, sometimes a distant cousin would inherit the estate, and any title that might accompany it. Because the Bennets have no sons, Mr. Collins, a cousin, has the rights to the entailment, a critical element of the plot of *Pride and Prejudice* and an additional motivation for the Bennets to hope that their daughters would marry.

Accomplishments and Eligibility

A woman especially, if she have the misfortune of knowing any thing, should conceal it as well as she can.
—*NORTHANGER ABBEY*

In Austen's day young girls were already being trained in the modest "accomplishments" that were to define middle-class femininity for most of the nineteenth century; the highest standards were to be expected only by such arrogant snobs as Miss Bingley from *Pride and Prejudice:*

No one can be really esteemed accomplished, who does not greatly surpass what is usually met with. A woman must have a thorough knowledge of music, singing, drawing, dancing and the modern languages, to de-

serve the word, and besides this, she must possess a certain something in her air and a manner of walking, the tone of her voice, her address and expressions, or the word will be but half deserved.

Elizabeth Bennet's incredulity about the existence of such paragons more closely approximates the actual expectations of female graces. Accomplished girls were expected to learn music, dance, drawing, all sorts of needlework, and perhaps a smattering of foreign languages, but they did not need to overdo. Sufficient accomplishment in music would be to sing and to play the piano "a little," "such as would have been / As quite impossible in Johnson's day / As still it might be wished" as Elizabeth Barrett Browning's Aurora Leigh later says. Elizabeth Bennet charms the savage breast of Darcy as he turns pages of music for her, just as half a century later Jane Eyre calms the still more savage breast of Mr. Rochester. As for drawings and other crafts, the expectations of Aurora Leigh's aunt at mid-century (allowing for new fashions in dance) were already the expectations in Austen's world at the turn of the century:

Celia Johnson, prim and demure, in a stage version of Pride and Prejudice

I drew . . . costumes
From French engravings, nereids neatly draped
(With smirks of simmering godship): I washed in
Landscapes from nature (rather say, washed out).
I danced the polka and Cellarius,
Spun glass, stuffed birds, and modelled flowers in wax,
Because she liked accomplishments in girls.

More important than such superficial accomplishments was everyday conduct. A girl must learn "general missionariness," or "angelic reach / of virtue" to be fully eligible for marriage. In fact, such virtue seems always to be inborn in such Austen heroines as Jane Bennet or Anne Elliot, but it was supposedly taught in the conduct books of the day, particularly in such works (ludicrous to the modern eye) as Fordyce's *Sermons,* which the absurd Mr. Collins fruitlessly attempts to read to the wayward younger sisters of Jane and Elizabeth Bennet. Ludicrous as the conduct manuals of the eighteenth and nineteenth centuries must seem to us, they must be understood if we are to appreciate the extent to which Jane Bennet, Anne Elliot, Fanny Price, and others are exemplars of female virtue and propriety. The eligibility of a bachelor, on the other hand, might tangentially involve his propriety of conduct but was much more emphatically centered on the value of his estate.

Veronica Leahy
on Conduct Literature

*I*n *Jane Austen's time there was no shortage of guides to female conduct, both written guides such as conduct manuals and living paradigms such as clerics. Austen characteristically makes fun of such guidance, as when she parodies both curates and conduct books by having the ludicrous Mr. Collins read to the bored Bennet girls from Fordyce's* Sermons. *The absurd pomposity of such bellwethers as Mr. Collins and the absurdly comical (to modern ears) advice of the conduct literature that Austen frequently parodied are the topic of Veronica Leahy's dissertation.*

A native of England, Veronica Webb Leahy received M.A. and Ph.D. degrees at Ohio State University in Columbus, Ohio. She is currently the chair of the English Department at the Columbus School for Girls.

NT: *Could you describe conduct books?*

VL: The conduct books that I researched and wrote about in my dissertation were the eighteenth-century equivalent of today's self-help books. They were texts addressed to middle-class women, and they offered advice on the proper education, manners, and behavior for young women, the ultimate goal being to attract, marry, and please men. These books were primarily written by men, but a few women also essayed conduct literature.

NT: *Does Jane Austen's characterization of good conduct draw on this literature? Are her characters guided by conduct books?*

VL: Anyone who has ever read Jane Austen will be aware that she is concerned with good conduct in her novels. Almost all her heroines are in need of education or reformation in some way before they can achieve the brass—or gold—ring. Her characters, however, are guided more by their own good sense, by experience, and/or by loving mentors than by conduct literature.

One of the underlying assumptions in most of the conduct literature is that women are naturally intellectually (and probably morally) inferior to men and that their educations should therefore be limited to the things that women should know in order to be pleasing wives, feminine accomplishments like music, drawing, dance, and the like. Conduct book writers advise limiting the experiences of young women and largely confining them to the domestic hearth.

Jane Austen's heroines all learn from direct experience, and most of them demonstrate that they are rational beings, capable of drawing their own conclusions when they are given the facts of a situation. Take Elizabeth Bennet, for example, after she has read Darcy's letter in the climactic scene of *Pride and Prejudice*. Despite her prejudices, for two hours she weighs circumstances, deliberates on the probabilities of each statement, reconsiders events, and ultimately changes her mind about Wickham and Darcy. Most of the conduct book writers would have considered women incapable of that kind of intellectual exercise.

NT: *Doesn't Austen mention a conduct book in one of her novels?*

ANNABELLA MILBANKE (LATER LADY BYRON) ON *PRIDE AND PREJUDICE*

I have finished the Novel called *Pride and Prejudice,* which I think a very superior work. It depends not on any of the common resources of novel writers, no drownings, no conflagrations, nor runaway horses, nor lap-dogs and parrots, nor chambermaids and milliners, nor rencontres and disguises. I really think it is the *most probable* I have ever read. It is not a crying book, but the interest is very strong, especially for Mr. Darcy. The characters which are not amiable are diverting, and all of them are consistently supported. May, 1813.

VL: In *Pride and Prejudice* one of Austen's most foolish characters, Mr. Collins, attempts to read Fordyce's *Sermons* to the Bennet family and is rudely interrupted by Lydia. This little scene identifies Mr. Collins with Fordyce and also illustrates that the kind of instruction Mr. Collins is trying to impart is not advantageous to many young ladies. After reading Fordyce's *Sermons* myself, I was struck by the similarity in the rhetoric of Fordyce and Mr. Collins, and I concluded that Jane Austen was parodying Fordyce when she created the character of Mr. Collins.

One might argue that Fanny Price in *Mansfield Park* is the epitome of conduct book propriety, but I examined the ways that Fanny is not the angel of the house that most perceive her to be and that trying to live up to a feminine code of conduct, as she does, is not compatible with youth and nature and can impair female energy and behavior. I believe that in this novel Austen shows the toll that conduct book prescriptions and proscriptions can take on a female character, and Fanny Price—Austen's least appealing heroine—is the result.

All this suggests that Austen read conduct books and rejected many of their assumptions and admonitions.

NT: *Do you think that Austen was a feminist?*

VL: For a long time critics viewed Jane Austen as a complacent conservative who accepted the values of her society even as she tweaked that society for some of its conduct. However, critical reevaluation has found similarities in her views about women and those of early feminists like Wollstonecraft.

Wollstonecraft's cause, it should be noted, was primarily advocacy of better education for women. She argued that women were probably not naturally intellectually and morally inferior to men but that the typical female education made them so. She attacked a number of the conduct book writers, most notably Fordyce and Rousseau, whom she held responsible for the "barren blooming" of women. Her main point was that an education designed solely to make women more pleasing to men deprived women of the opportunity "to unfold their own faculties and acquire the dignity of conscious virtue: and that it made women worse—not better—wives and mothers."

Take Mrs. Bennet, for example. We are told in the first chapter that she is a woman of "mean understanding" and "little information," and anyone who has read the novel is aware of her shortcomings as a wife and mother. When we are introduced to her brother, Mr. Gardiner, in Chapter Twenty-five, we learn that he is "a sensible, gentleman-like man, greatly superior to his sister as well by nature as education." Obviously Mrs. Bennet could never have been an intellectual giant, but a better education might have made her a more tolerable wife and responsible mother.

The differences in the Bennet daughters is partially explained by Elizabeth when she describes to Lady Catherine de Bourgh the desultory education available to them: ". . . such of us as wished to learn never wanted the means. We were always encouraged to read, and had all the masters that were necessary. Those who chose to be idle, certainly might." Lydia, who clearly falls into the latter category, is turning into a carbon copy of her mother: vain, empty-headed, and foolish. At the end of the novel Kitty, removed from the influence of her mother and sister Lydia and exposed to the rational discourse of her two oldest sisters and their husbands, becomes "less irritable, less ignorant, and less insipid." Clearly Austen believed that good education and the right environment and experiences could significantly improve women.

I might mention Mary Bennet here, the bookish sister. She is the perfect product of conduct book reading. She is plain but vain of her accomplishments; she is the only Bennet daughter to appreciate the foolish Mr. Collins; and she lacks all human compassion, substituting conduct book precepts for genuine emotion. Mary leads the sheltered life advocated for women by conduct book writers. She does not exercise her reason and learn from experience as Elizabeth does. Her character is fixed for readers in the second chapter when her father asks her a question and says, "... you are a young lady of deep reflection I know, and read great books, and make extracts." Austen then tells us that "Mary wished to say something very sensible, but knew not how." Conduct book reading has left Mary mentally impoverished.

Austen's novels are full of foolish and ignorant female characters, many of whom wreak havoc in the lives of the people around them and whose education or lack thereof had made them at least in part what they are.

MARTIN AMIS ON PRIDE AND PREJUDICE

*W*hen I was introduced to the novel at the age of fourteen, I read twenty pages and then besieged my stepmother's study until she told me what I needed to know. I needed to know that Darcy married Elizabeth. (I needed to know that Bingley married Jane.) I needed this information as badly as I had ever needed anything. *Pride and Prejudice* suckers you. Amazingly—and I believe, uniquely—it *goes on* suckering you. Even now, as I open the book, I feel the same panic of unsatisfied expectation, despite five or six rereadings. How can this be, when the genre itself guarantees consummation? The simple answer is that the lovers really are made for each other by their creator. They are *constructed* for each other: interlocked for wedlock.

Walking

J ane Austen loved walking, and throughout most of her life she managed to walk about six miles a day. She wrote: "The beauties of nature must for me be one of the joys of heaven." In her novels characters who walk are usually superior to those who ride. Unlike their undiscerning counterparts, Is-

abella and John Thorpe, Eleanor and Henry Tilney prefer walking to riding in a carriage. In *Pride and Prejudice* we learn that "Mrs. Bennet was not in the habit of walking" and that Mary could never "spare time" to walk. All the characters beloved by Austen herself, however, enjoy a country walk. Near the end of the book Bingley and Jane take a walk along with Darcy and Elizabeth. That Kitty joins them may hint at the possibility of her rehabilitation now that she has been separated from the influence of her risqué sister Lydia.

The belief that the walker is morally superior to the rider was shared with Austen by the Romantic poets of her time and by her eighteenth-century forebears. In his poem *The Task,* one of Austen's favorite poets, William Cowper, reminds us that "the sofa suits the gouty limb" but that he, the poet-narrator, has "loved the rural walk through lanes / Of grassy swarth, close cropped by nibbling sheep." John Gay, an earlier eighteenth-century poet whom Austen had read in her days at Steventon, dedicated a lengthy poem to the salubrious effects of walking as opposed to riding in coaches in his *Trivia; or, The Art of Walking the Streets of London.* The nineteenth-century poets rejected much of the philosophy of the eighteenth century, but they were fervent walkers. William Wordsworth may be the biggest champion of walking in all Romantic literature, and Jane Austen certainly read his poetry.

In *Pride and Prejudice* Elizabeth Bennet's walk to Netherfield to nurse Jane inspires Darcy's admiration. Bingley's sisters, the hyperfastidious Mrs. Hurst and Caroline Bingley, condemn her:

"She has nothing, in short, to recommend her, but being an excellent walker. I shall never forget her appearance this morning. She really looked almost wild."

"She did indeed, Louisa. I could hardly keep my countenance. Very nonsensical to come at all! Why must *she* be scampering about the country, because her sister had a cold? Her hair so untidy, so blowsy!"

"Yes, and her petticoat; I hope you saw her petticoat, six inches deep in mud, I am absolutely certain; and the gown which had been let down to hide it, not doing its office."

"Your picture may be very exact, Louisa," said Bingley, "but this was all lost upon me. I thought Miss Elizabeth Bennet looked remarkably well, when she came into the room this morning. Her dirty petticoat quite escaped my notice."

"To walk three miles, or four miles, or five miles, or whatever it is, above her ancles in dirt and alone, quite alone! what could she mean by it? It seems to me to shew an abominable sort of conceited independence, a most country town indifference to decorum."

"It shews an affection for her sister that is very pleasing," said Bingley.

By defending Elizabeth's walk, Darcy and Bingley discover that they may need to reassess their notions of decorum.

In *Emma* we find a similar situation in regard to walkers and walking. The tawdry Mrs. Elton rejoices in her barouche-landau, a symbol of her material values, whereas Mr. Knightley, our hero, is a great walker. Indeed, he is "too apt," in Emma's opinion, "to get about as he could, and not use his carriage so often as became the owner of Donwell Abbey." Emma's opinion at this point is similar to Mrs. Elton's, and she has to recognize and exorcise those snobbish traits before she can become a suitable match for Mr. Knightley. Ultimately she reaches her accord with Mr. Knightley and her acceptance of his offer of marriage as they are walking together, a contrast with the offer Mr. Elton made to her in a carriage. Generally in Jane Austen's novels the pedestrian possesses moral superiority.

"*Every time I read* **Pride and Prejudice** *I want to dig her up and beat her over the skull with her own shin-bone.*" *One wonders why Twain returned to the book repeatedly. Didn't he have other instigations to biliousness without taking down* **Pride and Prejudice** *yet once more?*
—MARK TWAIN, commenting on Jane Austen

❧ QUIZ: DO APPEARANCES DECEIVE? ❧

Who is being described?

1. "No sooner had he made it clear to himself and his friends that she had hardly a good feature in her face, than he began to find it was rendered uncommonly intelligent by the beautiful expression of her dark eyes."

2. "Her face was so lovely, that when in the common cant of praise she was called a beautiful girl, truth was less violently outraged than usually happens. Her skin was very brown, but from its transparency, her complexion was uncommonly brilliant; her features were all good; her smile was sweet and attractive, and in her eyes, which were very dark, there was a life, a spirit, an eagerness which could hardly be seen without delight."

3. "He was a stout young man of middling height, who, with a plain face and ungraceful form, seemed fearful of being too handsome unless he wore the dress of a groom, and too much like a gentleman unless

he were easy where he ought to be civil, and impudent where he might be allowed to be easy."

4. "Her height was pretty, just such as almost everybody would think tall, and nobody could think very tall; her figure particularly graceful; her size a most becoming medium, between fat and thin, though a slight appearance of ill-health seemed to point out the likeliest evil of the two. . . . It was a style of beauty, of which elegance was the reigning character."

5. "Her Countenance is absolutely sweet, & her voice & manner winningly mild. I am sorry it is so, for what is this but Deceit?"

6. "When they first saw him he was absolutely plain, black and plain: but still he was a gentleman, with a pleasing address. The second meeting proved him not so very plain; he was plain, to be sure, but then he had so much countenance, and his teeth were so good, and he was so well made, that one soon forgot he was plain."

7. "She was a good-humoured, merry, fat, elderly woman, who talked a great deal, seemed very happy, and rather vulgar. She was full of jokes and laughter, and before dinner was over had said many witty things on the subject of lovers and husbands. . . ."

8. "She was a tall, large woman, with strongly-marked features, which might once have been handsome. Her air was not conciliating, nor was her manner of receiving them, such as to make her visitors forget their inferior rank. . . . [w]hatever she said was spoken in so authoritative a tone, as marked her self-importance."

9. "She was looking remarkably well; her very regular, very pretty features, having the bloom and freshness of youth restored by the fine wind which had been blowing on her complexion, and by the animation of eye which it had also produced."

10. "That tooth of hers and those freckles! Freckles do not disgust me so very much. . . . I have known a face not materially disfigured by a few."

11. "Her reddened and weather-beaten complexion . . . made her seem to have lived some years longer in the world than her real eight and thirty."

12. "Her person was rather good; her face not unpretty; but neither feature, nor air, nor voice, nor manner, were elegant."

13. "[She] was a stout, well-grown girl of fifteen, with a fine complexion and good-humoured countenance. . . . [s]he had high animal spirits, and a sort of natural self-consequence."

14. "They found in the appearance of the eldest, who was nearly thirty, with a very plain and not a sensible face, nothing to admire: but in the

other, who was not more than two or three and twenty, they acknowledged considerable beauty; her features were pretty, and she had a sharp quick eye, and a smartness of air, which though it did not give actual elegance or grace, gave distinction to her person."

15. "[She] was a little, thin woman, upright, even to formality, in her figure, and serious, even to sourness, in her aspect. Her complexion was sallow; and her features small, without beauty, and naturally without expression; but a lucky contraction of the brow had rescued her countenance from the disgrace of insipidity, by giving it the strong characters of pride and ill nature."

ANTHONY TROLLOPE ON JANE AUSTEN

*M*iss Austen was surely a great novelist. . . . What she did, she did perfectly. Her work, as far as it goes, is faultless. She wrote of the times in which she lived, of the class of people with which she associated, and in the language which was usual to her as an educated lady. Of romance,—what we generally mean when we speak of romance—she had no tinge. Heroes and heroines with wonderful adventures there are none in her novels. Of great criminals and hidden crimes she tells us nothing. But she places us in a circle of gentlemen and ladies, and charms us while she tells us with an unconscious accuracy how men should act to women, and women act to men. It is not that her people are all good;—and certainly, they are not all wise. The faults of some are the anvils on which the virtues of others are hammered till they are bright as steel. In the comedy of folly I know no novelist who has beaten her. The letters of Mr Collins, a clergyman in *Pride and Prejudice,* would move laughter in a low-church archbishop. Throughout all her works, and they are not many, a sweet lesson of homely household womanly virtue is ever being taught.

Fay Weldon on Jane Austen

*F*ay Weldon is celebrated as "the critically acclaimed master commentator on the rivalry between men and women," according to the Times Literary Supplement. Like Jane Austen, she specializes in the funny, fraught, and fertile field of human relationships. In addition to her accomplishments as a novelist and a short story writer, Weldon has written several screenplays, including the script for BBC's 1985 version of Pride and Prejudice. Her book Letters to Alice on First

Reading Jane Austen *is a wonderful introduction to the enchantments of litera-ture, of writing, and of "The City of Invention" where writers create "Houses of the Imagination." Some of her best-known novels include* Female Friends, Praxis, The Life and Loves of a She-Devil, The Shrapnel Academy, The Heart of the Country, Life Force, Trouble, *and 1998's* Big Girls Don't Cry, *a pocket history of the feminist movement in novel form. Recent screenplays by Weldon include* The Bennet Boys *and* Sanditon.

NT: *Which came first, your screenplay for the BBC production of* Pride and Prej-udice *or your book* Letters to Alice on First Reading Jane Austen?

FW: I was no expert on Jane Austen to begin with. I was asked by the BBC to do an adaptation of *Pride and Prejudice.* I didn't hesitate. Rather rashly I then began to adapt it. I had not done a television adaptation before and didn't know how to set about it. My mother lent me her copy of *Pride and Prejudice* with the old illustrations, which she hated for some reason, so she took them out before she gave me the book. I first divided it up and did a page of mine for a page of hers so at least there would be some sort of shape to what I proceeded to do. But of course the system breaks down, and you end up having five episodes when it has to be reduced to four. I didn't have to invent anything. I just used the book. I came to love Austen amazingly because every line meant something. She's a very unwasteful writer.

Anyway, that done, I became in spite of myself an expert on Jane Austen be-cause many people would ask me about her and I felt apart from *Pride and Prejudice* they knew nothing at all about her. Then I was asked by a publisher to do a book. I agreed to do that for the simple reason that they were paying me a great deal of money. When I began to do this, I realized how little was known about Jane Austen. This was about thirteen or fifteen years ago. A great deal more has been put together since. The book in fact is semifiction because the writer in the book is real, and when I talk about being on a book tour in Australia, these things are true. In the book I am trying to persuade myself why Jane Austen is important, why people should study her. Never something I'm quite convinced of anyway. Writers don't write books to be studied; they write them to be read. They don't expect people to mull over them to find out what they mean. At the time I wrote *Letters to Alice* Jane Austen was still por-trayed as England's Jane, a very gentle, middle-class English lady. Hardly as a living, breathing writer with temperament, and will, and the difficult, scratchy nature she had.

I never did English literature myself; I studied economics. So I did not read Jane Austen actually until I was older.

NT: *Since you came to Jane Austen in mid-career, after you had already written about ten novels and many short stories, do you think that reading her had any influence whatever on you in terms of the craft of writing novels?*

FW: No, I don't think so. She writes in a way not dissimilar to me. I mean there's a kind of way of looking at the world that we have in common. She is a born writer. She's not trying to write anything; she writes because she wants to. It was not then a world in which writing was a fashionable thing to do, as it is today. She has an extraordinary pleasure in observing the world and up to a point joining in, but not necessarily. In many ways the world of the time prevented her from joining it. So her pleasure came from observing it, and shaping it, and turning it into form.

I have read some recent biographies with great pleasure. I just loved the Nokes one. He dramatizes everything, and it's got terrific energy. Claire Tomalin covers much the same ground. I like learning all about the relationship to the cousins and the sort of details about the mother, which presents a life so unlike what we've been traditionally led to believe.

NT: *Are you currently working on any new projects?*

FW: At the moment I'm doing for television a kind of reverse *Pride and Prejudice,* brought up-to-date, in which we have the Bennet boys rather than the Bennet girls. Mrs. Bennet is desperately trying to marry off the boys to get them out of the house. My theory is that women are able to earn money and have careers and are much more practical than boys are now. I keep Mrs. Bennet as the foolish mother and Mr. Bennet as the difficult but witty father. I have always had great sympathy with Mrs. Bennet. She was absolutely right about what would happen if she didn't get the girls married. You think of the impossible woman who is always misunderstood and indeed is foolish and embarrasses everybody, but her heart is in the right place. I find it just like me. Really. I'm like Mrs. Bennet.

NT: *Does your television script take place today?*

FW: Yes. It is set in contemporary time in a suburb of London. You can't write that script unless it is contemporary. You can't really bring *Pride and Prejudice* up to date without changing the gender of the children. In a way it is an illustration of how life has changed. It's called *The Bennet Boys.* There are four of them, not five, too many to cope with. And the boys don't take on the qualities of the Austen sisters because I don't want to be seen doing too close a thing or indeed any sort of parody or anything other than paying my respect for this classic invention of the family, which just continues in various forms. Now you want to marry sons off to some nice, comforting, earning persons who will have the energy to look after them.

Clergymen:
Ridiculous and Sublime

Knowing Austen to be the daughter of a clergyman, and the sister of two clerics, we might be prepared for generally positive portraits of the clergy in her novels, and indeed Henry Tilney and Edmund Bertram are laudable characters. Yet Austen spent at least as much time on a gallery of delightful clerical fools: Mr. Elton, Mr. Grant, and, most memorable, Mr. Collins.

Austen's depictions of clergymen fall chronologically between two other famous writers who spent much time describing the clergy, Henry Fielding and Anthony Trollope. In Austen's works the clergy are all genteel and on good terms with the landed gentry. In Fielding's novels the clergy are hangers-on like Thwackum or Trulliber or Parson Adams, who, in spite of his bouts of wisdom, is feckless and impoverished and lives in squalor. Writing only a little more than a hundred years after Fielding comes Trollope, with his riotously high-living ecclesiastics: the Stanhope family, which maintains a clerical living in England but spends years in Italy; the Proudies, who jockey for position with the Grantleys and lead wealthy, sumptuous lives. Trollope acknowledges the miseries of poor clerical families like the Quiverfulls, who try to raise fourteen children on forty pounds a year or the wretchedly poor perpetual curate of Hogglestock, the Reverend Josiah Crawley. His Reverend Obadiah Slope makes Mr. Collins seem unassuming and attractive.

Austen's clerics live neither in a bishop's palace nor in a curate's hovel. Most significantly her clerics—even Edmund Bertram—all lack what one might call spirituality or soulfulness. Although Mr. Collins is most anxious to minister to Lady Catherine de Bourgh, her needs are more secular than devotional.

Jane Austen's novels are more concerned with the clergy's attempt to find "livings" that will enable them to marry and lead comfortable lives than with their religious agons. These livings are highly coveted. Wickham, hardly our idea of a spiritual fellow, wants a living from Darcy; Sir Thomas Bertram has provided one to the Reverend Mr. Norris, his brother-in-law, who has no money of his own. When Norris dies, Sir Bertram sells the living to Dr. Grant, in order to have some ready cash to pay for his son Tom's extravagant debts. Colonel Brandon arranges one for Edward Ferrars. But we never see Austen's clergymen at their orisons or struggling with their flock the way we glimpse Fielding's gentle Parson Adams. For Austen, it would seem, being a clergyman was just another way to make a living.

Mr. Bennet

In the opening pages of *Pride and Prejudice* Mr. Bennet's character is shown to considerable advantage in counterpoint to his wife's glaring stupidity; his wry irony at Mrs. Bennet's expense reveals his intelligence and sense of humor, and his seeming indifference to the welfare of his daughters is belied as he reveals that he has already arranged for them to meet the newly arrived, eminently marriageable Mr. Bingley. Indeed, so favorable is the first impression made by Mr. Bennet that his ironic intelligence and even his willingness to advance the marriage plot seem to make him one with Austen's narrative voice.

A full reading of the novel, however, reveals serious shortcomings in his character. Late in the novel the moral limitations of his humor are apparent in his comment on his family's vulnerability to gossip: "For what do we live, but to make sport for our neighbors, and laugh at them in our turn?" Austen may share his satiric view of her neighbors, but he lacks her strong moral concern.

> On learning that someone wished to meet the lady who had written *Pride and Prejudice,* Jane wrote to Cassandra that "I am rather frightened by hearing that she wishes to be introduced to *me*. If I *am* a wild beast, I cannot help it."

Must we reexamine our first impression? Mr. Bennet's irony is after all at his wife's expense, and suggests first, a lack of marital love, and second, an inappropriate choice of a wife. Like all of Austen's novels, *Pride and Prejudice* is concerned with the dangers of making a poor marriage because of one's inability to recognize the real character of a potential spouse. Mr. Bennet, locked in a loveless marriage with a fool, epitomizes the error of mistaking a pretty face and a vivacious manner for a promising life partner.

The inadequacy of Mr. Bennet's character is also abundantly clear in his failure as a father to care for his daughters. He fails them not only materially, by overspending his income and leaving them without dowries or the possibility of independence, but also morally, by failing to inculcate proper values or supervise their behavior. He has encouraged catastrophe by allowing Lydia to go to Brighton, and he humiliates Mary in public by halting her performance with a sarcastic remark.

Mr. Bennet is partially redeemed by his eventual repentance of his carelessness, by his recognition of the sterling qualities of his eldest daughters, Jane and Elizabeth, and by his genuinely amusing irony, but he has a deeply flawed character, a textbook case that first impressions deceive.

"*Lizzy, I bear you no ill-will for being justified in your advice to me last May.*"
—MR. BENNET

The Liveliness of Your Mind

In the penultimate chapter of *Pride and Prejudice,* Elizabeth Bennet playfully asks Darcy "to account for his having ever fallen in love with her":

"I can comprehend your going on charmingly once you had made a beginning; but what could set you off in the first place?"

"I cannot fix the hour, or the spot, or the look, or the words, which laid the foundation. It is too long ago. I was in the middle before I knew I *had* begun."

"My beauty you had early withstood, and as for my manners—my behavior to *you* was at least always bordering on the uncivil, and I never spoke to you without rather wishing to give you pain than not. Now be sincere; did you admire me for my impertinence?"

"For the liveliness of your mind, I did."

In *Pride and Prejudice* the intelligent, lively woman is loved for her mind. If that is not exactly revolutionary, it must certainly be one of the reasons that this romance is so deeply satisfying for readers. Austen knows that men, and women, can fall in love for all the wrong reasons. Austen does *not* make a Cinderella fairy-tale story for Elizabeth because it is the flash of her intelligence, not her dancing shoes or her pretty face or the

Laurence Olivier as Darcy, succumbing to Greer Garson's depiction of the liveliness of Elizabeth Bennet's mind.

deus ex machina of a fairy godmother, that makes her worthy of his love. Darcy falls in love with a mind.

Is there a mind more lively in fact than Jane Austen's? In Elizabeth Bennet, Austen fans find the character most similar to their beloved Jane. Darcy's love for Elizabeth transcends the vulgarity of her relatives and the stupidity of his aunt Lady Catherine.

In a neatly geometrical congruity, in the first chapter of the book, Mr. Bennet, Elizabeth's father, tells his wife that his daughters are all "silly and ignorant like other girls; but Lizzy has something more of quickness than her sisters." Quickness? Liveliness? Can it be that Elizabeth is loved by both her father and her future husband for the same reasons? Quite possibly Lizzy (her father's nickname for her) has learned that the way to a man's heart is not through good looks and goodness (her sister Jane, manifestly good and good-looking, does not seem to have any special bond with her father) but through satiric discourse. She has won distinction in her father's eyes through the very same qualities that will win Darcy.

Does this mean that Darcy will be a father figure, that the Darcys will replicate the disastrous marriage of the Bennets? No, not at all. Elizabeth is attracted to the goodness and moral probity that Darcy displays in managing his estate, Pemberley. She is dismayed by the way her father has abnegated his paternal responsibilities. She chooses a husband who will love her for the same reasons her father loves her but who will also be a responsible citizen, someone who is not totally wrapped up in the cloak of ironic distancing. Although, interestingly, when Elizabeth first meets Darcy at the Netherfield ball he appears as sardonically misogynistic as Mr. Bennet. When Bingley suggests that Darcy dance with Elizabeth he retorts:

> "She is tolerable; but not handsome enough to tempt *me;* and I am in no humour at present to give consequence to young ladies who are slighted by other men. . . . You are wasting your time with me."
>
> . . . Mr. Darcy walked off; and Elizabeth remained with no very cordial feelings towards him. She told the story however with great spirit among her friends; for she had a lively, playful disposition, which delighted in any thing ridiculous.

Elizabeth's spirit provides her with some resiliency against the ludicrous posturings of others. But there is tension between the ironic distance her wit provides and her real need to be engaged by love. Elizabeth knows well that of his five daughters she is the only one who has managed to win her father's sincere love, and she dreads the thought that her proposed marriage to Darcy will pain him. She knows that Darcy is going to ask Mr. Bennet for her hand:

> In the evening soon after Mr. Bennet withdrew to the library, she saw Mr. Darcy rise also and follow him, and her agitation on seeing it was extreme. She did not fear her father's opposition, but he was going to be made unhappy, and that it should be through her means, that *she,* his

favourite child, should be distressing him by her choice, should be filling him with fears and regrets in disposing of her, was a wretched reflection, and she sat in misery till Mr. Darcy appeared again, when, looking at him, she was a little relieved by his smile. . . . . Her father was walking about the room, looking grave and anxious.

Note how unusual it is: This is perhaps the only time we catch Mr. Bennet "grave and anxious," undoubtedly a reflection of his true love for Lizzy.

"Lizzy," said he, "what are you doing? Are you out of your senses, to be accepting this man? Have you not always hated him? . . . Let me advise you to think better of it. I know your disposition, Lizzy, I know that you could be neither happy nor respectable, unless you truly esteemed your husband; unless you looked up to him as a superior. Your lively talents would place you in the gravest danger in an unequal marriage. You could scarcely escape discredit and misery. My child, let me not have the grief of seeing you unable to respect your partner in life. You know not what you are about."

Mr. Bennet hopes to dissuade his Lizzy from making the same kind of marital blunder he did. He shows a true paternal responsibility toward her in giving council to Elizabeth that the reader knows to be true: that she *must* be able to respect her partner. She *cannot* live like Charlotte Lucas in a marriage without esteem.

Although Mr. Bennet is wrong about Elizabeth's feelings and Darcy's character at this point, his general dictum is correct and sincere. Later, Elizabeth "had the satisfaction of seeing her father taking pains to get acquainted with [Darcy]." Mrs. Bennet's response is characteristic: She does not have the imaginative intelligence to transcend her own intransigent stupidity and she merely ooh-la-las over the "pin-money . . . jewels . . . and carriages" that her daughter will have, betraying the vulgar faith that carriages bring prestige and status, which is tantamount to happiness and an essential for conjugal bliss.

In his book *Erotic Faith: Being in Love from Jane Austen to D. H. Lawrence,* Robert Polhemus uses a dance metaphor that is reminiscent of Henry Tilney's comparison of marriage to a country dance. Polhemus says:

For Austen, love, like dance, ought to be a rational pursuit, leading to what is pleasurable, useful, and beautiful. Elizabeth and Darcy come at last to move in complementary harmony and rhythm—like Fred Astaire and Ginger Rogers . . . in their great number, "Never Gonna Dance," who begin by trying to keep from dancing, but end up joined together in fluid, unified, loving, and lovely motion. If we imagine Elizabeth, her friend Charlotte Lucas, and her wild sister Lydia in a dance, we get a precise image not only of the kind of dancing, but of the kind of love Austen values. Charlotte would move by rote, woodenly, without joy. Lydia would be all tawdry bounce and flounce, without grace. Elizabeth's motion would be both lively and elegantly poised. Like ballet, good and rational love is a balancing act.

In *Pride and Prejudice* Austen shows that learning to love a "lively mind" is good and rational, just as for Bingley and Jane loving a kind and gentle spirit can be also good and rational. The marriages that do not have the approbation of their author are founded on the frivolous, the material, and the base. Charlotte Lucas wants security and she wants to free her family from a financial burden; Mr. Bennet fell for a pretty face, and Lydia simply wants to have sex. She is precociously hormonally charged for a fifteen-year-old girl of her time. She babbles incessantly of lottery tickets, hats, and the joys of dressing up a soldier in women's clothing. Her desire to go to Brighton is expressed in this purple, almost lurid sampling of her imagination:

> A visit to Brighton comprised every possibility of earthly happiness. She saw with the creative eye of fancy, the streets of that gay bathing place covered with officers. She saw herself the object of attention, to tens and to scores of them at present unknown. She saw all the glories of the camp; its tents stretched forth in beauteous uniformity of lines, crowded with the young and the gay, and dazzling with scarlet; and to complete the view, she saw herself seated beneath a tent, tenderly flirting with at least six officers at once.

And, reader, you may ask does not Lydia display a lively mind in this fantasy? Indeed, it is a lively fantasy, but while it implies a veritable flow of redcoats descending upon Lydia's "tent" it is also a limited fantasy: The officers endlessly duplicate and reduplicate themselves in their tender flirtations, in their youth, their energy, and their dazzle.

Elizabeth's imagination is varied and diffuse whereas Lydia's imagination emerges from her gonads rather than her brain.

Darcy and Pemberley

Late in *Pride and Prejudice,* after all the engagements have been made, Jane asks Elizabeth when she first fell in love with Darcy. Elizabeth answers that it was when she saw Pemberley. Is Elizabeth mercenary after all? Hardly. In Austen's world much was revealed about a man by the way he managed his estate. The country estate indeed was a cornerstone of the social order in her world. It was crucial to the economic structure of the countryside since most of the farming was handled by tract farmers, who paid rent to the squire and moreover depended upon him for the maintenance of their farms and lands. The law was largely enforced by country squires who also acted as magistrates. Even religion was to a great extent controlled by the estate, since the clerical positions of the local churches were usually filled by the squire's appointment. In fact, Darcy's refusal to appoint the dissolute Wickham to a living, though first held against him by most of the characters, turns out, when Wickham's real character is revealed, to indicate Darcy's wise management.

WHITE SOUP

*C*harles Bingley is waiting only the completion of sufficient white soup to give his first ball at Netherfield. White soup is similar to syllabub in its marriage of cream and sweetened-liquor, but it is more fortifying in that it also includes meat stock, egg yolks, and ground-up almonds. Served hot, this cholestorol-laden treat must have added to the general euphoria of a ball, especially when followed by a quaff of syllabub.

Further, Elizabeth initially formed a negative opinion of Darcy when seeing him in effect out of his native element—away from his estate and separated from his social role. At Pemberley she sees the beautiful grounds and the well-stocked library, which help maintain the essential elements of English culture at its best. She sees that Darcy is a loving brother to his younger sister, Georgiana, a fair and genial employer of his servants, and even a loved and respected landlord. Pemberley reveals Darcy as caring and generous and not at all guilty of the excessive pride for which she had first condemned him.

Jane Bennet

The eldest of the Bennet sisters, Jane, epitomizes the perfect young lady of Austen's day. She is tactful and sensitive to others, generous in her judgments, and, to top it off, both intelligent and beautiful. Jane is superior even to her sister Elizabeth, the novel's heroine, because she is more beautiful and because she would never be guilty of the indiscretions Elizabeth commits in her conversations with Wickham and in her prejudice against Darcy.

Ironically, however, her virtues are the source of her difficulties in the novel. First, her perfect manners and absolute propriety prevent her from showing her love for Bingley. Consequently Bingley believes she is indifferent to him and breaks off his courtship. In addition, her generosity makes her incapable of recognizing the scheming natures of Bingley's sisters, and of course, like everyone else, she fails to recognize the true nature of the dastardly Wickham. Upon agreeing to her engagement with Bingley, Mr. Bennet says: "You are each of you so complying, that nothing will ever be resolved on; so easy, that every servant will cheat you; and so generous that you will always exceed your income."

In Jane Bennet, Austen presents the very perfection of female propriety as her age defined it, but in presenting her vulnerability, Austen is indirectly criticizing the ideals of the age.

*P*ride and Prejudice *seems to be an updated retelling of* Shakespeare's Much Ado About Nothing. *Not only are there the sparring future lovers resisting their attraction that's so obvious to everyone else, but there's also the subplot of Benedick/Darcy rescuing a young female relative of Beatrice/Elizabeth from a highly unsuitable relationship with a bounder: Claudio/Wickham.*
—TIFFANY HOLMES

Elizabeth Bennet

Elizabeth Bennet, the heroine of *Pride and Prejudice,* is probably the most beloved of all Austen's heroines. Less a paragon of virtue than her older sister, Jane, she is witty and vivacious and appeals to modern readers because she has enough daring and individuality to rebel slightly against her age's ideal notion of the acquiescent, genteel, accomplished young lady. She nevertheless remains generally within acceptable limits of female propriety, and even in Austen's time readers would have applauded the independence of spirit that prompts her to walk three miles in the rain to inquire after her sick sister. Despite the dirtying of her petticoat, few readers would have agreed with Caroline Bingley in censuring her behavior as indecorous.

Further, Elizabeth's often critical judgments are not characteristic of a virtuous young lady's proper tendency to be so unconscious of evil that she would see no evil, hear no evil, etc. But for the most part her judgments of

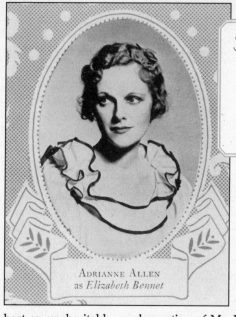

Adrianne Allen's doe-eyed Elizabeth Bennet from the 1935 theatrical production of Pride and Prejudice

ADRIANNE ALLEN
as *Elizabeth Bennet*

character are in accord with the narrator's and impress readers as a demonstration of good sense.

Still, Austen makes it clear that Elizabeth's vivacity leads her beyond the bounds of propriety. As Elizabeth herself eventually realizes, her pride in her independent judgments leads her to what is at best an uncharitable condemnation of Mr. Darcy's character. More seriously, her social verve leads her into improper, even compromising conversational intimacies with Wickham. Undoubtedly readers are right to excuse Elizabeth's mistakes as the pardonable excesses of youthful impetuosity.

Mary Bennet

Mary Bennet is a relatively minor character in *Pride and Prejudice,* but in her few appearances she is mercilessly exposed as a witless, pompous bore. Her declaration, for example, about the distinction between pride and vanity is ponderously pedantic, delivered on the authority of learned authors, but without wit or tactful response to the others involved in the discussion. Moreover, when given the opportunity to display her accomplishments, specifically her musical abilities, she selects music too solemn and onerous for the occasion, music that requires diligent practice but whose performance displays more study than natural taste.

The third of the five Bennet daughters, Mary lacks the beauty and intelligence of her older sisters, but she also lacks the excessively high spirits and moral carelessness of her hoydenish younger sisters. Mary's admiration for the pompous Mr. Collins definitively establishes her as a ridiculous character.

Still, she is more to be pitied than derided. She is isolated by the natural pairings of Jane and Elizabeth as confidantes and Kitty and Lydia as playmates. Mary is the only Bennet who does not have at least one other family member in sympathy with her, and thus she is a real outsider. Her father is not delighted by her intellectual achievements, which may after all have been undertaken to please him; they could hardly have been calculated to foster attention from her mother. Mary's faults are the result of trying too hard to compensate for her lack of the intelligence and beauty possessed by her older sisters. Her excessive study and tendency to parade her knowledge and accomplishments set her apart from the morally careless behavior of her frivolous younger sisters. In short, she is the quintessential middle child.

> *Mrs. Bennet (stupid, prattling, vulgar, greedy), is one of the greatest comic nightmares in all literature, yet we are scarcely less restrained than she in our fretful ambition for her daughters. Jane Austen makes Mrs. Bennets of us all.*
>
> —MARTIN AMIS

Dr. Samuel Johnson

Dr. Samuel Johnson (1709–1784) was Austen's favorite prose writer. He was also an exceptionally prolific and energetic poet, critic, moralist, and lexicographer. The late eighteenth century is frequently called the Age of Johnson, which points to his preeminence in shaping the literary milieu in which Austen grew up. Like Cowper, Crabbe, and Austen herself, Johnson was not born into a life of opulence. The son of a Staffordshire bookseller, the infant Johnson developed scrofula, also known as the king's evil because of an idea that a touch from royalty could cure it. Johnson was taken to London to be "touched" by Queen Anne in 1712, when he was thirty months old. According to fable, Johnson was the last person in England to be touched by royalty in order to cure a case of scrofula. He developed into a robust child, perhaps thanks to the touch of Queen Anne. After spending some time at Oxford and some time comtemplating various careers, Johnson decided that he could make a living only in literature, so he moved to London and flourished. His essays in the *Rambler* and the *Idler,* along with *Rasselas,* a philosophical romance (which he composed hastily to meet the funeral expenses of his mother), secured his fame, which was permanently sealed by the titanic *Dic-*

tionary of the English Language. His *Prefaces to Shakespeare* and *Lives of the Poets* remain major commentaries on their subjects.

The title Doctor was awarded to him in the form of honorary degrees from Trinity College, Dublin, and Oxford. Dr. James Battersby comments:

> Between Austen and Johnson, there is a compatibility of sentiment and feeling, a companionable appreciation of subtle distinctions, a marked preference for hard realities over comforting myths, and a habit of testing professions against practices. On the level of style, we find in both a reliance on balance and clarity of expression. On the less than totally admirable side, there is in both a strong penchant for the devastating riposte or the cruel but witty rejoinder, though, in fairness, it must be noted that both are specialists in the sort of wit and irony that strikes cleanly home without destroying sympathy or empathy for the one impaled, that lacerates the peccadillo but leaves room in our esteem for the person under scrutiny. To maintain sympathy with our fellow journeymen in life's struggles, even as we relentlessly pursue the ironical and satiric implications of their actions and beliefs, is an uncommon skill, one possessed in superlative degree by both Johnson and Austen. In Austen's work, Johnson is not so much quoted as echoed and reflected, and that not infrequently.

Both Austen and Johnson resisted trends in literature and resisted easy solutions and formulas to complicated human problems. Austen's narrative voice is consistently reminiscent of Johnson's. Johnson believed that authors should not merely delight but instruct, and instruct by the example of morally exemplary characters whom the readers can imitate. These characters must be virtuous but not so saintly that their example is beyond the emulation of readers. Many critics have pointed out that such characters as Henry Tilney and Fanny Price read, refer to, and rely on Johnson

> ⊶∞⊷
>
> *I*f Hamlet is the first son of English arts and letters, Elizabeth Bennet is the daughter most dear. Female readers of Jane Austen's *Pride and Prejudice* immediately see themselves in the second sister. Not the angelic oldest, Jane, but the next girl, the one with fine eyes and spirited seeing. She is her father's favorite and her author's favorite, too: "I must confess that I think her as delightful a creature as ever appeared in print."
> —LAURA JACOBS

for their ideas of morality. Anne Elliot counsels Captain Benwick to read more prose of "our best moralists" and less Byron in his melancholy state. Certainly she must have Johnson in mind.

Mansfield Park

A woman can never be too fine when she is all in white.
—EDMUND BERTRAM

Mansfield Park is to Jane Austen's oeuvre what the problem plays are to Shakespeare's. Published only a year after *Pride and Prejudice,* it lacks the sparkle and verve of its predecessor. Where *Pride and Prejudice* is witty and lovable, *Mansfield Park* is profound and rather homiletic. It was the first new novel that Austen worked on and completed after her move to Chawton as well as the first novel that she worked on after having become a published author. It therefore is the first of her novels to have been wholly conceived and written during her mature period.

Mansfield Park is the story of Fanny Price, an impoverished niece of Sir Thomas and Lady Bertram of Mansfield Park, who is offered an opportunity, at age nine, to come live with them and enjoy the benefits of wealth and education. The Bertrams have four children of their own, Tom, Edmund, Maria, and Julia, all of whom are older than Fanny. Only Edmund, the second son, is particularly kind to the young Fanny. She is tormented by Mrs. Norris, another aunt, who lives nearby, and is neglected by the rest of the family. Her rare moments of pleasure, when she is not shy and miserable, occur with Edmund and with her own brother William, who has embarked on a naval career and is occasionally invited to visit her at Mansfield Park.

The novel's main crisis begins when Fanny is sixteen. Sir Thomas has to leave Mansfield Park for an extended business trip to Antigua. New neighbors arrive. Henry and Mary Crawford arrive from London, trailing clouds of sophistication, to live with their sister, wife of Dr. Grant, the local rector. Mrs. Norris influences Maria to become engaged to a wealthy but idiotic local squire, Mr. Rushworth, who has an estate, Sotherton. Henry Crawford flirts outrageously with both Maria and Julia, in spite of Maria's engagement, and Edmund appears to be falling deeply in love with Mary Crawford, much to Fanny's distress, even though Mary is supercilious about his ambition to become a clergyman.

The group of young people, augmented by Mr. Rushworth and Mr. Yates, a vacuous friend, decide to engage in a home theatrical. They select a mildly racy play called *Lovers' Vows,* a perfect vehicle for Henry to continue his flirtation with the now-engaged Maria and for Mary to attempt to bewitch Edmund. Abetted by Mrs. Norris, they rehearse and transform Sir Thomas's study into their theater. Despite the urging of everyone, even Edmund, Fanny resolutely refuses to take part in the play. Sir Thomas returns and is appalled to find the home theatricals in full swing. It is a "moment of absolute horror."

Maria marries, and Henry decides to play court to Fanny. He wants to marry her, and the Bertrams all rejoice at the splendid offer. Fanny, once more resolute, refuses him. Sir Thomas decides to send her home to Portsmouth, where her family live in ramshackle, noisy indigence. Much as Fanny misses Mansfield Park and the Bertram family, she does everything in her power to improve the condition of her family in Portsmouth, imposing some order amid the chaos. When Henry Crawford cames to call on her there, she is almost attracted to him. He has helped her beloved brother William to rise in the naval ranks after all. Perhaps he is redeemable.

The reader feels some real conviction that Fanny may well end up marrying Henry, just as Edmund and Mary seem destined to marry. But disaster strikes. Tom Bertram becomes dangerously ill as a result of his dissipated ways, Henry runs off with Maria, who is of course another man's wife, and Julia elopes with Mr. Yates, who originally introduced the idea of the home theatricals to Mansfield. Sir Thomas and Lady Bertram send for Fanny; they realize that they cannot live without her, that she is in effect their "true" daughter. Fanny returns to Mansfield with her sister Susan, who will follow Fanny's model in becoming a "daughter of Mansfield," one who is guided by moral principles rather than desire and vanity.

Edmund is horrified by Mary Crawford's lack of moral horror at the adultery within their families. Edmund sees that Fanny is not only the true daughter of Mansfield but the one who should be his wife:

Scarcely had he done regretting Mary Crawford, and observing to Fanny how impossible it was that he should ever meet with such another woman before it began to strike him whether a very different kind of woman might not do just as well—or a great deal better; whether Fanny herself was not growing as dear, as important to him in all her smiles, and all her ways, as Mary Crawford had ever been; and whether it might not be possible, an hopeful undertaking to persuade her that her warm and sisterly regard for him would be foundation enough for married love.

Ultimately they marry at a time specified by Austen only as "exactly the time when it was quite natural that it should be so."

Q. D. Leavis, the influential early twentieth-century literary critic, thought that *Mansfield Park* was the "first modern novel," one that anticipates the work of George Eliot and Henry James. Douglas Bush believes:

Mansfield Park is certainly the book in which Jane Austen conducted her deepest explorations of the human heart and head. It may be that, on the threshold of middle age and for reasons unknown to us, she felt a special need of getting some things said about her world. . . . [I]n its corrective conservatism *Mansfield Park* remains true to the traditional ethos of comedy, but it also shows the maintenance of inward order against worldly pressures, and the tragic flaws and waste that attend the lack of such order, on a level well above the comic.

THE THREE SISTERS

*J*ane Austen freqently has a triangulation of sisters in her novels, and that seems to be the perfect geometrical figure to play off various traits and experiences, sundry harmonies, and counterpoints upon one another. *Mansfield Park* begins with a description of the three Ward sisters: Miss Maria, who had "the good luck to captivate Sir Thomas Bertram of Mansfield Park," Miss Ward, the older sister, who married the Reverend Mr. Norris; and Miss Frances Ward, who wed a "Lieutenant of Marines, without education, fortune, or connections. . . . She could hardly have made a more untoward choice." This sororal troika has many permutations in the pages of Jane Austen. In *Mansfield Park* it is echoed in the fact that Fanny Price becomes a de facto sister to the two Bertram daughters, Maria and Julia, and becomes a moral force in the lives of her two sisters back home in their impoverished apartment in Portsmouth, Susan and Betsey. *Sense and Sensibility* features three Dashwood sisters; in addition to Marianne and Elinor, there is the thirteen- year-old Margaret, and there is also an unpleasant alternative in their selfish sister-in-law, Fanny.

In *Pride and Prejudice* the romantic action is monopolized by the three Bennet sisters who marry: Jane, Elizabeth, and Lydia. In *Persuasion* the Elliot sisters provide another trio. In this case Anne, the middle sister, is highlighted because of her inherent goodness, a sharp contrast with the conceited Elizabeth and the querulous Mary.

The Unbearable Loneliness of Being Fanny Price

Fanny Price is Austen's only major character whom we see in detail as a child. She is only ten years old at the beginning of the novel. Chapter 2 of *Mansfield Park* poignantly shows the plight of the young outsider, forlorn and overwhelmed by Sir Thomas Bertram's "most untoward gravity of deportment," the "grandeur of the house," the maidservants who "sneered at her clothes," and her female cousins, who "hold her cheap" and mock her deficient education. This portrait of the misery of the young Fanny, who tries so hard to overcome her terrors, cannot help being heartrending for the reader. In this early chapter Austen engages us completely with sympathy for Fanny and appreciation of Edmund's understanding of her sufferings. In no other novel does she so fully examine the idea that the "child is father to the man." For we see not only the suffering and loneliness of Fanny, but how spoiled her

cousins Maria and Julia are. They are pampered and flattered by their aunt Norris. They make Fanny a "generous present of some of their least valued toys," indicating that they have already adopted materialistic values since they seem to have an abundance, really a surplus, of toys and gowns. Fanny's unprivileged status should endear her to readers. She has a special place in Austen's heart as well; near the end of the book Austen refers to her as "My Fanny," a term of endearment of a personalization that she extends to none of her other characters. Since Austen viewed her books as her own dear children, she must have had a special sense of Fanny as an exceptionally vulnerable and needy child, most deserving of her mother's affections.

The Servant Problem

All respectable families of Austen's time kept servants, and though there was a deep gulf set between the middle and the serving classes, resident servants nevertheless lived in a strange kind of intimacy with their employers;

someone after all had to empty the chamber pots and clean the linens. Under the circumstances it was important to maintain one's position and a measure of privacy from the domestics. The loose-tongued Lydia Bennet, for example, might well compromise her family's honor by speaking too freely in front of the servants (who might easily communicate family secrets to the Lucas servants and hence to the Lucases themselves), but the more discreet members of a family always withheld any significant family information until the servants were out of the room.

MARY CRAWFORD'S THOUGHTS ON EDMUND BERTRAM'S CHOSEN PROFESSION

⸻

*M*iss Crawford began with, "So you are to be a clergyman, Mr. Bertram. This is rather a surprise to me."

"Why should it surprise you? You must suppose me designed for some profession, and might perceive that I am neither a lawyer, nor a soldier, nor a sailor."

"For what is to be done in the church? Men love to distinguish themselves, and in either of the other lines, distinction may be gained, but not in the church. A clergyman is nothing. A clergyman has nothing to do but to be slovenly and selfish— read the newspaper, watch the weather, and quarrel with his wife. His curate does all the work, and the business of his own life is to dine."

Edmund Bertram's opinion: "As the clergy are, or are not what they ought to be, so are the rest of the nation."

Since servants lived at the expense of the family, care had to be taken when servants, such as those of *Persuasion*'s two Musgrove families, dressed themselves too lavishly or were inclined to "gad about." Such behavior could be demoralizing and dangerously alluring to the more strictly kept servants of other families in the neighborhood and could cause suspicion that because the Musgroves did not discipline their servants, their morals might be generally too lax.

The lower classes are not obtrusive in Austen's novels, but the comforts of the middle class are largely dependent upon them, and thus our understanding of the domestic life of the Bennets and Bingleys and so forth involves an understanding of class relations and of the care and treatment of the serving class.

The invisibility of servants in Austen's novels probably reflects the invisibility of the servant in the well-run household. Only in the chaotic Portsmouth home of the Prices, in *Mansfield Park,* is the incompetence of a servant an issue. In wealthier homes, such as Emma's, one servant, Serle, is actually mentioned by name because of his facility with soft-boiling eggs. Serle is singled out because he provides a valuable service in a uniquely adroit way for his master, the valetudinarian Mr. Woodhouse. General Tilney in *Northanger Abbey* may redeem himself somewhat to modern readers since he has renovated his kitchen and "every modern invention to facilitate the labour of the cooks had been adopted within this, their spacious theatre."

In *Mansfield Park* Mrs. Norris provides several glimpses of her noxiousness as she deals with the servants. And Baddely, Sir Thomas Bertram's butler, even has the triumph of one-upping Aunt Norris when he tells Fanny that Sir Thomas wishes to speak with her in his own room:

> "It is me, Baddely, you mean; I am coming this moment. You mean me, Baddely, I am sure; Sir Thomas wants me, not Miss Price."
>
> But Baddely was stout. "No Ma'am, it is Miss Price, I am certain of its being Miss Price." And there was a half smile with the words which meant, "I do not think you would answer the purpose at all."

The reader is therefore led to concur with the opinion of a servant and to "half smile" along with Baddely at his successful little dig at the deplorable aunt Norris.

Finally, Lizzy Bennet is much moved in favor of Darcy by hearing the testimony of Mrs. Reynolds, the housekeeper at Pemberley. Lizzy thinks: "What praise is more valuable than the praise of an intelligent servant?"

Mark Conroy on Jane Austen's Popularity

Mark *Conroy is the author of* Modernism and Authority: Strategies of Legitimation in Flaubert and Conrad *and the forthcoming* Graven Image: Fictions of American Mass Culture. *His teaching interests include literature and intellectual history and the nineteenth- and twentieth-century novel. He has been a professor at Louisiana State University, Yale University, and the Ohio State University.*

NT: *Why is Jane Austen so popular? Is it the doing of Hollywood or are there deeper forces at work?*

MC: I think there are deeper forces at work, which are three: the intrinsic quality of Austen's writing; and her moral sensibility, the ordered universe that her writings seem to our eyes, to occur in, so comforting to those of us afflicted with modern anomie; and a subtler point but equally important for at least part of the audience: Her works negotiate the sort of issue that women raised in sheltered privilege often face when contemplating marriage—i.e., how to embark on a new life without in the end really leaving home.

NT: *Which of Austen's novels do you find most appealing?*

MC: I like *Emma* the most because it strikes me, as a twentieth-century person and therefore inevitably post-Freudian, as one of the few pre-Freudian literary texts that explicitly dramatize the ways in which people willfully ignore their own most fundamental desires, projecting them promiscuously on to others (and of course ruining their lives, or threatening to, in the process).

NT: *What kind of influence do you think Austen had on later novelists? Was she innovative?*

MC: Curiously, she has had almost no direct influence, although I've long thought that *Middlemarch* may have owed indirectly to the milieu that her works depict, along with some of Arnold Bennett's provincial novels and works of Mrs. Gaskell. Where she was innovative is seemingly minor but portentous as it has worked out, and that is in the use of free indirect discourse. Indeed, one could argue that she broaches for English letters the territory Gustave Flaubert is lauded for exploring on behalf of French fiction. Why is Flaubert so well known for it, Austen so little? Could it be just a lot of plain old sexism?

NT: *Do you think that you like* Mansfield Park *in spite of or because of Fanny Price?*

MC: Essential to the drama of my reading *Mansfield Park* was in fact the very tension about how to view Fanny: Was she just a nervous Nellie whose Christian charity in the end came from timidity, or was she made of genuine better stuff? It is for me a drama far superior to the more conventional questions about Darcy in *Pride and Prejudice*. One of the interesting things for me about *Mansfield Park* is precisely the question of whether I was liking it because or in spite of its heroine. Ultimately, I guess, the answer is yes. Perhaps I hew to an outdated ideal of "true womanhood" obsolete in the late twentieth century.

NT: *What advice would you give to new readers who have enjoyed the film and television programs and want to embark on reading the novels?*

MC: Start at the beginning; go until you get to the end; then stop. Then do it all over again. This I think says it all.

*E*very Janeite is like the Princess and the Pea.
—MARTIN AMIS

Chawton: An Intense Burst of Writing

Jane Austen spent the last eight years of her life at Chawton House, a seventeenth-century house in the small village of Chawton. It was the first settled home she had had since her parents left the Steventon Rectory in early 1801. Jane and Cassandra, along with Mrs. Austen and Martha Lloyd, moved into the house, which had been inherited by their brother Edward, in July 1809. Within a few weeks Jane wrote a congratulatory verse to her brother Frank upon the birth of his son. At the end of the poem she bursts into an enthusiastic encomium upon the new house:

Our Chawton home, how much we find
Already in it, to our mind;
And how convinced, that when complete
It will all other Houses beat
That ever have been made or mended,
With rooms concise, or rooms distended.
You'll find us very snug next year,
Perhaps with Charles & Fanny near,
For now it often does delight us
To fancy them just over-right us.—

A couple visits Chawton House, as it appears today. The woman appears to be pointing to the information plaque, a contemporary addition to the exterior of the house.

MARTHA LLOYD

⟨⟨⟨○⟩⟩⟩

*M*artha Lloyd was a close friend of the Austen family. Martha and her younger sister Mary moved to Steventon with their widowed mother in 1789, when Jane Austen was thirteen. Although Martha was ten years older than Jane, they became close friends. The friendship must only have been cemented when Mary became the second wife of James Austen, Jane's eldest brother, in 1797. Jane never seems to have liked Mary very much—she was not a reader, among other failings—but Martha was probably her most cherished lifelong friend. When Martha's mother died, she was invited to join the female household of Mrs. Austen, Cassandra, and Jane. She lived with them first in Southampton and then joined them at Chawton. Jane told Cassandra that she loved Martha dearly. They seemed to get along very well, laughing, joking, occasionally sharing a bed. Martha was not afraid of criticizing Jane and disapproved of her dedication of *Emma* to the Prince Regent, writing that Jane had been influenced by "the most mercenary motives." Martha helped nurse Jane in her illness and remained at Chawton with Cassandra and Mrs. Austen, helping to nurse Mrs. Austen in her final illness. In 1828, at age sixty-three, Martha agreed to marry Frank Austen, a widower with ten children, ranging in age from seven to twenty-one. Cassandra was then alone at Chawton. Martha died in 1843.

The Chawton years were productive and happy for Austen; she hit her stride as a writer and had her first successes with publication. While living at Chawton, she revised *Sense and Sensibility* and *Pride and Prejudice,* wrote *Mansfield Park, Emma,* and *Persuasion,* and began work on *Sanditon.*

At Chawton, Austen led a fairly predictable and well-regulated life, which provided the consistent stability one would need to sustain writing a novel. Each morning she arose before Cassandra and played the piano for a while, and then she was in charge of seeing to the family breakfast of tea and toast. Attending to the day's first repast was essentially her only household chore. Cassandra and Martha took care of the rest of the work, aided by a servant and a cook. Claire Tomalin describes how Jane Austen "managed the day-to-day routines of a novelist with an efficiency and discipline worthy of her naval brothers." Her nephew J. E. Austen-Leigh, in his *Memoir of Jane Austen,* writes about her methods of composition:

[S]he had no separate study to retire to, and most of the work must have been done in the general sitting-room, subject to all kinds of casual interruptions. She was careful that her occupation should not be suspected by servants, or visitors, or any persons beyond her own family party. She wrote upon small sheets of paper which could easily be put away, or covered with a piece of blotting paper. There was, between the front door and the office, a swing door which creaked when it was opened; but she objected to having this little inconvenience remedied, because it gave her notice when anyone was coming.

Austen-Leigh describes her writing process as "mystic," an adjective that goes far toward the Austen family image of Aunt Jane managing to compose, revise, and complete five novels in five years under such conditions. Most critics today agree that she must have been able to find sustained private time in which to work uninterrupted. Austen was overjoyed finally to see her work in print when *Sense and Sensibility* was published. Her housemates must have shared in her joy and must have taken good care not to interrupt her work. Of course it must have been constantly on her mind. Austen's niece Marianne recalls that her aunt would sit quietly beside the fire, "saying nothing for a good while, and then would suddenly burst out laughing, jump up and run across the room to a table where pens and paper were lying, write something down, and then come back to the fire."

Chawton has become a magnet for lovers of Austen since the doors were opened to the public by T. Edward Carpenter, who endowed it as a museum in 1949. The public has flowed in increasing numbers to this Hampshire village to admire, among other relics, Austen's writing desk, a patchwork quilt made by Jane, Cassandra, and their mother, the two topaz crosses given to his sisters by Charles (which is echoed in William Price's gift of an amber cross to his sister Fanny in *Mansfield Park*) and to purchase tea towels and books in the gift shop. In recent years there has been an average of about 25,000 visitors to Chawton House, but in 1996 that number expanded to 57,482, and 1997 was an even greater year. Tourist buses full of Janeites from as far away as Japan pull into the parking lot. These travelers take tea at Cassandra's Tea Parlor or fortify themselves with stronger potations at the pub across the street from Chawton House.

BARBARA PYM ON HER VISIT TO CHAWTON

11 August, 1969. Visit to Jane Austen's house.... I put my hand down on Jane's desk and bring it up covered with dust. Oh that some of her genius might rub off on me! One would have imagined the devoted female custodian going round with her duster at least every other day. Then to the site of Steventon Rectory, the place of her birth—now a field overgrown with nettles and docks. We went into Steventon Church—very cool inside. Steventon Manor is deserted and overgrown, not beautiful but sad, almost romantic. Such enormous beech trees and that *silence*—a few miles away the road from Basingstoke to London and the traffic roaring by.

Anna Massey

*A*nna Massey has had an illustrious career on the stage, on television, and in films. Her theatrical experience extends from playing Ophelia in Hamlet *to* Lady Teazle *in* School for Scandal *to* Annie Sullivan *in* The Miracle Worker. *Her work in film includes* A Doll's House, Mountains of the Moon, Impromptu, Angels and Insects, *and* Grave Indiscretions. *For television she has starred in* The Pallisers, The Mayor of Casterbridge, Sakharov, Rebecca, *and* Mansfield Park, *in which she depicted Aunt Norris.*

Anna Massey

NT: *Tell me some of your memories of playing Aunt Norris in* Mansfield Park?

AM: I read the book several times to prepare. No actor would approach a part without having read the novel at least once and probably many more times. I most enjoyed playing the role, but we used multiple video cameras in the filming, so I never felt that the characters were completely registered in the film. I didn't think it achieved its goal terribly well. There were many more details in such a dark and complicated novel than could be handled in one film. I felt it was not always the deepest of renditions.

NT: *Viewers loved your performance of a character that they love to hate.*

AM: Yes, but Mrs. Norris is really pathetic. She is not evil in any way; she is pathetic. She is not out to damage anybody; she is just out to be in control and interfering.

NT: *Do you have a favorite among the novels?*

AM: *Persuasion* is almost a flawless novel. The character of Anne Elliot is the most complicated. Her journey is complicated, her character is completely evolved, and her journey is impeccably told.

NT: *Tell me about recording the novels for Books on Tape?*

AM: It is very consuming work because you have to use the minimum of different voices for different characters and the minimum of interpretation because it takes away from the concentration of the narrative. You have to find subtle ways of differentiating between the characters, and that takes hours and hours of thought and preparation.

NT: *How long does it take you to record a book?*

AM: There is quite a lot of homework before you get to the hard reading. I prepare for at least twenty hours and average about a hundred pages a day normally. But with Jane Austen's novels the sentences are so complicated that I read about seventy pages a day.

NT: *Which of the novels have you recorded?*

AM: I have recorded *Northanger Abbey* more than once and all of the rest of them, but funnily enough, I haven't recorded *Mansfield Park*.

❧ QUIZ: FOOD IN JANE AUSTEN ❧

---

*G*ood apple pies are a considerable part of our domestic happiness.
—JANE AUSTEN, letter to Cassandra, October 1815

Answer the following questions:

SENSE AND SENSIBILITY

1. Who tries to cure the inconsolable Marianne Dashwood with olives, dried cherries, Constantia wine, and sweetmeats?

2. Who believes that the Dashwoods deserve no more than "presents of fish and game, and so forth, whenever they are in season?"

3. Who stuffs "sugar plums" into the "violently screaming" mouth of Lady Middleton's three-year-old daughter, Annamaria?

MANSFIELD PARK

4. Which character feels ill from "the milk," which is a "mixture of motes floating in thin blue"?

5. Who takes home "jellied candies" in her pockets, supposedly to give to her maid?

6. Which gourmand "brought on apoplexy and death, by three great institutionary meals in one week"?

7. Which two characters argue about apricots?

8. Who played the harp when sandwiches were served?

EMMA

9. What kind of food does Miss Bates claim that her mother loves more than any other?

10. Who ate Stilton and North Wiltshire cheeses with celery and beetroot?

11. Who sends a sack of apples to Mrs. and Miss Bates every year?

12. Who brings a "basket with pink ribbon" to pick "the best fruit in England," strawberries, at Donwell Abbey?

13. Which character "hopes to influence" others against eating wedding cake?

SANDITON

14. Which character never eats "for about a week after a journey"?

15. Who prides himself on his ability to toast bread?

16. What drink "acts like poison" upon Arthur Parker and "takes away the use of his right side for several hours"?

T. Coraghessan Boyle

Crawford was waiting for me in the ragged shadows of the trees, turned to face me like a bayed animal. I felt a surge of power. I wanted to call him a son of a bitch, but, in keeping with the times, I settled for cad. "You cad," I said, shoving him back a step, "how dare you come sniffing around here after what you did to Maria Bertram in Mansfield Park? It's people like you—corrupt, arbitrary, egocentric—that foment all the lust and heartbreak of the world and challenge the very possibility of happy endings.

—T. CORAGHESSAN BOYLE, "I Dated Jane Austen"

Mary Park has said that *"skinny, earringed, satanically goateed, T. Coraghessan Boyle is the trickster fixture of American letters. Part court jester, part holy fool, he slips in and out of various narrative disguises as it suits him." A professor at the University of California at Los Angeles, Boyle is the author of novels that combine history, parody, and protopunk points of view, with high literary seriousness. His novels include* Water Music, World's End, The Road to Wellville, The Tortilla Curtain, *and* Riven Rock. *He has also published a number of short stories, including "I Dated Jane Austen."*

NT: *So you dated Jane Austen?*

TCB: I don't generally like kiss-and-tell stories, and I very rarely pull the plug on my dates, disastrous or otherwise, but in the case of "I Dated Jane Austen," my baser instincts took over, I'm afraid. You see, I'd admired her from afar—she was famous, after all, and I was just starting out, having published maybe two dozen stories or so—and I was surprised when she agreed to go out with me at all. She was a bit older, you understand. But since age in such circumstances is such a touchy subject, I never pressed her to reveal just how much older than I she was.

I got the sense that she was inwardly toting up my shortcomings (hair, dress, accent, that sort of thing) and that I wasn't really doing too well. She was funny, I guess, in a very dry, Englishy sort of way, but she had cute eyes, and those curls and mobcap just killed me. But as you can see from my account, it was Cassandra whose candles I really lit. With her, I might have had a chance. Unfortunately I was unable to pursue it. For one thing, and I never revealed this to Jane, though she would have secretly thrilled to know it, I was already engaged.

NT: *Do you have a favorite humorous moment in Austen's novels?*

TCB: Yes. When Mr. Elton makes his intentions known to Emma Woodhouse.

NT: *Has she influenced your own writing in any way?*

TCB: Jane has, I think, but not so much as her predecessor Henry Fielding and her successors Charles Dickens, Anthony Trollope, and the modern British novelists. My Ph.D. is in nineteenth-century British, so I've read a few three-volume novels in my day. I suppose they've all had an influence on my own novels, especially *Water Music, World's End,* and *Riven Rock.*

Home Theatricals: *Lovers' Vows*

Fanny Price is surely Jane Austen's most morally rigorous heroine, so much so that many readers see her as a prig, particularly in her objections to the home theatricals staged by the young Bertrams and Crawfords during Sir Thomas's absence from Mansfield Park. Fanny's objections, however, are entirely reasonable on several grounds. In the first place, the selected play, Kotzebue's *Lovers' Vows,* is not quite proper, depending as it does on seduction and illegitimacy. Even its happy ending is problematic since it reconciles the illegitimate son with his father, a baron, and implies that the baron's title and estates will pass to an illegitimate line and consequently undermine the whole social order based on familial history.

But Fanny has still more pressing reasons for objecting to the play. It is clear to her, as it is to readers, that the performances of the various roles would put the actors in situations of unwarranted intimacy. Fanny particularly dreads a scene in which her beloved Edmund and the scheming Mary Crawford would perform together: "The whole subject of it was love—a marriage of love was to be described by the gentleman, and very little short of a declaration of love be made by the lady." Ultimately, however, Fanny's strongest objection is to playing a role herself. Her repeated statement, "I cannot act," must be taken seriously. It is not just that she *will* not act but that she *can*not; it is not possible for her to be, or even seem to be, anyone but herself. Fanny's objection in the end is an objection to all artifice, especially to playing at being in love, a technique used by unscrupulous women in the practice of husband hunting. Indeed, as it turns out, the characters that play at being in love find themselves inappropriately and disastrously falling in love with their fellow performers. The scheming Crawfords of course do not fall in love because they have been playacting all along. Fanny's rigor on this point must be understood as the moral opposite of the dangerous hypocrisy underlying the playfulness of Henry and Mary Crawford. Austen herself delighted in home theatricals and played Mrs. Candour in *The School for Scandal.*

It is his objections to the proposed private theatricals that finally establish Edmund as repulsive. . . . We are right to expect from Edmund something more intelligent, more liberal, more manly . . . and a cursory reading will show that Lovers' Vows *is in fact innocuous rubbish. This being so, his eventual reluctant consent to participate, which we are invited to see as the tragic overthrow of a noble mind worked on by Mary Crawford, becomes a squalid and ridiculous belly-flop.*
—KINGSLEY AMIS, on Edmund Bertram

Phoebe Spinrad on Mothers and Fathers in Austen's Novels

*C**aptain Phoebe Spinrad, a renaissance woman, is a highly decorated veteran of the Vietnam War. She is the author of* The Summons of Death on the Medieval and Renaissance English Stage *and has many published poems to her credit. She is also the author of extensive articles on Shakespeare, Donne, and Marvell, among others. She is a professor of English Literature at the Ohio State University.*

NT: *I have heard you comment on the role of parents in Jane Austen. Do you have any generalizations about the parents in her novels?*

PS: It seems that in every one of the novels we're presented with wonderful examples and horrible examples of how to be a family member. Several of the main characters have either no mother or no father. A number of the characters do have surrogate parents in some way, whether they have a living parent or not. Anne Elliot, for example, whose mother has died, has really been raised more by Lady Russell than by her own father. Some characters have living parents who have given them to others to be raised. Frank Churchill, for example, has been raised by his aunt and uncle even though he has a living father. Yet we also have some very close family members. It's very hard to make generalizations except that there are so many variations on the family structure.

NT: *Which of the mothers in the novels do you think might be the best, which the worst, and why?*

PS: One set of parents is head and shoulders above the rest: Mr. and Mrs. Morland in *Northanger Abbey*. These two are, hands down, the best parents. Mrs. Morland is very commonsensical. She's raised a huge family and raised them well; they're honest, straightforward people who care about others. She's never pressured any of her children into doing things they don't like or aren't capable of. Yet she has insisted on their getting good educations. When Catherine in her childhood decided she wanted to play the piano, Mrs. Morland immediately found the money to get her a piano master. When Catherine then decided she didn't like it, there was no question of going on; she stopped having the piano lessons. She was made to learn her lessons, but she was not forced into anything that wasn't going to do her any good.

When Catherine has a chance to go to Bath and have a good time, Mrs. Morland isn't worried that she's going to get into terrible scrapes and doesn't make a melodrama out of their parting. She just tells Catherine to be a good girl. Mr. Morland gives her a small but adequate amount of money and tells her to ask for more if she needs it.

What I think is wonderful about Mrs. Morland is the way she handles the situation at the end. Here comes her daughter in very humiliating circumstances, turned out of General Tilney's house, sent home alone in the equivalent of a Greyhound bus, and Mrs. Morland finds something good in it: Well, that's very strange of General Tilney, but at least we know that Catherine can take care of herself. In effect she turns the humiliation into a compliment to Catherine. What wonderful parents the Morlands are. They're no-fuss parents who have obviously gained the deep affection of their children, without the melodrama that we see in some of the other families.

I think that Mrs. Bennet is evil.

NT: *Evil?*

PS: It must be terrible to be her daughter, and even Elizabeth (dear Lizzy!) occasionally remarks that years of happiness will not make up for some of the humiliations she and her sister Jane have suffered through her mother's ignorant and loudmouthed behavior in public. But we tend to write that off because Austen has made Mrs. Bennet so very entertaining to read about.

And we think she's just dumb, just stupid. Well, Mrs. Bennet may not be malicious—although she sometimes is in a narrow-spirited way toward the Lucas family and Mr. Darcy—but I use the word "evil" about her because she condones her daughter's vice. Now, this is a horrible thing. This isn't just a matter of embarrassment; it's a matter of teaching her daughters to sleep around. The way she welcomes Lydia back into her household afterward as though she'd done something wonderful by managing to get Wickham to marry her. The way she shows Lydia off around the neighborhood after the marriage as though the circumstances were something to be proud of: "Here's my wonderful daughter, the slut." (No, she doesn't say that; I'm expressing my own outrage.) The only thing she seems to be worried about during the affair is what the neighbors will say, but after the marriage she seems to assume they'll be just as delighted as she is with the outcome and forget the prelude or accept it as good. Lydia has now become her favorite daughter because Lydia is the first to get married. But she's teaching her other daughters—or would, if Lizzy and Jane didn't have some morals in spite of her—that sleeping around is a good way to catch husbands, and everyone will admire you and pamper you afterward. This is a terrible thing for a mother to teach her children.

We have two sets of aunts and uncles for the Bennet girls. We have Aunt Phillips, who's another of those fluffy-headed, giddy, let-the-girls-get-into-trouble-if-it's-fun types. But we also have Mr. and Mrs. Gardiner, whom Lizzy is proud to show off before Darcy. So there are some intelligent good relatives after all. The Gardiners are also good examples of what parents can be. They have children of whom they're obviously very fond and who are very good children.

NT: *Speaking of surrogates, Aunt Norris . . .*

PS: Oh dear, oh, my. And oh, yes, I haven't mentioned the *Mansfield Park* parents yet, have I? Lady Bertram, as a mother, is just sort of . . . not there. And Aunt Norris? If she were a mother, I might put her in second place to Mrs. Bennet. In fact, she might be tied for worst, considering how willing she is to fob Maria off on Mr. Rushworth even though she knows that Mr. Rushworth is terrible and that Maria can't possibly be happy with him. All she cares about is the money, the connection, and the establishment. Yes, if she were a mother, I'd rank her right up there (or down there) with Mrs. Bennet. Of course she's also a ghastly aunt.

NT: *Do you have a favorite father in the novels, and conversely, do you have one you think is the worst?*

PS: Putting aside Mr. Morland, who is the best father, I select Sir Thomas Bertram. I know that may sound like an unusual choice because he seems very forbidding and he also has a daughter who gets into trouble. But he's such a domestic person. He has that sense of responsibility. When he comes back from Antigua and discovers that Mr. Rushworth is a clod and that even Maria seems to look upon him with disdain, he offers to free Maria from the engagement. He really doesn't want to; it'll be publicly embarrassing for him to break off the engagement, and the Rushworth connection would be financially and socially a very good one for the family. But he still offers to let go of the connection and to take the full burden of the disengagement on himself to save Maria the embarrassment if the marriage will make her unhappy. He also takes pains with Fanny. Even though he's uneasy over the possibility that she may fall in love with one of her cousins, he still brings her into his home and educates her along with his own daughters. Sir Thomas says straight out that once he takes responsibility for Fanny, he takes it for life; he's going to raise her to be a gentlewoman. There's no question of just giving her an education and then turning her back to some other kind of life. Once he's said yes, it's yes for life—even when he's angry with her for not wanting to marry Henry Crawford.

One scene that really illuminates Sir Thomas's character is the evening of his arrival home from Antigua. That picture of his genuine happiness as he sits looking around with deep pleasure at his whole family gathered together just leaps off the page. Moreover, he calls for Fanny, who's been reluctant to "in-

---

FIRST TRANSLATIONS

⁂

*I*n 1815 Austen was first translated into a foreign language: Appearing in France was *Raison et Sensibilité, ou les Deux Manières d'Aimer. Traduit librement de l'anglais, par Mme Isabelle de Montolieu.* In 1816 *Le Parc de Mansfield, ou Les Trois Cousines* appeared, followed by *La Nouvelle Emma, ou les Caractères anglais de Siècle.*

trude" on his "real" family; he says, "Where is Fanny?" He has not forgotten her. Once he does realize he's made a mistake, he's not like Mr. Bennet; he doesn't just make a sardonic joke about it and go back to business as usual. He tries to make up for what he's done.

NT: *Speaking of fathers, Fanny's natural father is no prize.*

PS: Here we come to the competition for worst father. Mr. Price is a terrible father, and once again my immediate impulse might be to say he's the worst. Partly because he ignores her but partly because he makes her the

---

WHAT IS A HA-HA?

*R*eaders of eighteenth- and nineteenth-century novels often meet with strange words. What exactly are bathing machines and ha-has? And how could Japan fit into Northanger Abbey? The bathing machines, which are referred to in *Sanditon,* were large, covered, horse-drawn wagons, which ensured some privacy so that ladies could take the seawaters and maintain their pudency. The horses actually trotted several feet into the ocean.

The Japan at Northanger Abbey was a large, black cabinet: "Japan" is a hard varnish that gives wood a glossy finish.

In *Mansfield Park* a party visits the Rushworths' home, Sotherton, and Edmund, who is walking with both Mary Crawford and Fanny Price, leaves Fanny on a bench overlooking a ha-ha. Poor Fanny is abandoned to the view of the ha-ha since Edmund urges her to rest while he promenades with the robust Mary. Ellen Jorden of the University of Newcastle, Australia, provides us with a definition:

> The idea of a ha-ha was to keep cattle/deer/people out of an area without ugly fences breaking up the vista. A ditch was dug and a fence of some sort placed at the bottom. The way across was by an unditched area closed off by a wrought iron gate. These gates usually had further barriers stretching from the gatepost to the edge of the ditch shaped rather like a quarter of a bicycle wheel with spokes and with spikes protruding beyond each spoke. This is the barrier that Henry Crawford and Maria climb around in *Mansfield Park* while poor Mr. Rushworth has hurried off to get the key to the gate that will let them into the park.

The ha-ha in this case also serves as a reminder of Maria's impending "imprisonment" in her marriage to Mr. Rushworth. She remarks that "unluckily that iron gate, that ha-ha, give me a feeling of restraint and hardship." At Henry Crawford's suggestion, she slips through the gate, foreshadowing her fling with Henry, which will free her from her marriage to Rushworth but leave her to live in scandal and isolation.

subject (as Austen tells us) of a coarse joke in front of his male friends, which is deplorable. The whole house is chaotic, partly through Mr. Price and partly through Mrs. Price. They're both slovenly in their own ways. But William has turned out well, and Susan is turning out well. So I'm not sure I'd place either of those parents as the worst, in spite of Mr. Price's coarse joke.

NT: *We haven't discussed Mr. Bennet or Sir Walter Elliot of* Persuasion.

PS: I was saving the worst for last. First, Mr. Bennet. Again, even though we find his wisecracks entertaining, I'd say he's not a good father. When he sees the way his daughters are going, he should step in as Sir Thomas Bertram would do and try to get them shaped up. But the worst of all is Sir Walter Elliot. Worse than Mr. Price with his coarse joke. Worse than the irresponsible Mr. Bennet. Sir Walter can't be excused on the grounds of unthinking stupidity or being backed into a corner or giving up in despair on a bad marriage or even the prevailing mores of his society. Sir Walter Elliot is cruel. He's stingy; he thinks about no one but himself. The only reason he seems to like his eldest daughter, Elizabeth, at all is that she's so much like him. Mirrors, constant mirrors. That's the way I think about him: as surrounded by mirrors. When Admiral Croft rents the house, the first thing he does is take out all the mirrors. When someone can't be a good mirror for Sir Walter, he discards her. I definitely would have to say that Sir Walter is the worst father. I can find no redeeming qualities in him. None. Zero.

NT: *Which of the novels would you recommend to the reader who has not yet experienced Austen?*

PS: I suppose that the one I would recommend to someone who hasn't read Austen before would be *Pride and Prejudice* because it's, as Austen herself said, the most light and sparkling, and you certainly do get the most of that ironic tone of voice. Also, you get an introduction to many different types of characters, and it has a very clear-cut happy ending. And the heroine is delightful. Dear Lizzy. Wouldn't you love to have her as a friend?

The British Empire

First-time readers of Jane Austen frequently ask why none of her characters seems to work for a living. In fact, some do, though we never actually see the various clergymen delivering sermons or the various soldiers at war, but the impression of a leisured society is not inaccurate. Austen famously centers her novels on a few country families whose estates are inherited and whose sources of wealth are generally kept out of sight. During the period when Austen was writing, the gap between the wealthy county families and the rural poor who paid them rent was growing wider, and glimpses across that gap are rarely offered. We are, however, made aware that Darcy has tenants, and in *Emma* we are actually introduced to one of Mr. Knightley's tenant farmers, the admirable Robert Martin.

Still, the main source of British wealth in Austen's time was the British Empire, and in various ways the genteel life of Austen's emphatically English county gentry was made possible not by the wealth of the local agricultural community but by the commercial wealth of the Empire. In part British wealth, specifically the wealth of the Bertram family in *Mansfield Park*, was based on the labor of slaves on the plantations of the British West Indies.

THE SPECIAL DIMPLE

*V*ladimir Nabokov, an Austen enthusiast, has described Austen's use of irony as "a special dimple" that is "achieved by furtively introducing into the sentence a bit of delicate irony between the components of a plain informative statement." He gives several examples: "Lady Bertram was a woman who spent her days in sitting nicely dressed on a sofa, doing some long piece of needlework, *of little use and no beauty,* thinking more of her pug than her children.". . . and "Mrs. Price in her turn was injured and angry; and an answer which comprehended each sister in its bitterness, and bestowed such very disrespectful reflections on the pride of Sir Thomas, *as Mrs. Norris could not possibly keep to herself,* put an end to all intercourse between them for a considerable period."

Though Austen's novels seem to represent a timeless, placid way of life in England's "green and pleasant land," it is possible to glimpse very occasionally the lower level of the economic pyramid and the powers that preserve the status quo. The poor families visited by Emma and Harriet, for example, were a regular feature of the landscape, not just a temporary prop to enable Emma to showcase her charity, and the troops continually moving through Meryton were not simply providing an endless supply of dashing officers for the younger Bennet sisters but were going about the military business of making Great Britain the world's most powerful nation.

Further, Austen's beloved navy was not just a way to make Admiral Croft and Captain Wentworth wealthy and to set Fanny Price's brother William on the road to prosperity. It was the primary military power that kept order in the world's most extensive empire and made it safe for Sir Thomas Bertram and others to own and occasionally to visit plantations worked by slaves in Antigua and elsewhere.

Fanny Wars

Perhaps no controversy excites and divides lovers of Jane Austen as much as that surrounding Fanny Price. Certainly no other character, not even Emma, has met with such mixed reactions. Many readers are uncomfortable with or just plain dislike the poor relation Fanny Price and her "Cinderella-like" transformation; she is the only Austen heroine who comes from a sordid background. Some readers may find the villains more attractive and compelling than the virtuous heroine in this novel, in a way that is reminiscent of Milton's *Paradise Lost,* where Satan seems more attractive than God. Fanny Price is Austen's most "perfect" heroine insofar as she never seems to misjudge a situation or succumb to temporary folly. Elinor Dashwood comes close, and Anne Elliot has made few mistakes, but Fanny is infallible. Kingsley Amis called her "a monster of complacency and pride," yet Fanny is the only character in the novel who is never misguided. Fortunately the novel has enough comically grotesque characters to leaven the lump of her virtue. Fanny's moral perfection may be irritating to readers who enjoy the process of the heroine's learning about herself and becoming a better person. Some readers think Fanny is anemic and mouselike; others think she is impeccable in her instincts and admire her steadiness.

Just mention the name [Fanny Price] and stand back, whatever else is being discussed falls by the wayside.
—EDITH LANK

I pity, approve, respect, and admire her, but I neither desire her company nor am greatly concerned about her destiny.
—A. C. BRADLEY

Fanny is the only character in the novel who has no clear social understanding or identity, but . . . this timid outsider is the only one who has a wise and consistent moral identity, who has "all the heroism of principle." She . . . maintains the true or ideal character of Mansfield Park. And this is the novel that is said to have a fatal lack of irony!
—DOUGLAS BUSH

*He wished, in short, to be Fanny Price in **Mansfield Park**, not, of course, in her creep-mouse days, but in her time of flowering, when her full worth is known and her single-mindedness and sincerity have made her loved by all. . . . She is overtly virtuous and consciously virtuous and therefore almost impossible to like. But I like her.*

—LIONEL TRILLING

Into Fanny, Jane Austen, to counterbalance her apparent insignificance, has put really nothing except rectitude of mind; neither passion, nor physical courage, nor wit, nor resource . . . her very love is only calf-love—a schoolgirl's hero-worship for a man who has been kind to her when they were both children, and who, incidentally, is the least attractive of all Jane Austen's heroes.

—C. S. LEWIS

The quietest and most mundane of visionaries, she remains also one of the firmest: her dedication is to the future of Mansfield Park as the idea of order it once seemed to her.

—HAROLD BLOOM

When I tried reading this novel some years ago, I gave up about two thirds of the way through because I could not endure the company of meekly mousy Fanny Price for one more page.

—JEREMY KINGSTON

Her immobility, her refusal to be "moved" are not symptoms of mule-like stubborness or paralysed fear, but a measure of her integrity, her adherence to her own clear evaluation of how things stand. She speaks for the "inner light" in a world of falling worldly standards. . . . We see her as a lonely conscience—ignored, despised, bullied, at times besieged by the forces of worldly persuasion, yet finally recognized as the true preserver of the values represented by Mansfield Park.

—TONY TANNER

Mansfield Park is a great novel, its greatness being commensurate with its power to offend.

—LIONEL TRILLING

Squalor in Portsmouth

Fanny Price's family home in Portsmouth is Austen's only extended study of a family living in somewhat squalid conditions. Portsmouth was the birthplace of Charles Dickens, and his early life may well have been similar to the fictional life of the Price family. There was undoubtedly a good deal of transience and activity in Portsmouth as a major port city, as opposed to the settled world of Mansfield Park. Fanny's parents live in an "abode of noise, disorder, and impropriety. Nobody was in their right place, nothing was done as it ought

BLUSHING

Blushes and other physical displays play an important role in Austen's novels, since they communicate by involuntary body language what the characters might have preferred to keep to themselves. How does the reader interpret who did what and why when Darcy and Wickham meet on the street in Meryton, and "Both changed colour, one looked white, the other red." As the narrator asks, "What could be the meaning of it?" Austen's readers are still pondering the question, but an alert reader will take notice of the telltale blushes, breathlessness, sighs, and moans of the characters as a clue to what is going on in their minds. The blush is a sign of virtue in Austen. In *Pride and Prejudice,* when Wickham and his bride, Lydia, make their triumphal wedding visit to Longbourn, some of her sisters are shocked by their laughter and their "easy assurance." Elizabeth "blushed, and Jane blushed; but the cheeks of the two who caused their confusion suffered no variation of colour." Fanny Price, more than any other heroine, blushes frequently. In *Emma* the full nuances of blushes and the subtle language of blushing are most explored. Emma is much more self-assured than Fanny, and we expect that she will blush less often. She prides herself on detecting what she thinks are telltale blushes in others; she is certain that Jane Fairfax has a "blush of guilt" at the name of Colonel Campbell. She thinks that she is an adept at interpreting Harriet's blushes, but in fact, she misunderstands them as often as not. Moreover, at the Box Hill picnic Emma is unrepentant when Miss Bates blushes upon hearing Emma's unkind cut about her loquacity.

Perhaps the most delightful convergence of blushing in all of Austen's novels comes at the end of *Persuasion,* when both Anne Elliot and Frederick Wentworth are blushing at their joy in having reached an understanding. Their cheeks glow in unison as their spirits dance "in private rapture."

to be." Family life there is disorganized, compared with the "repose" that Mansfield Park offers. Fanny believes that Sir Thomas Bertram desires "the repose of his family circle." In contrast, her own father has "coarser" manners than she is prepared for. He "swore and drank, he was dirty and gross." Her siblings squabble. Although Fanny does her very best to bring greater order and tranquillity to the Portsmouth home, she finds that she is homesick for Mansfield Park, which has become the home of her spirit. "The elegance, propriety, regularity, harmony—and perhaps, above all, the peace and tranquility of Mansfield, were brought to her remembrance every hour of the day, by the prevalence of every thing opposite to them *here*," she thinks about her Portsmouth home.

In Portsmouth Fanny cannot even eat properly. The "hashes, brought to table as they all were, with such accompaniments of half-cleaned plates, and not half-cleaned knives and forks," constrain her to the point that she cannot eat and has to rely on her brothers to bring her "biscuits and buns" in the evenings. Although Fanny cannot do much about the grease, stains, and dirt of her home (perhaps the all-carbohydrate diet has weakened her), she is able to do something to improve the mind of her sister Susan. She introduces Susan to books and to Mansfield Park values. Throughout her stay in Portsmouth, Fanny is comforted by literature. She quotes Cowper to herself, she gets books from the circulating library, and she thinks of Dr. Johnson. The implication is very much that books and a knowledge of literature can sustain one in miserable circumstances.

When Fanny returns to Mansfield, she is delighted to be able to rescue Susan from the squalor of Portsmouth. Susan claims Fanny's previous role as general factotum to Lady Bertram, and Fanny claims the role of "the daughter" that Sir Thomas "always wanted."

Emma

Emma is the climax of Jane Austen's genius and the Parthenon of fiction.
—RONALD BLYTHE

I am going to take a heroine whom no one but myself will much like.
—JANE AUSTEN, on Emma

No exception to the general rule of Jane Austen's fiction, *Emma* is the story of a young woman discovering her capacity for love and discovering further that the course of true love never does run smooth. Unlike the heroines of the other novels, however, Emma does not appear at the outset to be in need (or in want) of a husband. As the justly famous opening sentence makes clear, she is entirely independent and happy: "Emma Woodhouse, handsome, clever, and rich, with a comfortable home and happy disposition, seemed to unite some of the best blessings of existence; and had lived nearly twenty-one years in the world with very little to distress or vex her." Though the conclusion of the sentence is ominous with impending vexation, Emma herself maintains throughout most of the novel that unlike others, she is not likely to be distressed or vexed by the conditions of the marriage market. As she tells her young friend and protégée Harriet Smith: "I have none of the usual inducements to marry. Were I to fall in love, indeed, it would be a different thing! but I never have been in love; it is not in my way, or my nature; and I do not think I ever shall." And "without love, I am sure I would be a fool to change such a situation as mine. Fortune I do not want; employment I do not want; consequence I do not want."

Without needing to arrange her already comfortable life, Emma devotes herself to "the greatest amusement in the world," the management of other people's lives, particularly through the art of matchmaking. As the novel opens, she is congratulating herself upon the marriage for which she takes credit between her much-loved governess and friend Miss Taylor and an affable neighbor, Mr. Weston. Despite the advice of her querulous father and wise neighbor, Mr. Knightley, she is already beginning to plan a match between Harriet and the handsome, gregarious clergyman Mr. Elton. The first obstacle in arranging the bliss of the young couple arises when Emma learns of Harriet's existing attachment to a worthy young farmer, Robert Martin. Characteristically Emma decides that Martin is not socially worthy and creates a good deal of mischief by persuading Harriet that a marriage to him would be a "degradation." Having successfully talked Harriet out of loving Martin, she easily talks her into loving Elton.

Most of the plot twists in *Emma* revolve around Emma's overestimation of her own cleverness in reading people. She has genuinely convinced herself that Elton is in love with Harriet and builds up Harriet's hopes accordingly. Emma learns that she has seriously misread Elton's intentions when the slightly inebriated clergyman professes his desperate love for Emma herself. Though Austen drops abundant clues to alert the reader to the true state of affairs and to Mr. Elton's fundamental vulgarity and upwardly mobile goals in marriage, Emma was "clueless" and is astonished and mortified to learn that Mr. Elton could have imagined himself close enough to her social level to propose marriage to her. Emma's behavior throughout this fiasco is that of a complete snob and a heartless busybody. Austen makes it very clear that her schemes have serious repercussions for both Harriet and Robert Martin.

At the same time Emma is seen in the wider context of her social and family activities. Her relationships to the rich cast of characters in and around her village of Highbury reveal that despite her serious mistakes, she is indeed both clever and loving. Most obviously she is shown in a good light in her constant, loving attention to the "gentle selfishness" of her absurdly hypochondriacal and needy father. In addition, her good qualities are apparent by the respect shown her by the unquestionably worthy and discerning characters that know her best, Mr. Knightley and Mrs. Weston. Even the amiable but comically talkative, sometimes irritatingly verbose Miss Bates has a high opinion of Emma that carries some weight. In addition, Emma's regrets about misleading Harriet show that she has acted at least in part from affectionate motives. Perhaps most important, Emma has the virtue of a teachable disposition. Her regrets are partially motivated by the blow to her own self-esteem but are mostly brought about by her concern for Harriet: "That was the worst of all. Every part of it brought pain and humiliation of some sort or other; but, compared with the evil to Harriet, all was light; and she would gladly have submitted to feel yet more mistaken—more in error—more disgraced by misjudgment than she actually was, could the effects of her blunders have been confined to herself." Still, Emma does not learn her lesson all at once. Because of her keen sense of social distinctions, she continues to view Robert Martin as unworthy of Harriet and is determined to prevent their renewing their attachment.

Just as Emma's matchmaking folly is at its climax, she herself is set up by circumstances as a likely match for Mr. Weston's son, Frank Churchill, who is expected soon to visit Highbury. Frank has been essentially adopted by Mr. Weston's wealthy in-laws after the death of the first Mrs. Weston, so he is of an appropriate social class to woo Emma, and Austen provides very clear clues to the reader to expect this courtship: "It so happened that in spite of Emma's resolution of never marrying, there was something in the name, in the idea of Mr. Frank Churchill, which always interested her. She had frequently thought . . . that if she *were* to marry, he was the very person to suit her in age, character, and condition." Though we are invited to anticipate a romance between Frank and Emma, a subtler hint of other possibilities is raised by the apparently unreasonable dislike that the "idea of Mr. Frank Churchill" inspires in the usually magnanimous and kind Mr. Knightley. Experienced readers of Jane Austen might suspect an element of jealousy in such an attitude.

Once Frank Churchill arrives in Highbury all the characters seem to be enacting a conventional marriage plot. The friends of both Emma and Frank fondly imagine that they will marry, and she herself flirts with the idea that she might be in love with him. Fortunately for her own peace of mind and for her determination never to marry, she comes increasingly to the conclusion that although Frank may be very much in love with her, she is certainly not more than a little bit in love with him.

While the romance between Emma and Frank is developing, Austen raises the comic level of the novel by sending Mr. Elton out of town and bringing him back with a preposterously presumptuous wife, Miss Augusta Hawkins, who represents herself in Highbury as the crème de la crème of high society in Bath, though she is actually from an upstart family with no just pretensions of social prestige. The Eltons work together to humiliate the already humbled Harriet. Another new addition to Highbury society is the niece of Miss Bates, Jane Fairfax, who, like Frank Churchill, has been raised in a wealthy family but who has no material expectations and seems fated to resign herself to the socially degrading position of governess. Though lower than Mrs. Elton in economic status, Jane Fairfax far outclasses her in manners, abilities, and true elegance, so a major element in the social comedy of *Emma* involves the outrageousness of Mrs. Elton's patronizing behavior to Jane.

The characters of *Emma* exhibit their manners and expose their true characters in a variety of social occasions, including dinners, balls, luncheons, and two memorable excursions, one to Mr. Knightley's estate, Donwell Abbey, and one to the picturesque Box Hill. Emma's limitations in particular are revealed in her wicked and totally unfounded gossip about Jane Fairfax, her overflirtatious manner with Frank Churchill, her continued interference between Harriet and Robert Martin, and finally, her outrageous insult of the good-hearted and defenseless Miss Bates at Box Hill.

The plot seems to be developing toward the marriage of Frank and Emma, the sacrifice of Jane Fairfax to the governess trade, and the sacrifice of Harriet to Emma's ill-considered manipulations. A complication develops when Emma decides that she does not love Frank and becomes determined to match him up with Harriet. The ultimate twist in the plot occurs, however, when it is revealed that Frank and Jane have been secretly engaged all along and that both have been acting a part in all their social relations. As a result, all plots seem to come undone. These include the Westons' plot to match up Frank and Emma, Emma's plot to match Frank with Harriet, and apparently even Austen's plot to bring about the marriage of her heroine.

As it turns out, Emma has characteristically been mistaken about Harriet and learns that her friend has thought herself in love not with Frank but with Mr. Knightley. Emma discovers from her own reaction to this news that she herself has been in love with Mr. Knightley all along. Now Harriet and Robert Martin are free to find each other, and the marriages of the three couples resolve all difficulties for everyone and produce an entirely happy ending.

"Handsome, Clever, and Rich"

These three adjectives capture beautifully the cadence of Jane Austen's writing; they could no more be rearranged than could Shakespeare's "friends, Romans, countrymen." Emma Woodhouse, like the words "handsome" and "clever" and the name Knightley, is a trochee, or falling meter: a long stress followed by a short one. (trociness?). In none of Austen's other novels do we find such a plethora of trochees: Campbell, Churchill, Dixon, Elton, Fairfax, Goddard, Hawkins, Martin, Suckling, Taylor, Weston, Hartfield, Donwell, Randalls. Only Miss Harriet Smith and Mrs. and Miss Bates break the trochaic pattern of the major characters' names. Jane Austen loved poetry, and her writing reveals a superb ear for the language. Does so much of *Emma* take place in falling meter as a counterpart to the fall of Emma herself into self-knowledge?

Emma is both delightful and infuriating and causes almost as much controversy among readers as does Fanny Price. Many readers identify with Emma's desire to control a disordered world. When she learns her limitations, she admits to herself that she has not always spoken and behaved as she ought to have done. Readers find this self-recognition familiar, if not endearing. Humility is a bitter pill to swallow, and Emma takes her dose with elegance. Unlike the mousy and infallible Fanny Price, Emma is handsome and all too fallible. She gets herself into more trouble with her precipitate judg-

An Exchange of Letters with James Stanier Clarke

From James Clarke, March 27, 1816
Dear Miss Austen,

I have to return you the thanks of His Royal Highness, the Prince Regent, for the handsome copy you sent him of your last excellent novel [*Emma*]. . . . The Prince Regent has just left us for London; and having been pleased to appoint me Chaplain and Private English Secretary to the Prince of Coburg, I remain here with His Serene Highness and a select party until the marriage. Perhaps when you again appear in print you may chuse to dedicate your volumes to Prince Leopold: any historical romance, illustrative of the history of the august House of Coburg, would just now be very interesting.

Believe me at all times,
Dear Miss Austen,
Your obliged friend,
J. S. Clarke

To Clarke, April 1, 1816
My Dear Sir,

I am honoured by the Prince's thanks and very much obliged to yourself for the kind manner in which you mention the work. . . . You are very kind in your hints as to the sort of composition which might recommend me at present, and I am fully sensible that an historical romance, founded on the House of Saxe Coburg, might be much more to the purpose of profit or popularity than such pictures of domestic life in country villages that I deal in. But I could no more write a romance than an epic poem. I could not sit seriously down to write a serious romance under any other motive than to save my life; and if it were indispensable for me to keep it up and never relax into laughing at myself or other people, I am sure I should be hung before I had finished the first chapter. No, I must keep to my own style and go on in my own way; and though I may never succeed again in that, I am convinced that I should totally fail in any other.

I remain, my dear Sir,
Your very much obliged, and very sincere friend,
J. Austen

ments, her matchmaking proclivities, her thoughtless flirtations, and her cattiness, which borders on malice, than we would expect of an Austen heroine. How does she explain herself? How does she redeem herself? The plots of most Austen novels pivot around the heroine and the hero's coming to a mutual understanding. Emma, much more so than Lizzy Bennet, is obliged to know herself and to realize that being "handsome, clever, and rich" does not guarantee perfection.

Joan Wolf on the Regency Period

*J**oan Wolf is the author of more than thirty-five novels, representing several
different genres, including the historical novel, the Regency romance, and
the historical romance. Her books include* The Reindeer Hunters, The Road to
Avalon, The Rebel and the Rose, The Horsemasters, Daugher of the Red Deer,
Highland Sunset, The Counterfeit Marriage, A Double Deception, Fool's
Masquerade, Beloved Stranger, A Fashionable Affair, Wild Irish Rose, Lord
Richard's Daughter, *and* The American Duchess.

NT: *Could you tell me what the Regency period was?*

JW: The Regency period is the first part of the nineteenth century up until the
Prince Regent became king upon the death of George III in 1820. The term
"Regency" is usually extended through the end of his own reign as George IV
until 1830. King George III was declared incompetent by reason of insanity,
and so his eldest son, George, was appointed to be Regent for him. In other
words, he was king in everything but name. He could not officially become
king until his father died, but he had all the responsibilities of the kingship.

The Regent was a playboy, if you want to talk about him in today's language.
He liked to have a good time. He liked women, and he was not very honorable
with regard to them. He liked drinking, the theater, clothing, hanging about
with his group of pals. His father had been much more of a "nose to the grind-
stone" kind of person.

NT: *Did the Regent's attitude toward pleasure and fun influence the country in
general?*

JW: It had an influence on the upper class. When we talk about the Regency,
we are really talking about the upper class, a very small segment of English society. The people in the lower class were struggling to make a living, and they
did not have any chance at all to live like the Regent.

The Regent built the huge palace in Brighton, the Brighton Pavilion, and
that became a place to be for the aristocracy and the upper classes. Later in his
career he may have become more an object of ridicule than admiration for the
nobility, but during his heyday he certainly did lead society.

NT: *Three of Jane Austen's novels are situated in part in Bath, but she sent only
Lydia Bennet to Brighton. Was Brighton not fashionable during her time?*

JW: Jane Austen did not move in the top level of society. The level of society
that she moved in would tend more toward Bath. Lower upper class, I suppose, is what you would call her. The high fliers, what we would call the in
crowd, went to Brighton with the prince. The rest of society still went to the

other watering holes. Bath certainly did not fold because of the popularity of Brighton.

NT: *So Brighton Pavilion was the Trump Tower of its time?*

JW: Yes, or Monte Carlo. It was the glittery place to be, where all the golden people went.

NT: *You have written many popular Regency romance novels. Have Jane Austen's writings been an inspiration to you?*

JW: I think she is a fabulous, fabulous writer. Anybody who writes Regency I am quite sure is indebted to her. Her use of language is so wonderful; her wit is so wonderful; her apprehension of character is really amazing. She is dealing with a very narrow segment of society in a very small space, and she manages to suggest so much about good and evil within these confines. She was true to herself. She had a very good sense, artistically, of what she was doing.

THE BRITISH POST OFFICE

The Post Office has a great charm
at one period of our lives.
—*EMMA*

*D*uring the seventeenth century the first government proclamations made regular mail service a reality. "No age has shown more strikingly than our own that communication is paramount to progress," said William Dockwra, founder of the London penny post. The mail coach was initiated in 1784 in England. After three centuries of foot posts and horse posts, suddenly the modern mail coach could deliver the mail at speeds of up to ten miles per hour. In *Emma* the importance of the mail is stressed. Jane Fairfax depends upon it for her communications with Frank Churchill and says: "The post-office is a wonderful establishment . . . the regularity and dispatch of it! If one thinks of all that it has to do, and all that it does so well, it is really astonishing!" Jane Austen herself relied upon the postal service to keep her in touch with her family whenever they were separated.

POST CARD

*J*ane Austen persistently and politely declined to take upon herself the book topics suggested by the Reverend James Stanier Clarke, who was domestic chaplain and librarian to the Prince of Wales, then the Regent of Great Britain. A few months earlier Clarke had suggested to Austen that she write a book about an English clergyman. In this book she should "describe him burying his own mother—as I did—because the High Priest of the Parish in which she died—did not pay her remains the respect he ought to do. I have never recovered the Shock. Carry your Clergyman to Sea as the Friend of some distinguished Naval Character about a Court." Clarke had, not surprisingly, been a Naval chaplain earlier in his career. He evidently fancied himself an excellent subject for treatment by Austen!

*C*onsider . . . the great opening sentence of Austen's **Emma**: "*Emma Woodhouse, handsome, clever, and rich, with a comfortable home and happy disposition, seemed to unite some of the best blessings of existence; and had lived nearly twenty-one years in the world with very little to distress or vex her.*" There is a delicate play of modern irony about the psychological perimeter of this sentence that is almost impossible to arrest and define. It is an atmospheric rippling, an undulating vocal convection. The sentence contains the whole novel. Rhetorically, it is a glissando from eighteenth-century to nineteenth-century style. The grand public oratory of "handsome, clever, and rich" sinks down to the small, homely "vex," the thorn that will prick the bubble of Emma's pride. As the sentence ends, we hear the new obliqueness of modern writing and almost see the author's hidden smile. . . . Emma, like Dorian Gray, enchants by a double-sexed charm, to which not all readers are susceptible. But it is the mysterious iridescence of Emma's half-repellent character that has evoked from commentators on the novel a body of criticism unusual in its fineness. **Emma** is a reactionary work of Augustan assumptions, and its heroine presides from a tribunal of privilege. Emma's well-bred aggression becomes crasser in Rebecca Sharp, the upwardly mobile adventuress of Thackeray's **Vanity Fair.**
—CAMILLE PAGLIA, on *Emma*

*E*mma is, with Jane Austen, what **Hamlet** is with Shakespeare. It is the book of hers about which her readers are likely to disagree most; they tend either to praise it extravagantly, or to find it dull, formless, and puzzling. The reason for this, I believe, is that, just as in the case of **Hamlet**, there is something outside the picture which is never made explicit in the story but which has to be recognized by the reader before it is possible for him to appreciate the book. . . . [s]ome readers, like Justice Holmes, who was certainly a connoisseur of fiction yet who wrote that . . . "bar Miss Bates," he was "bored by Emma," never succeed in getting into the story because they cannot see what it is all about. Why does Emma take up her two protégées? Why does she become so much obsessed by her plans for them? Why does she mistake the realities so and go so ludicrously long to reach the obvious rapprochement with Knightley?

The answer is that Emma is not interested in men except in the paternal relation. Her actual father is a silly old woman: in their household it is Emma herself who, motherless as she is, assumes the functions of head of the family; it is she who takes the place of the parent and Mr. Woodhouse who becomes the child. It is Knightley who has checked and rebuked her, who has presided over her social development, and she accepts him as a substitute father; she finally marries him and brings him into her own household, where his role is to reinforce Mr. Woodhouse.

—EDMUND WILSON, on *Emma*

---

*A*fter I read the book I realized these people are not as wealthy as you think they are. They're not free to make any choices at all. Their lives are all circumscribed by duty and responsibility. I appreciated Austen's sense, for want of a better word, of morality. And I don't mean she was a prude. I just realized that at the heart of Emma is a character who is at times distinctly unlovable. And Austen's sense of mischief in writing that and sustaining that for a 400-page novel is absolutely brilliant. Because, of course, you love Emma, but she'd drive you fucking mad, and you suffer with her mistakes as you go along."

—JEREMY NORTHAM, who played Mr. Knightley to Gwyneth Paltrow's Emma

---

I have likewise read one of Miss Austen's works, Emma—read it with interest and with just the degree of admiration which Miss Austen herself would have thought sensible and suitable—anything like warmth or enthusiasm, anything energetic, poignant, or heartfelt, is utterly out of place in commending these works: all such demonstrations the authoress would have met with a well bred sneer, would have calmly scorned as outré and extravagant. She does her business of delineating the surface of the lives of genteel English people curiously well; there is a Chinese fidelity, a miniature delicacy in the painting: she ruffles her reader by nothing vehement, disturbs him by nothing profound: the Passions are perfectly unknown to her; she rejects even a speaking acquaintance with that stormy Sisterhood; even to the Feelings she vouchsafes no more than an occasional graceful but distant recognition; too frequent converse with them would ruffle the smooth elegance of her progress.

—CHARLOTTE BRONTË, on *Emma*

Judith Martin: "Miss Manners" on Jane Austen

Miss Manners

A graduate of Wellesley College and the recipient of honorary degrees, Miss Manners was "born a perfect lady in an imperfect society." She "considers it her duty and privilege to lead the way to a more civilized—and possibly even more pleasant—society." Judith Martin is the author of many books, including Miss Manners' Guide to Domestic Tranquility; Miss Manners Rescues Civilization from Sexual Harassment, Frivolous Lawsuits, Dissing and Other Lapses in Civility; Miss Manners' Guide for the Turn-of-the-Millennium; and the Miss Manners' Basic Training series, which includes Communication, Eating, and The Right Thing to Say. She has also written two novels, Gilbert: A Comedy of Manners and Style and Substance. Her newspaper column is widely syndicated.*

NT: *Miss Austen is hard on those who break the rules of civilized social intercourse and is scathing in her presentation of characters who boast unduly or who speak cattily of others. Clearly, not everyone was well mannered in the early nineteenth century. Do you think Austen portrayed the manners of her time accurately?*

JM: That was not a surprise to me, not even when I first read Miss Austen, because human beings have always been human beings. In her era you don't have to look very far to find people who defied the standards of the time. Her patron, George IV, was not exactly a model of behavior, was he? But this has been happening since the world began. It is also true that manners have evolved and changed over the years and centuries and that every generation has thought that the next generation is not as well behaved as itself. This requires a lot of select memory and too often the mistaking of change for deterioration. When people transgressed manners in Miss Austen's time, they generally realized they were doing so; whether they obeyed them or not, they all bought into the idea that manners were a desirable thing. The reaction we had in the sixties was not totally unprecedented. The reason I do not think we are approaching complete doom now is that a generation later people who have experienced an almost manners-free world react against it. Everybody is talking about civility, so I am full of hope that one of these days everyone will do more than just talk about it. I am not surprised that people in the past disobeyed manners; if nobody were inclined to do that, you really would not have to have any rules.

NT: *Do you think that Miss Austen's resurgence of popularity and public recognition may be, at least in part, due to your allusions to her in your column?*

JM: Well, if I thought that, I would be extremely proud. It would veer into arrogance, but it would be nice to think so. I am certainly a tremendous enthusiast, but I am far from the only one. Miss Austen was never unpopular, like Trollope, for example, who virtually disappeared and then came back. I think that great surge of new popularity has to do with the reaction against the rudeness and abrasiveness of our own society, resulting from the feeling

COOL BRITANNIA: APPLES IN JUNE

*I*n *Emma* Austen refers to the apple trees as blossoming in June. Austen lovers and scholars have always thought that this infelicitous inaccuracy is atypical of Austen. As it turns out, Austen was writing *Emma* during an uncharacteristically chilly summer in 1814. Euan Nisbet, professor of geology at Royal Holloway College, London University, has noted that climatic data of the summer of 1814 indicate that Jane Austen accurately recorded an unusual phenomenon. Professor Nisbet says that "meteorology shapes *Emma*, reflecting the twists and turns of the plot. Drizzling rain signals impending misery; when the weather turns hot and sultry, romance and danger loom. Perhaps the novel is an allegory on nature itself."

that we should all behave naturally and not follow any manners. I am glad to see the popularity, and I have seen a lot of misplaced enthusiasm—people who believe that everybody behaved perfectly in those days. Once I was interviewed for a television show about the Jane Austen movies by someone who was going on and on about the Victorians. She did not actually say that the Victorians hadn't heard of sex, but that is what she was implying, and I said, "Do you think Jane Austen was a Victorian?" The Georgians were hardly prudish. This is a false nostalgic admiration that I hope leads some people to discover the real Jane Austen, who, I needn't tell you, is biting, satirical, and very well aware of what is going on.

NT: *Which is your favorite of Jane Austen's novels and why?*

JM: *Emma.* I love them all, but I love *Emma* the best. Perhaps identifying with someone who goes around giving advice to people, I adore Emma herself. Her manner is not arrogant, but her assumptions are. In all Jane Austen, but I think particularly in *Emma,* the relationship between surface manners, which I refer to as etiquette, is distinct from manners itself, the principles behind etiquette. It is not enough to have a good heart. Emma does have a good heart. You must also translate that into behavior that conveys respect and all the other qualities of manners that constitute good behavior. This is the very opposite of the rationale for getting rid of etiquette on the ground that if you mean well, everything will be fine. Emma does mean well. But everything is not fine because she keeps messing up—not only in the scene with Miss Bates but in her attitude toward Harriet and Harriet's suitors.

Miss Austen provides, I suppose, the best demonstration we have ever had of social dynamics and the role of learned cultural behavior. It is a wonderful antidote to the idea of being spontaneous. In Jane Austen the complications of social dynamics even on her "two inches of ivory" do not have to present the dramatic extreme of society. This is what civilization is all about.

One thing she and I certainly share is the idea that the whole subject and, for that matter, all human behavior is funny. If you can't enjoy watching it, what's the point?

> *E*mma is the snob's *vade mecum*. The art of the book lies in discriminating between the Eltons' vulgar snobbery, which is so distressingly crude and gross, and Emma's own snobbery, which, like Austen's, acts as a form of satire. The book both invites and reproves our complicity with its style of social condescension. The most memorable characters are all monsters of egocentricity.
> —DAVID NOKES

Who Is Vulgar and How to Avoid Vulgarity

The following checklist reveals telltale attributes of the vulgarians who provide mirth and a measure of zaniness in the novels. Each vulgar character is given an E, or Elton rating for vulgarity, the E being a unit of boorishness named in honor of the Eltons, from *Emma*.

Although it is tempting to distribute Eltons as lavishly as award shows give out Emmys and Oscars, the critic must exercise restraint (a very nonvulgar attribute, but calling attention to it is itself vulgar) and award a maximum of five Eltons to any one character.

How does one accumulate Eltons?

There is no one clear path to an Elton; it can be earned in several ways. Grammatical solecisms, the use of slang, presumption, self-importance, complaining, materialism, vanity, hypocrisy, pretended intimacy, the inappropriate use of nicknames, first names, or surnames, avarice, meanness, hubris all are strategies to gain E points.

5 E CHARACTERS:

Augusta Hawkins Elton

Lady Catherine de Bourgh

Sir Walter Elliot

Aunt Norris

General Tilney

4 E CHARACTERS:

The Denham family

Fanny Dashwood

Robert Ferrars

Lucy Steele

Mr. Price

Mr. Collins

Mrs. Bennet

Lydia Bennet

Mr. Wickham

John Willoughby

John Thorpe

Isabella Thorpe

William Walter Elliot

Reverend Philip Elton

Mrs. Ferrars

Maria Bertram Rushworth

3 E CHARACTERS:

Elizabeth Elliot

Louisa Bingley Hurst

Caroline Bingley

Mrs. Ferrars

2 E CHARACTERS:

Henry Crawford

Mary Crawford

Frank Churchill

Harriet Smith

Mary Bennet

Lady Middleton

Mrs. Palmer

Anne Steele

Mary Musgrove

Lady Bertram

1 E CHARACTERS:

Emma Woodhouse

Marianne Dashwood

Mr. Palmer

Mrs. Jennings

Let's examine the above Elton ratings. Only five characters merit the full laurels of vulgarity because they have a noxious mix of power, position, and pretension and their vanity knows no limits. They edge out all other competitors by extremes of bad behavior and by crude despotism. General Tilney ousts a young lady from his home and sends her off without protection. Mrs. Norris makes every effort to be nasty and punitive to Fanny Price and constantly reminds her of "the nonsense and folly of people's stepping out of their rank and trying to appear above themselves. . . . [R]emember wherever you are, you must be the lowest and last." Lady Catherine thinks of dear Elizabeth Bennet

Regency dancing girls from First Impressions. This chorus line was intended to exemplify vulgarity.

as a pollutant, a besmirching of the family escutcheon. Sir Walter goes out to count the number of ugly "frights" that pass him on the streets and is satisfied with human beauty only when he gazes in the mirror. Augusta Hawkins Elton has raised affectation and mean-spiritedness to an art form. She sweeps into Highbury determined to take precedence and to take over. Her apotheosis of the Sucklings of Maple Grove rivals Lady Catherine's esteem for the Shades of Pemberley. Her "ease without elegance" condemns her to eternal vulgarity.

Those characters that boast of four Eltons have manifold vulgarities, but they don't have the range or power of the holders of five Elton points. They generally have one enormous flaw that makes it impossible for us to approve of them. Each of them determinedly hurts others in his or her quest for gratification. Each is also boorishly self-righteous about this flaw. Some of them, such as Maria and Lydia, are too ebullient and are prodded to excesses by runaway hormones. But they should better govern their own impulses. Some, like Mr. Collins and Mr. Elton, are driven by ambition. Others, like Lucy Steele and Isabella Thorpe, hear the siren song of money.

Three Elton points are awarded to those that are annoying, usually by virtue of excessive personal vanity and class pride. These are characters that might commit sins of omission but that have sufficient conscience to prevent them from any real sins of commission. They generally do not have the power to commit true malfeasances, but they are often derelict in the duties of social politeness.

Two Eltons are awarded to those characters that are vulgar in some way but may have some redeeming features. They can sometimes be likable, good-hearted, generous, fun to be with, amusing, and enthusiastic, but their two degrees of Eltonness disqualify them from being heroes or heroines. Each of them suffers from an excess. Henry and Mary Crawford might have been redeemed, but they could not sufficiently curb their animal vitality. Frank Churchill, on the other hand, has earned his two Eltons for his chicanery. Marriage to Jane Fairfax will set him straight, however, and those Eltons will disappear. We already see them starting to pack up and leave in the long mea culpa letter he writes to Mrs. Weston near the end of *Emma*. Harriet Smith is also likely to shed her Eltons as she learns steadiness in her marriage to Robert Martin. Lady Bertram has earned her Eltons through excessive indolence, but she does not have a bad heart. Some characters earn their two Eltons simply by being stupid.

One Elton is a flaw, but not a fatal flaw. Such characters can redeem themselves and rid themselves of the point, as Emma Woodhouse and Marianne Dashwood do in the process of maturation. When they learn how to be polite—or less dictatorial, to be blunt—they will be stripped of their Eltons. Mr. Palmer even knows when to be appropriately concerned, compensating for his habitual rudeness. But the rudeness of silence is not so noxious as the rudeness of raillery. Mrs. Jennings is really a kind, good-natured woman, but her laughter and her jokes have earned her one Elton.

Hermione Gingold as Mrs. Bennet in First Impressions. Perhaps she is celebrating the day she "got rid" of her daughters, or maybe she is getting ready to welcome Wickham as her first son-in-law.

TEN SUREFIRE WAYS TO BE VULGAR

1. If you are a woman, refer to a man by his last name only. Imitate Isabella Thorpe who speaks of Tilney and Morland. Remember how quickly Mrs. Elton refers to Knightley? Such address will establish your social superiority as well as your popularity.

2. Make sure that you gossip plentifully so that people will know how much you know. Be sure to exaggerate for added impressive effect. John Thorpe is able to have quite a chummy conversation with General Tilney based on his willingness to reveal a much-inflated estimate of the Morland family income. Be sure to add twice as much "for the grandeur of the moment," and triple the amount of any private fortune. Such detailed knowledge of private fiduciary concerns

will establish you as an authoritative expert and stress your intimacy with the subject of the gossip. Also, when you gossip, make sure you know all the latest slang so that you can quiz people or pick out quizzes in the crowd. As Lydia Bennet says, "A little sea-bathing would set me up forever." Some nifty turns of phrase will set you up forever!

3. Be bossy. Very, very bossy. Emma has an Elton point because of her bossiness mixed with her snobbery. When she first meets Harriet, she loses "no time in inviting, encouraging, and telling her to come very often." Make note of this sequence. If people don't respond to invitations, give them orders. The order indirect is also an excellent art to master. Remember when Lady Middleton manipulates Lucy Steele into making a basket for little Annamaria by first assuring Lucy that she need not finish it so quickly and then dwelling on the disappointment that would be incurred in the small breast of Annamaria if the work were not to be done immediately?

4. Don't be coy about the number of beaux you have! Let everyone know which beaux are pursuing you. Also, don't hesitate to call any eligible man a beau. Mrs. Elton herself calls Mr. Woodhouse "an old beau" of hers at first meeting.

5. A little learning is a dangerous thing and a sure path to vulgarity. Recollect Robert Ferrars's discourse on cottages and Lady Catherine's general knowledge of everything.

6. Don't keep your knowledge and your opinions to yourself. Make sure that you disseminate them widely. You know enough to advise anyone about anything. Imitate Lady Catherine de Bourgh, who has the candor to proclaim, "There are few people in England, I suppose, who have more true enjoyment of music than myself, or a better natural taste. If I had ever learnt, I should have been a great proficient." Also use your discernment to point out general and specific flaws in the appearances or backgrounds of people. Don't neglect to bewail your cousin's freckles or your sister's gap-toothed ugliness. Remember the gracious example of Sir Walter Elliot, who reminds us that Lord St. Ives is the son of a "country curate, without bread to eat."

7. Have a prominent relative or at the very least a connection with a person of prominence. Make sure the world knows the fortune and influence of your family connections. Be sedulous in your attentions. Emulate Mr. Collins, for example, who tells Lady Catherine that her daughter seems "born to be a duchess, and that the most elevated rank, instead of giving her consequence, would be adorned by her." Or follow the fulsome example that Sir Walter Elliot provides in his attentions to the Dowager Viscountess Dalrymple.

8. Have the best coach around equipped with the fastest horses. Make certain that everyone knows about it; do not trust to people's powers of observation.

9. Be cutting edge avant-garde. Be the first person to adorn your bonnet with apricots or strawberries (in season). Or explore the possibilities of gender bending as Lydia does in *Pride and Prejudice*: "We dressed up Chamberlayne in woman's clothes, on purpose to pass for a lady,—only think what fun!"

10. Laugh too much, even if you don't understand why you are laughing. Peals of laughter cascade from the mouth of Mrs. Palmer, who laughs all the time and thinks that her husband's taciturn ways are particularly risible. Robert Ferrars laughs when he hears that his brother intends to enter the clergy. Lydia Bennet is always ready to "die of laughter" and assumes that her family will just "laugh" when they find out about her elopement with Wickham.

Mrs. Goddard's School

Most of Jane Austen's heroines are educated at home, and certainly Austen herself preferred her own education at home to those miserable months at the Abbey School. Yet Austen clearly believes that women should cultivate their minds, in the way that Elizabeth Bennet has. Only one school is more than cursorily featured in the novels, and that is Mrs. Goddard's establishment in *Emma*:

> Mrs. Goddard was the mistress of a school—not of a seminary, or an establishment, or anything which professed, in long sentences of refined nonsense, to combine liberal acquirements with elegant morality, upon new principles and new systems, and where young ladies for enormous pay might be screwed out of health and into vanity, but a real, honest, old-fashioned boarding-school, where a reasonable quantity of accomplishments were sold at reasonable price, and where girls might be sent to be out of the way, and scramble themselves into a little education, without any danger of coming back prodigies. Mrs. Goddard's school was in high repute, and very deservedly; she had an ample house and garden, gave the children plenty of wholesome food, let them run about a great deal in the summer, and in winter dressed their chilblains with her own hands.

Mrs. Goddard's school seems to be relatively benign; Austen's irony is gentle. True, Harriet Smith is not an intellectual giant, but she is not unhappy at school and is not learning the insidious values of snobbery that Rosamond Vincy picked up at Miss Lemon's odious establishment in George Eliot's novel *Middlemarch*. Austen speaks of Mrs. Goddard with a good deal of approbation—for the ampleness of the grounds and the free time the students are afforded. She seems to detest those costly establishments that value teaching refinement above teaching "a little education."

A Fling at the Slave Trade

In a letter to Cassandra, Jane Austen declares herself to be "in love with" Thomas Clarkson, author of *The History of the Rise, Progress, and Accomplishment of the Abolition of the African Slave Trade by the British Parliament*. Of course the comment may not mean much. Austen writes of several literary infatuations in her letters. She also allows that she is in love with Claudius Buchanan, who wrote *Christian Researches in Asia*, and with Captain Pasley, author of *Essay on the Military Policy and Institutions of the British Empire*, as well as with James and Horatio Smith, brothers who wrote *Rejected Addresses*, the comic sensation of the season. All we can conclude is that Austen was widely read in a number of different types of literature. The book by Clarkson tells of the great sufferings of the victims of the trade in human flesh. Clarkson was absolutely repulsed by those who supported the slave trade on the ground of its economic benefits for England.

Certainly Austen would have been aware of the poet William Cowper's antislavery writings as well. In "Pity for Poor Africans," he sarcastically laments:

> *I pity them greatly, but I must be mum,*
> *For how could we do without sugar and rum?*
> *Especially sugar, so needful we see?*
> *What, give up our desserts, our coffee, and tea?*

In *Emma* the slave trade is mentioned indirectly by Jane Fairfax, who is looking for a position as a governess: "There are places in town, offices, where inquiry would soon produce something—Offices for the sale—not quite of human flesh—but of human intellect." Mrs. Elton responds with her typical knee-jerk reply in which the Sucklings of Maple Grove are cited with panegyrics: "Oh! my dear, human flesh! You quite shock me; if you mean a fling at the slave-trade, I assure you Mr. Suckling was always rather a friend to the abolition."

Mrs. Elton may be unwittingly implicating Mr. Suckling as a participant in the slave trade. Certainly his name is often on her tongue, but she seems to have associated him immediately with Jane's phrases about the sale of humans. Her family comes from Bristol, one of the major centers of the trade:

> Miss Hawkins was the youngest of the two daughters of a Bristol—merchant, of course, he must be called; but, as the whole of the profits of his mercantile life appeared so very moderate, it was not unfair to guess the dignity of his line of trade had been very moderate too. . . . Part of every winter she had been used to spend in Bath, but Bristol was her home, the very heart of Bristol. . . . And all the grandeur of the connection seemed dependent on the elder sister, who was *very well married* to a gentleman in a *great way*, near Bristol, who kept two carriages!

Mr. Hawkins, who has settled a full ten thousand pounds on his *younger* daughter is no ordinary merchant; the richest merchants were making an average annual income of only twenty-six hundred pounds per annum in 1803.

How could the family have become so wealthy? The above paragraph fairly drips with sarcasm and innuendo: "merchant, of course, he must be called," "as the whole of the profits of his mercantile life appeared so very moderate, it was not unfair to guess the dignity of his line of trade had been very moderate too." Bristol is mentioned four times in a relatively short passage, and Mrs. Elton comes from the "very heart of Bristol." Could that be a "heart of darkness," in the Conradian sense of a place where people take advantage of people weaker than themselves? The clincher is the name Hawkins. Sir John Hawkins had introduced the slave trade to England. Austen does not write polemics. Her devastating portrait of Mrs. Elton as a parvenu, a ruthless narcissistic arriviste who is cruel to Harriet Smith and infuriatingly

WAYNE BOOTH ON *EMMA*

*A*sk whether any character in this novel is perfect. You cannot answer that question without asking at the same time where your standard of perfection comes from. And obviously no character, not even Knightley, provides all of that standard. It is derived not from any male, after all, but from that great woman, the implied Jane Austen, the dauntingly mature human being who underwrites every act of imagination she takes us through. It is she who provides an accompaniment of both understanding and love to Emma's *almost* detestable meddling. And it is she who provides the subtle clues to Knightley's own egotism. More subtly, she creates for us the imaginative and witty vitality of Emma herself, as a criticism of the somewhat stodgy wisdom and stately power of Knightley. She teaches us that although Emma's imagination is obviously dangerous, it is also an admirable loveable grace in a world contaminated most by fools, knaves, and clods. And finally she provides, at scores of points, a commentary that corrects any naive over-identification that we are tempted to commit.

complacent about her role as lady patroness of Highbury, is, however, her implicit condemnation of those who are indifferent to the trade in human flesh.

"Caro Sposo"

A little Italian is a dangerous thing. . . .

In a letter written on May 26, 1801, Austen in her dry, playful way advises Cassandra to get ready "due scraps of Italian & French" in order to talk to one Miss Holder, who has heard that Cassandra is "remarkably lively." Mrs. Elton, who is remarkably lively, entertains us with her unstable knowledge of Italian. Evidently her oft-repeated "caro sposo" was a fashionable phrase during the 1770s and the 1780s, making her slang badly out of date. She also shows her inability to remember gender agreement, first by calling her husband "Cara Sposa" (feminine for "dear bride") and then by mixing her genders and calling him Cara Sposo. Finally she gets it right and on her third try calls him Caro Sposo, correctly marrying gender and word ending. Perhaps someone has corrected her; more likely she just blundered into the correct usage. Mrs. Elton also occasions the derision of Emma and readers by calling her husband Mr. E., yet another indication of her vulgarity.

On Becoming a Governess

Governesses and their sorry plight are a staple of nineteenth-century literature. Jane Eyre, Agnes Grey, the nameless heroine of *The Turn of the Screw*, and Mme. Vine in *East Lynne* are just a few examples. In *Emma* we are introduced to a governess, Miss Taylor, who, at the very beginning of the novel marries a local squire, Mr. Weston. Miss Taylor has been a true member of the family and much more of a friend than a subordinate to Emma. Although she moves to her own household and becomes a mother by the end of the novel, Mr. Woodhouse never stops lamenting the fate of "Poor Miss Taylor that was." Readers must laugh at Mr. Woodhouse's idea that it is better to be a governess in his home than to find a husband and happiness for oneself.

One of the most poignant features of the plight of Jane Fairfax, however, is that she seems destined to become a governess. The reality of course is that few governesses find themselves as comfortably situated as "Miss Taylor that was." Probably even fewer actually marry the master of the establishment, as does Jane Eyre. Most governesses were paid very poorly and had no natural allies in a home. They were regarded as servants, in spite of being educated. They were not necessarily accepted by their fellow servants, as indicated by Mrs. Blenkinsop in Thackeray's *Vanity Fair.* "They give themselves the hairs and hupstarts of ladies and their wages is no better then you nor me." Nor were they necessarily treated well by their charges. Anne Brontë's *Agnes Grey* describes the bratty ungovernability of the young children she is forced to teach. The discerning reader understands

REGINALD FARRAR ON *EMMA*

———⊗⊗⊗———

*O*nly when the story has been thoroughly assimilated can the infinite delights and subtleties of its workmanship begin to be appreciated, as you realise the manifold complexity of the book's web, and find that every sentence, almost every epithet, has its definite reference to equally unemphasized points before and after in the development of the plot. Thus it is that, while twelve readings of *Pride and Prejudice* give you twelve periods of pleasure repeated, as many readings of *Emma* give you that pleasure, not repeated only, but squared and squared again with each perusal, till at every fresh reading you feel anew that you never understood anything like the widening sum of its delights. But, until you know the story, you are apt to find its movement dense and slow and obscure, difficult to follow, and not very obviously worth the following.

For this is THE novel of character, and of character alone, and of one dominating character in particular. And many a rash reader, and some who are not rash, have been shut out on the threshold of Emma's Comedy by a dislike of Emma herself.

that Mrs. Elton's officious meddling with Jane Fairfax is bad enough, but that her scheme to find Jane employment as a governess with one of her vulgar friends would be an untenable position for the sensitive Jane.

*J*ane Austen has a special appeal for those of us living in Los Angeles; as society collapses around us in filth and appalling violence, it is thrilling to encounter stories in which rudeness is a sin. Her appeal is undeniable, especially in a city built on self-delusion and vulgarity, both of which Jane Austen understood better than anyone. I love Los Angeles—don't get me wrong—but the reason I love it is the reason I love Jane Austen, too. Risible pretense built Hollywood, so it only makes sense that Hollywood would embrace Jane Austen, who was so finely attuned to the niceties of pretension in all its forms.
—JOHN C. HARRIS

Is Emma Gay?

Two members of the British nobility, Emma Tennant and Lady Rachel Billington, who are otherwise friends, have had a literary feud regarding their respective sequels to, or continuations of, *Emma*.

Emma Tennant is half sister to Lord Glenconner, a particular friend of Princess Margaret. Her late father-in-law, Henry Green, wrote remarkable novels that focus on dialogue and have been called the literary equivalents of the visual works of Monet and Picasso. Tennant has written sequels to *Sense and Sensibility, Pride and Prejudice, Tess of the d'Urbervilles,* and *Gone with the Wind*. The book jacket to *Emma in Love* asserts that Tennant "has created a new literary genre, now much emulated, the classic progression." Tennant says of her new book:

> I am not taking any liberties. *Emma* is known as the lesbian book in Jane Austen's *oeuvre*. It has strong lesbian overtones and undertones. In the original, Emma absolutely adores Harriet Smith, her protégée and spends a lot of time with her. There's a passage where she describes how Harriet's soft blue eyes are just the type of eyes that Emma loves. I am not the first to draw out her lesbianism. Serious academics have found many clues to it in *Emma*.

I confess that, man and boy, I have been in love with Emma. I stood with Mr. Knightley by her father's Hartfield fireside watching her scheme with the emotions of her friends. As each scheme dissolved in her hands, I scolded, but felt for her anger. Other people's love seemed so wayward. Emma might be bored, selfish, malicious, a snob, but she was never quite a fool. She took each defeat hard but returned philanthropic to the fray, to set her microcosm of the world on the path to happiness, shipshape and Emma-fashion.

—SIMON JENKINS

Lady Rachel Billington also boasts a pedigree both aristocratic and literary. She is the author of fourteen novels and is the daughter of the late Lord Longford and the sister of Lady Antonia Fraser, the acclaimed biographer. Lady Billington has said that Emma Tennant is resorting to "sensationalism": "Suggesting that Emma was lesbian is silly really. You can't take it that seriously. It's all that post-Freudian analysis where you can read anything you like into anything. I couldn't do this book in such a light-hearted way." Lady Billington's analysis is persuasive. Female admiration for female beauty is commonplace in literature and need not suggest a sexual desire. The same is true for deep female friendships. Aside from explicit sexual activity (which never occurs in Austen's works) there was no real notion in Austen's time of gay or lesbian personality "types." Lord Byron was omnisexual and was known to have had many sexual liaisons with men yet was not regarded as a homosexual, merely as "mad, bad, and dangerous to know."

In the last decade of the nineteenth century the new study of "sexology" began characterizing people according to their sexual practices. Prior to that, people do not seem to have developed their sense of identity according to their sexual proclivities. Obviously latent sexual desires can be read into many texts and may be an informative avenue of inquiry but can hardly prove any points definitively. Emma may have had erotic feelings for women, but there was no context in which she could have named herself a "lesbian" and no context in which Austen could have labeled her character a lesbian. On the other hand, since Austen knew that she would have to dedicate this novel to the Prince Regent, it is possible that the subversive within her spirit decided to add a level of ambiguity that she knew would pass right over the Regent and his unctuous librarian, James Stanier Clarke.

The closeness of many female friendships portrayed in literature is so intense because among other reasons, there was little or no awareness of sexual passion or tension that might have caused a heroine in a novel, or an author, to recoil into a guarded self-consciousness.

Emma in Love may also disturb readers who do not expect Miss Bates to speak in four-letter words.

The story of Emma is, of course, vomitously dire, a moral husk of a tale larded with empty snobbery and vain civility. The original "it girl" whose crass attempts at genetic engineering fall apart when everybody settles happily into their allotted social strata, a result that is pitifully obvious.
—A. A. GILL

Why Does Frank Churchill Change His Name?

This case is analogous to the one in which Austen's brother Edward changed his surname to Knight. The Knights, wealthy and childless, adopted Edward, when he was about sixteen years old. The Austens could hardly have denied such a magnificent future to their son. Although he changed his name, he continued to have friendly relations with his family, who enjoyed visiting his estate, Godmersham. He also inherited Chawton Estate and Chawton Cottage, the home in which he was able to install his sisters and mother. Edward and his family had constant friendly intercourse with the Austens, even after he had to change his name to Knight. Frank Churchill, on the other hand, has spent very little time with his father since his adoption by the Churchills. They seem to have preempted all his time and attention. Fortunately Mr. Weston is a genial man of goodwill who, although very proud of his son, is unwilling to press him for too much attention, in contrast with the Churchills, who seem determined to monopolize his time.

> *I*rving Howe writes that *Emma* has the "greatest picnic in literature." In quiet novels, where "nothing" happens, it becomes convenient for the writer to gather together his/her characters in a sort of bunch ... and force a confrontation of temperaments or needs. A convenient way of doing this is to arrange a picnic, since, after all, no one can question or undermine the verisimilitude of a picnic: it has a built-in probability. People come to a picnic with a certain mild expectation: they don't think they'll be swept off their feet, or knocked down, but "something" may happen.

What Is a Natural Child?

Emma's friend Harriet Smith is a "natural child." Not many "natural children" darken the pages of the novels; Colonel Brandon's ward, and niece, Eliza is another "natural child." What are they? Do they anticipate the offspring of a match between Carole King's Natural Woman with R. Crumb's Mr. Natural? Or perhaps one thinks of naturists and wonder if refugees from nudist camps have populated the novels of Jane Austen.

A "natural child" is, bluntly, an illegitimate child, a marginal figure in society. To succeed in marrying Harriet Smith to the snobbish Mr. Elton would thus have been an impossible triumph, even for the determined Emma. Harriet's illegitimacy is one of the many reasons she speaks formally to Emma, calling her Miss Woodhouse, while Emma calls Harriet by her first name. In this class-bound society Harriet can marry a farmer, but the expectations Emma gives her of making a finer marriage are unrealistic. Harriet "proved to be the daughter of a tradesman, rich enough to afford her the comfortable maintenance which had ever been hers, and decent enough to have always wished for concealment—Such was the blood of gentility which Emma had formerly been so ready to vouch for! . . . The stain of illegitimacy, unbleached by nobility or wealth, would have been a stain indeed." Of course the comments on the "stain" of illegitimacy are Emma's and do not necessarily represent Austen's views. Once Emma has ascertained, too late, that Harriet is not the fairy princess she once hoped her to have been, she finds that their intimacy must "sink" and "their friendship must change into a calmer sort of goodwill." In fact, had Robert Martin not been so persistent, Emma would have ruined Harriet's life.

Edith Lank on Jane Austen

*E**dith Lank exemplifies the Jane Austen devotee par excellence. A collector of Austeniana, she has more than six hundred books, tapes, videos, and movie posters, an Austen autograph, and a first edition of* Emma. *Her collection of Austen's works in translation includes German, Dutch, Italian, French, Spanish, Catalan, Turkish, Icelandic, Russian, and Finnish. Lank has written seven books on real estate and is the author of "House Calls," a widely syndicated weekly newspaper column.*

NT: *What kind of man was Jane Austen's father?*

EL: Everybody says he was a scholar. He was handsome and a very sweet man. He handled the first offer of publication of a manuscript for her. We know that when a circulating library was started, he paid for a subscription in her name. He took boarders into his house and prepared them for entrance to Oxford; he was what was called a crammer.

NT: *So it does not seem to you that Jane Austen's father was a model for any of her literary fathers?*

EL: If you take *Northanger Abbey* as the first serious effort, Catherine's father was a sensible man, and General Tilney was part of the burlesque of the Gothic. Austen makes a real effort to present Catherine as the kind of girl who lives next door to you, and nothing about her is like a Gothic heroine. She has a perfectly decent father. I think in spite of herself, Austen began to be a real novelist there. I don't think she set out to do that; I think she was writing another burlesque for the pleasure of her family, and then her talent took over.

Generally Austen stays off the subject of mothers. Catherine Morland has a sensible mother to go with her sensible father. She is the only one who does.

You know, I have a much higher regard for Mrs. Bennet than most people do. Jane Austen says the business of her life was to get her daughters married, and quite properly it *was* her life. She can't help it if nature has endowed her with very little to work with. But she was right to plot and scheme. If she had not sent Jane off on horseback to get a bad cold so that she had to stay over at Netherfield, Jane might never have married Bingley and I don't think Elizabeth would have married Darcy. And you'll notice that in spite of her husband's teasing her, he had already waited on Mr. Bingley at the first opportunity. He just was not going to give her the satisfaction of admitting it. But with very little help from her husband and very little help from her own intelligence I think she was rightly concerned with just what she should have been, and if the young Jane Austen did not admire it, I think perhaps the older one would have. At age forty you would really worry about those girls.

NT: *Has your real estate specialty given you any special insights into Austen's world, or has Austen given you insights into real estate?*

EL: She understood land, finance, and the law. She understood entails and rents. She understood the relationship with landlords. Land, at the beginning of her writing, was just about the only source of wealth. By the time we hit *Persuasion* we begin to see other sources emerging. In *Emma* we see the newly rich, and they are not getting all their money from land. There are plenty of hints that Mrs. Elton's family got their money from the slave trade. And we see the navy, which Austen saw in her own life as a method of advancement for those who are not landed.

NT: *Do you think that any of Austen's characters would make a good real estate agent today?*

EL: Mr. Shepherd was about as clever an agent as you can imagine when negotiating Sir Walter Elliot's acceptance of Admiral Croft as a tenant. It is an exquisite example of negotiation. Willoughby would have made a good salesman, but I imagine of expensive imported cars rather than real estate.

NT: *Which characters might you invite to a dinner party?*

EL: I would invite the Crofts to dinner. I like them, and I like their marriage. I certainly would not invite Fanny and Edmund. I can't imagine a duller evening.

Edith Lank: A Theory on Harriet Smith's Parentage

"THE WORD WAS BLUNDER: WHO WAS HARRIET SMITH'S MOTHER?"

More than one critic has noted that *Emma* may be read as a mystery story, pure and simple. Hints, deftly woven into the fabric of the novel, can easily pass unnoticed, so that each rereading yields one more delighted "Of course. Why did I never notice that before?"

Yet in 170 years' study of the book, no one has ever caught the clue, mischievously left in plain sight by Jane Austen, to the identity of Harriet Smith's mother.

Perhaps modern readers miss it because they forget the convention governing the naming of daughters in Jane Austen's world. The first girl was properly named for the mother. Thus Jane's older sister bore the name of Cassandra, and their cousin Jane Cooper was named for *her* mother, Mrs. Austen's sister Jane Leigh.

As Jane Austen's novels move away from the early burlesques, we find the convention more and more strictly observed. Miss Frances Ward becomes the mother of Fanny Price, and Miss Maria Ward's first daughter is Maria Bertram. Lady Elizabeth Elliot, dead before *Persuasion* opens, has given her name to her oldest daughter, and Jane Bates has left Jane Fairfax. Isabella Woodhouse's oldest daughter is Bella, and "Poor Miss Taylor that was," referred to as Anne or Anna, names her infant Anna Weston.

Lady Susan follows the rule, for her daughter Frederica bears the middle name of Susanna. Even an illegitimate child carried her mother's name; witness Colonel Brandon's lost love, his cousin Eliza Williams, whose daughter Eliza is eventually seduced and abandoned by Willoughby.

This brings us to the only bastard with whom we are personally acquainted, innocent, blooming Harriet Smith, the natural daughter of somebody.

It should be noted first that Jane Austen has no objection to using and reusing the same Christian names, including her own, in her stories. Thus we know of Elizabeth Bennet, and in other novels Elizabeth Martin, Elizabeth Elliot, Elizabeth Watson. Besides Anne Elliot, we know Anne Steele, Anna Weston, and even an Anne Thorpe. Mary Crawford, Mary Musgrove, and Mary Bennet never meet, however, because they live in different books. Neither do

Charlotte Lucas and Charlotte Heywood, Emma Woodhouse and Emma Watson.

Clearly, repetition of the same name *within* a novel is intended to signify mother and daughter.

When Emma Woodhouse pays her penitent call on the Bateses, to find all in disarray, worthy old Mrs. Bates flutters about and, "I hope you find a chair. I wish Hetty had not gone," she says.

Hetty?

Why does Jane Austen take the trouble to name Miss Bates for us? And is that name a diminutive for Harriet?

The chronology, carefully constructed as always by Jane Austen, easily allows for a visit by the secretly pregnant Miss Bates to her dying sister, for Jane Fairfax was three years old when her mother dies, and is not quite three years older than Harriet Smith. The child is born far from Highbury, and Lieutenant Fairfax's widow, the only witness, dies soon after. Moreover, as old Mrs. Bates complains, nobody tells her anything.

We are never told about Harriet Smith's infancy, but she was undoubtedly placed, like the Austen children themselves, with a country nurse who kept her until she was old enough to attend the establishment of the Bateses' friend Mrs. Goddard. Miss Bates, whose warm heart and undemanding intellect resemble those of Mrs. Goddard—and of Harriet Smith herself—could keep a contented eye on the child without raising any comment while her maternal feelings found an outlet in the Fairfax child who had become her "fondling."

Jane Fairfax would have been too young to understand the significance of the infant—if indeed she ever saw it. In any event, Jane's discretion is well established. If we assume she knew that the parlor boarder at Mrs. Goddard's was indeed her cousin, we have ironclad confirmation of the relationship.

Many a scholar has argued, from a complete lack of evidence, that "such universal silence on the matter clearly strengthens my thesis." And mannerly Jane Fairfax, who knows so well how to keep a secret, *never once speaks a single word to Harriet Smith.*

ENVOI

Of course, as Frank Churchill reminds us, sometimes one conjectures right and sometimes one conjectures wrong. There is always the distant possibility that "Hetty" was meant as a diminutive for Henrietta.

Enough. As Emma says reassuringly (and not quite convincingly), it is "all in a joke . . . a mere joke among ourselves."

Mr. Woodhouse

It may be possible to do without dancing entirely. Instances have been known of young people passing many, many months successively, without being at any ball of any description, and no material injury accrue either to body or mind.
—MR. WOODHOUSE

Mr. Woodhouse, Emma's father, is one of the most generally loved characters in Jane Austen's fiction, though whether such a man would be loved or lovable outside fiction is another question. The key to Mr. Woodhouse's character is presented in the opening pages, and his essential characterization remains unmodified throughout the novel: "[H]aving been a valetudinarian all his life, without activity of mind or body, he was a much older man in ways than in years; and though everywhere beloved for the friendliness of his heart and his amiable temper, his talents could not have recommended him at any time." Austen puts it gently, but Mr. Woodhouse, though concerned for the welfare of others, is a generally inert, somewhat imbecilic hypochondriac, always preoccupied with preserving his own health, safety, and comfort. His "habits of gentle selfishness" are gentle in that he attempts to preserve others from harm, and therefore from change of any kind, but are selfish because he can't imagine or sympathize with a self different from his own; he was never "able to suppose that other people could feel differently from himself." As a result, he opposes everything from marriage to dinner parties to roast pork, not only for himself but for everyone, on the grounds that they do not suit the nervous system or the digestive system. His idiosyncrasies are the source of much gentle comedy, as Jane Austen expresses his absurd reliance on his medical adviser, Mr. Perry, his crotchets about many sources of harmless pleasure for his healthier acquaintances, and such small but telling points as his refusal to believe an infamous rumor that Mr. Perry's children had been seen with slices of an "unwholesomely rich wedding cake."

His querulousness is forgiven since it takes the form of compassionate concern rather than rebuke or reproach, even though his feelings are outraged when, for example, Miss Taylor exposes herself and him to dangerous change by leaving his house to marry Mr. Weston. He constantly refers to her as "Poor Miss Taylor," presumably because she is undergoing the ordeals of marriage and pregnancy. In truth, however, his "gentle selfishness" is selfishness still, a failure of the empathy necessary to comfortable social existence.

For Emma, all considerations are sacrificed to the one paramount need of keeping her father comfortable, and it is her loving devotion more than his "gentleness" that makes his and her social world bearable. Though his resistance is gradually overcome by appeals to his own desire for increased security, he even opposes Emma's marriage to Mr. Knightley out of a selfish desire to keep her to himself, and he in fact makes it necessary for Mr. Knightley to give up his own residence and perform the highly unorthodox move of living with his bride at *her* house. Hence he becomes not only Emma's husband but another guardian and caretaker of Mr. Woodhouse. Ultimately Jane Austen's representation of Mr. Woodhouse reveals the gentle, loving dispositions of Emma and Mr. Knightley and the willingness of good people to tolerate and forgive even serious foibles if they are motivated by even the limited sort of neighborly love of which Mr. Woodhouse is capable.

Phyllida Law on Mrs. Bates

Phyllida Law played Mrs. Bates in the 1996 production of Emma starring Gwyneth Paltrow. She played the central character, Elspeth, in The Winter Guest. Her other film appearances include Much Ado About Nothing, Peter's Friends, *and* Leo Tolstoy's Anna Karenina. Her television roles include The Barchester Chronicles, The House of Eliott, Degrees of Error, *and* The Unpleasantness at the Bellona Club.

NT: *What was the most memorable aspect of playing Mrs. Bates?*

PL: I didn't have any lines to memorize! I enjoyed acting with my daughter [Sophie Thompson, who played Miss Bates], and I certainly realized how many women still live today in the same way that Mrs. Bates and Miss Bates do. I felt very sympathetic to their situation.

NT: *Did you first have the idea of being in the film together with your daughter, or were you approached?*

PL: We both went up at different time for Miss Bates, oddly enough. But I remember saying to Doug McGrath [the director] that I'm too old for Miss Bates. And Sophie was too young for Miss Bates, in fact. So we were falling between two stones really. I think that you should feel that Miss Bates has missed it, but not exactly by miles. You know that she missed her chance to marry. You should feel that and see it very clearly. I was just too old, as I said to Doug McGrath. I got called in again to see if I would play Mrs. Bates. And my daughter made herself look frumpy so she got the part of Miss Bates. But we did not suggest it, not at all. I think that Sophie was very touching. And I greatly admired Gwyneth Paltrow's being able to produce such an exquisite English accent; that was very clever, I thought.

NT: *You must have enjoyed it?*

PL: Yes, very much. I didn't have to learn any lines. I went to lovely places. I had a very nice gown, not too grand, of course. It was great fun.

An awful lot of English people have been brought up on Jane Austen and read the novels over and over again in their lives, but of course everyone goes back to reread the novel when they have been cast. Jane Austen is so particular that I don't think she can be captured completely on film because of her extraordinary background comments. Like Anthony Powell, to bring in a contemporary writer, the dialogue is not always what is so brilliantly funny but the comments by the author, the author's voice. It is almost impossible to get that on film. All you get is a slice of Jane Austen from the very surface.

I think the better the book, the less likely you are going to get the sense of it. I think maybe if the film interests people that they would go to the books with more delight, don't you? I mean if somebody has not yet read Jane Austen and they like the film, they might think, "Oh, I might read that boring old person." Then they would find all that delicious writing that makes you squeal with laughter. You just can't get that narrative voice in the film.

NT: *But some of the films have done really well at suggesting her delicately ironic insights.*

PL: Yes, absolutely. It is very difficult, though, I must say. *Emma* is a glorious book. It is one of my favorites. She was my brother's favorite authoress, and he used to sit there howling and reading them again and again, which I also do. We all adore her in my family!

NT: *You told me that when you played Mrs. Bates you thought a lot about her position in society?*

PL: Yes. I had just looked after my elderly mother, so I took a lot of her into it. My elderly mother could not see very well; she was almost blind, so a great part of my experience was applicable. We have got plenty of Mrs. and Miss Bates lying about. I feel for them very deeply. We don't pay them enough attention. And in Jane Austen's days it must have been just frightful. No money, no anything for women. I think it is terribly touching that Jane Austen noticed that. She did notice the money situation for women.

NT: *Do you have a favorite among the novels?*

PL: I used to like *Emma* best. I don't know that I have a favorite now. All her letters of course are divine. When we were filming *Emma,* we all dashed off to the Jane Austen places. Oddly enough, I have not been to her grave, but my daughter [Emma Thompson] has, of course.

NT: *I think you are to some extent the mother of the current Jane Austen industry, with both of your daughters' work. Sophie also was in* Persuasion, *and Emma won a screenwriting award for* Sense and Sensibility. *I have a theory that Jane Austen's popularity in the United States comes from the fact so many people confound your daughter Emma with Jane Austen and think that they are interchangeable.*

PL: Oh, that never occurred to me. It would be interesting, wouldn't it? Her subject was English literature. She loves it. But it was an American who commissioned her to write it, Lindsay Doran. She was the one who thought of Emma, so maybe there is a sort of Englishness about her that reminds Americans of the Austenian qualities still remaining in our strange land.

NT: *In your own career, what have been some of your most memorable roles?*

PL: I have been acting for about forty years, so there has been a lot of fun in there. I have even played the back end of a cow! There's a lot to choose from. I loved doing *The Winter Guest* because I am Scottish, and it all made great sense to me. The language is mine, the rhythms are mine. I am Glaswegian; I am not really English. I have a different music altogether. So I have enjoyed doing all the Scottish things I have done very much. I once played the Madame in *Measure for Measure* as a Glaswegian. That was good fun. Of course Mrs. Bates was voiceless.

NT: *It is a real tour de force not to have any lines but still to make such an impression on the audience.*

PL: It is great fun; the greatest fun in the world. It was a relaxing gift just to focus on the expression of your face and the stance of your position and not to have any lines. Very good fun. Don't let anybody tell you anything else about acting. It is just gorgeous!

Prunella Scales on Miss Bates

Prunella Scales *played Miss Bates in the 1996 ITV and A&E production of* Emma. *She has also enthralled viewers in her roles as Sybil Fawlty in* Fawlty Towers, *Miss Mapp in* Mapp and Lucia, *and Mistress Page in the BBC production of* Merry Wives of Windsor. *She has appeared in television's* Coronation Street, Breaking the Code, *and* The Rector's Wife *and in the films* Howards End, Boys from Brazil, The Lonely Passion of Judith Hearne, Consuming Passions, *and* A Chorus of Disapproval, *among many others. She has taped several of Austen's novels. With her husband, the actor Timothy West, Miss Scales heads Snipe Productions, Ltd.*

NT: *Tell me about playing Miss Bates.*

PS: Miss Bates's part had to be severely cut, to fit in with the time schedule, which was the most frustrating thing for me personally. As her chief characteristic is her garrulousness, it was sad, as an actress, not to be able to indulge it to the full! I was lucky to win a tiny battle with our brilliant adapter, Andrew Davies, about Miss Bates's famous line on Box Hill. He had very much simplified it, and I persuaded him to restore the original line "Three things very dull indeed, that will just do for me, you know. I shall be sure to say three dull things as soon as ever I open my mouth, shan't I—do not you all think I shall?," which I find much more touching without any modification.

Of course, having already recorded the book both for "Cover to Cover" and for Penguin Books, I was very familiar with the full text. I am sure that no actor that I know would ever dream of attempting to play any of Jane Austen's characters without having read the entire book beforehand and also as many of the other novels as possible, together with any relevant contemporary history and literature.

My husband, Timothy West (who has recorded all the Barchester and Palliser novels of Anthony Trollope), always says that the joy of taping an entire novel is that it is like setting up a production and then casting yourself in all of the parts!

Nieces and Nephews

When Jane Austen died, she had thirteen nieces and eleven nephews living. She took her "auntly" duties very seriously. She spent a great deal of time with her nieces and nephews and corresponded with them when they could not be together. She jokingly enjoyed thinking of herself and Cassandra as "the formidables" in relationship to the younger generation. The three children of her eldest brother, the Reverend James Austen, were particularly devoted to her memory and did the most to keep it alive by providing posterity with biographical information. With the help of some cousins, particularly the children of Charles Austen, the Reverend James Edward Austen-Leigh collected the material for his *Memoir of Jane Austen*, the scaffolding on which all biographies of Austen have been built. James Edward, known as Edward as a child, was sixteen years old when he was let in on the family "secret," that the lady who had written *Sense and Sensibility* and *Pride and Prejudice* was none other than his aunt. He sent her a poem to commemorate the occasion:

TO MISS J. AUSTEN
No words can express, my dear Aunt, my surprise
Or make you conceive how I opened my eyes,
like a pig Butcher Pile has just struck with his knife,

> *When I heard for the very first time in my life*
> *That I had the honour to have a relation*
> *Whose works were dispersed through the whole of the nation.*
> *I assure you, however, I'm terribly glad:*
> *Oh dear, just to think (and the thought drives me mad)*
> *That dear Mrs. Jennings' good-natured strain*
> *Was really the product of your witty brain,*
> *That you made the Middletons, Dashwoods, and all,*
> *And that you (not young Ferrars) found out that a ball*
> *May be given in cottages never so small*
> *And though Mr. Collins so grateful for all*
> *Will Lady de Bourgh his dear patroness call,*
> *'Tis to your ingenuity really he owed*
> *His living, his wife, and his humble abode.*

And so on. The poem ends with a couplet hoping that Jane Austen might marry that fop the Prince Regent, which undoubtedly struck her as a very infelicitous conceit.

Fanny Knight, the eldest daughter of Edward Austen Knight, was born in 1793, the same year as her cousin Anna. Fanny and her aunt Jane had an extensive correspondence, and in 1817, when the novelist was ill, she wrote to Fanny:

> You are the delight of my Life—You are worth your weight in Gold, or even in the new Silver Coinage. . . . You are the Paragon of all that is Silly & Sensible, common-place & eccentric, Sad & Lively, Provoking & Interesting.—Who can keep pace with the fluctuations of your Fancy, the Capprizios of your Taste, the Contradictions of your Feelings? . . . It is very, very gratifying to me to know you so intimately.

Although this sounds like a fairly mixed assessment of Fanny, it is a teasingly affectionate effusion. Did Fanny retain the "fluctuations of fancy" that so pleased her aunt Jane? Later in her life she lacks generosity and kindness in her posthumous appraisal of her aunts Jane and Cassandra. As Lady Knatchbull she wrote to her sister Marianne:

> It is very true that Aunt Jane from various circumstances was not so *refined* as she ought to have been from her *talent*, & if she had lived 50 years later she would have been in many respects more suitable to *our* more refined tastes. They were not rich & the people around with whom they chiefly mixed, were not at all high bred, or in short anything more than *mediocre & they* of course tho' superior in *mental powers & cultivation* were on the same level as far as *refinement* goes. . . . Aunt Jane was too clever not to put aside all possible signs of "common-ness" (if such an expression is allowable) & teach herself to be more refined, at least in intercourse with people in general. Both the Aunts (Cassandra & Jane)

were brought up in the most complete ignorance of the World & its ways (I mean as to fashion &c) & if it had not been for Papa's marriage which brought them into Kent . . . they would have been, tho' not less clever & agreeable in themselves, very much below par as to good Society & its ways. If you hate all this I beg yr. pardon, but I felt it at my *pen's end* & it chose to come along & speak the truth.

It is possible that the lively young Fanny Knight, the apple of her aunt's eye, became a fusty Victorian prude and a snob, who winced at her recollections of her aunt's letters describing body func-

A pencil portrait, reputedly by Jane Austen herself, of Fanny Knight, her niece

tions, fleas, and bad breath. Perhaps she simply came to deplore her less wealthy connections. Or perhaps she came to value female reticence and decorum over published novels and glittering wit.

When Anna Lefroy had her first child in 1815 and Austen became a great-aunt, she wrote to her niece Caroline, who was, at age ten, becoming an aunt for the first time herself: "Now that you are become an Aunt, you are a person of some conse-quence & must excite great Interest whatever you do. I have always main-tained the importance of Aunts as much as possible, & I am sure of your doing the same now."

Many of Austen's nieces and nephews started to write poems and stories at an early age, and Austen was a generous reader, critic, and commen-tator. Caroline lived until 1880 (Austen also had two nieces who lasted until 1896 and 1897, almost making the twentieth century), and one of her comments on her aunt Jane is much worthier than the snarky, snobby com-plaints of Lady Knatchbull. Caroline wrote: "Every country has had its great men, whose lives have been and are still read—with unceasing interest; and so in *some* families there has been *one* distinguished by talent or goodness, and known far beyond the home circle, whose memory ought to be preserved through more than a single generation—Such a one was my Aunt—Jane Austen." Austen herself, however, might have preferred Fanny's snideness. It goes against the grain of the rest of the family's determined hagiography of Aunt Jane, the Always Good Christian, and is the kind of "fluctuation of fancy" that might have made Jane laugh.

Persuasion

All the privilege I claim for my own sex (it is not a very enviable one, you need not covet) is that of loving longest, when existence or when hope is gone.
—ANNE ELLIOT

Persuasion, the last of Austen's completed novels, has an autumnal feel to it. It is poetic and slightly world-weary in spirit, even with its happy ending. Henry Austen spoke of the "many perusals" that his sister went through in revising her books, and it seems likely that Austen had not absolutely determined that the novel was complete at her death; the title, for example, was chosen by her brother from several possibilities.

Anne Elliot, Austen's oldest heroine at twenty-eight, is the only worthy member of her family. Ministering to the narcissistic, hypochondriacal demands of her father and sisters, Anne seems doomed to a life of martyred spinsterhood. She has, at age twenty, yielded to the advice of Lady Russell, a family friend and adviser who has taken over the function of maternal adviser since the death of Anne's own mother, and rejected a suitor, Frederick Wentworth, who is not sufficiently wealthy, although Anne loves him. Eight years later her father, Sir Walter, is forced to find a less expensive way of living, and everyone agrees that he should rent out the family estate, Kellynch Hall, and spend some time in Bath, where his expenses will not be so great. Kellynch is rented by Admiral and Mrs. Croft, who is Frederick's sister. Since Anne has not immediately followed her father and older sister, Elizabeth, to Bath but has stayed in the neighborhood to minister to her needy sister Mary Musgrove, she meets Frederick again. She shyly and unhappily observes that he seems to be courting Louisa, one of Mary's sisters-in-law, and appears indifferent to her.

A general party is made up to visit Lyme Regis. Some of Frederick Wentworth's friends are living there: Captain Harville and his family, and Captain Benwick, who is mourning the death of his fiancée, Harville's sister Fanny. While walking along the historic Cobb, Louisa impulsively insists that Frederick catch her as she jumps. She lands, apparently "lifeless," and requires a long period of recuperation, during which she stays with the Harvilles. Frederick is mortified and guilty, the more so when he realizes that people are expecting him to marry Louisa just when he is thinking that perhaps he does have hopes of winning Anne Elliot's hand after all. Captain Benwick, in the meantime, falls in love with Louisa. She is on her sickbed, they are engrossed in the reading of romantic poetry together, and their affection turns to love and a marriage proposal. Relieved to find out that he has no moral responsibility to Louisa, Frederick goes to Bath, where Anne is now staying with her family. He is annoyed to discover that Sir Walter's heir, William Elliot, is evidently courting Anne and that Lady Russell is championing his cause! Still, overhearing Anne telling Captain Harville that women's affections are constant and long-lived, Frederick dares hope that perhaps she still loves him. He proposes to Anne again, and she accepts with deep joy and rapture.

Persuasion shows the reader the interior life of Anne Elliot more sharply than that of any other heroine in Austen's novels. Anne is more isolated even than Fanny Price in terms of being unappreciated by her own family, who think her "nothing." She is the indispensable Jane-of-all-trades to the large and sometimes rather feckless Musgrove family. Both necessary and invisible, needed and unappreciated, she has entered every sort of stewardship and caretaking with all the people in her life and is determinedly self-effacing. Anne Elliot is possibly Jane Austen's most respected heroine. Her Christianity is suffused with idealism; she is indeed a picture of perfection. Although remarkably free of self-pity, she is full of self-doubt, which prevents her from seeing that Wentworth still loves her.

More so than any other of the novels, *Persuasion* is suffused with class anxiety. The British navy has created successful men whose families are not represented in the *Baronetage* or the *Peerage*. The novel shows us how superannuated, decayed, and decadent the Elliots of "old money" have become. They have not even been able to hang on to their money, and their estate, Kellynch Hall, must be rented to Admiral Croft and his wife, Sophie, Wentworth's sister, both of whom possess superb administrative ability.

Marlene Longenecker on Jane Austen and Feminism

Marlene Longenecker is a feminist scholar, a specialist in the Romantic period, and a professor at the Ohio State University.

NT: *A lot of people think that Jane Austen could not have been a feminist. Her heroines do not seem to aspire to anything but marriage. Do you see anything in her life or in her writings that might make you think she could have been a feminist?*

ML: I think "feminist" is a term that needs to be put in historical context. By late-twentieth-century standards, she is probably not a feminist in that she never imagined much in the way of a "public" role for women, nor did she directly address issues of political, economic, or even social equality. She did confine her interests—and those of her heroines—largely to the home and to women's domestic roles.

However, by late-eighteenth-century standards, many of her concerns could be called feminist. First, she was of course famously critical of the marriage market, in which women were reduced largely to objects of exchange between men, almost like commodities on the trade market. Mothers and fathers who attempt to marry their daughters off to the highest bidder come in for serious sanction in her novels; at the same time she is sympathetic to women whose only hope for economic security is a good marriage, if not a passionate one (Charlotte Lucas is the most famous example).

Secondly, like the most famous feminist of her day, Mary Wollstonecraft, Jane Austen firmly believed in what was called rational marriage—marriage based on friendship and on quality and equality of mind, not on mere passion or "sensibility." Like most of the intellectual women of her day, Austen knew that "romance" generally did more harm than good to women, and because women were thought to be nearly incapable of rational thought, claiming "reason" for them became itself a feminist act. All of Austen's heroines (and other female characters she approves of) are women who learn to understand their own emotions and to reason out their choices. And their choices involve serious moral questions: not *merely* the question of which man to marry but questions about loyalty and duty and obligation and sacrifice and community and integrity. (Think of Elizabeth Bennet's confrontation with Lady Catherine de Bourgh.)

Though Austen uses stereotypes of flighty and silly and "romantic" women, it is only to disapprove of them and to suggest that they are not appropriate models.

Finally, although she does not imagine careers other than wives (and presumably mothers) for her heroines, she herself of course had one. She risked the very public role of woman author (and businesswoman as well) and claimed her right to write when it was still very difficult for a woman of her class to pursue any work other than domestic duties.

NT: *Do you think her final novel,* Persuasion, *is different from her earlier novels in terms of feminism, insofar as Anne Elliot is older than any of Austen's other heroines by at least seven years?*

ML: I do think it is more feminist because the choice of a mature and reflective heroine (extremely unusual at that time in novels, virtually unknown) gave Austen the chance to explore things that the earlier novels did not. Anne is of course the most self-aware and self-analytical of all of Austen's heroines, and she controls the point of view of the novel almost exclusively, so we see the world through her eyes and experience her emotions much more intensely than we do those of the heroines in the earlier novels. Some of this is the effect of Romanticism on her work, the influence of Wordsworth and Byron and Scott (whom Anne discusses in the novel with Captain Benwick), whose work all focuses heavily on the interior self—but almost always from a male point of view.

Austen is one of the first to give a woman what Wordsworth called the "hard task" of analyzing a soul. In addition, Anne is an opportunity for Austen to explore what it means to be a "spinster" in her society. Anne and her sister Elizabeth are what would then have been called old maids, and the differences between the ways they cope with this status are instructive: Elizabeth, following the lead of her father, tries to attract the appropriate aristocrat, while Anne, having refused two offers of marriage, seems, until Captain Wentworth's return, settled into being "useful." The novel also explores all the ways she really *is* useful to her family and to Lady Russell.

Anne is melancholic, but she is not grasping at every man who comes her way. Then, of course, there is the famous conversation at the end in which Anne and Captain Harville discuss gender differences and Anne actually says what are probably the most "feminist" words in any of Austen's novels: that women are more faithful and more constant than men—but largely because they have nothing else to do!

Austen in that conversation also points out that all previous "stories" about men and women have been written by men, so Harville is not allowed to bring them in as evidence of his own theory that men are the most loyal and loving. Making Anne Elliot older means too that unlike Elizabeth Bennet or Emma, Anne is never silly and never has to transcend her prejudices and her egotism. She has done all that before the novel opens, and as Austen says, now she must learn romance.

NT: *Are Austen's novels significantly different in their approach to what we might call feminist issues than other novels by women during the same period?*

ML: Most novels written by Austen's female contemporaries were either conventional romances, in which heroines achieve marriage after a series of adventures that nearly compromise their integrity and honor, or Gothic romances in imitation of Ann Radcliffe, in which heroines also achieve marriage after a series of dreadful encounters with evil men who lock them up in ruined castles to fend for themselves against ghosts, potential rapists and robbers, corpses, and other assorted horrors.

But there were a number of serious novelists at the time who took up many of the same themes Austen did: Radcliffe herself, whose Gothic novels—unlike those of many of her imitators—always feature very adventurous and assertive heroines.

Though Austen makes fun of Radcliffe's *Mysteries of Udolpho* in her first novel, *Northanger Abbey*, the parody is also a tribute. Catherine Morland does not find a murderous villain at the abbey, but she does find, in General Tilney, a patriarchal snob who humiliates her largely because she hasn't got any money. Austen domesticates the Gothic and takes away the ghosts but leaves the reader with the evil man who must be resisted.

But Austen is not as radical as Mary Wollstonecraft or Mary Shelley, who were way ahead of their time in terms of feminist issues. It could be argued (and has been) that Austen's more conservative approach was in fact more effective since it reached a wider audience. That of course is debatable, since Mary Shelley's *Frankenstein*, in which feminism is deeply embedded, has lasted at least as well as Austen's novels. Between them they perhaps represent the two poles of what women novelists could do at the beginning of the nineteenth century.

❧ QUIZ: READING AND READERS IN JANE AUSTEN ❧

---

*Shakespeare one gets acquainted with without knowing how.
It is part of an Englishman's constitution.*
—HENRY CRAWFORD

---

1. Which character from *Mansfield Park* says: "Cut down an avenue! What a pity! Does not it make you think of Cowper? 'Ye fallen avenues, Once more I mourn your fate unmerited.'"

2. Who has been "frequently almost driven . . . wild" by the poetry of William Cowper?

3. In which of the juvenilia is a character judged harshly because "we were convinced he had no soul, that he had never read the Sorrows of Werther . . ."?

4. Who asks Anne Elliot "whether *Marmion* or *The Lady of the Lake* were to be preferred, and how ranked the *Giaour* and *The Bride of Abydos*"?

5. Who is of the opinion that "Novels are all so full of nonsense and stuff; there has not been a tolerably decent one come out since *Tom Jones* except *The Monk*"?

6. Who alludes to Milton's "L'Allego" by saying of her spouse: "I used to say to a certain gentleman in company in the days of courtship, when, because things did not go quite right, did not proceed with all the rapidity which suited his feelings, he was apt to be in despair and exclaim that he was sure at this rate it would be *May* before Hymen's saffron robe would be put on for us!"?

7. Speaking of Milton, who quotes *Paradise Lost* in describing "the blessing of a wife" as "Heaven's *last*, best gift"?

8. Which characters in *Sense and Sensibility* commence a group reading of *Hamlet*?

9. "'The course of true love never did run smooth'—A Hartfield edition of Shakespeare would have a long note on that passage." Which character says this about which putative romance in *Emma*?

10. Which character from which late novel enthuses: "Do you remember Scott's beautiful lines on the sea? Oh! what a description they convey! . . . That man who can read them unmoved must have the nerves of an assassin!—Heaven defend me from meeting such a man unarmed"?

*G*ilbert Ryle, British philosopher, when asked if he still read novels said "Yes, all six every year," referring, of course, to Jane Austen and showing the confident self-sufficiency of British culture.
—ARISTODES

*V*irginia Woolf detected two problems with Jane Austen: "First, that of all great writers she is the most difficult to catch in the act of greatness; second, that there are 25 elderly gentlemen living in the neighborhood of London who resent any slight upon her genius as if it were an insult offered to the chastity of their maiden aunts."
—VIRGINIA WOOLF, on Jane Austen

Jan Fergus on
Whiners and Complainers

*J*an Fergus *is professor of English at Lehigh University, Bethlehem, Pennsyl-
vania. She is the author of* Jane Austen and the Didactic Novel *and* Jane
Austen: A Literary Life *and several articles on publishing, bookselling, and readership in late-eighteenth-century England. Her presentations on male and female
whiners and complainers in Austen's novels are a perennial attraction at the annual meeting of the Jane Austen Society of North America.*

NT: *How did you become interested in working on Jane Austen?*

JF: I was given *Pride and Prejudice* to read at fourteen. Ever since, she has
been my favorite writer, though for years (once I chose her as my dissertation
topic) not only could I not read her, but I couldn't even bear to hear her *mentioned*! It took me six years to write the dissertation.

NT: *What constitutes a whiner?*

JF: A whiner is manipulative, usually unconsciously. We whine in order to vent
our discontent and to manipulate others into lessening it, usually by giving us
what we want, since our whining generally blames *them* for our unhappiness.
A genuine whine is also frequent; repetition is essential to the whine.

NT: *Who is your top female whiner in the novels?*

JF: Mary Musgrove, no question! Mary Musgrove wins as a whiner because
she can't open her mouth without blaming someone. She is always convinced
that everyone else has found the best seat, the best place at table, the best
sweetbread, the best of whatever is going; she therefore feels deprived at all
times, writing to Anne, for instance, about how horrible it is to suffer dirty
lanes at Uppercross while Anne is in Bath "with your nice pavements." Her
first speech to Anne, her first speech in the novel, is something like "There
you are *at last*," arraigning Anne for not having come sooner. She is ever alert
for slights, for insults, for indications that she is not getting her due, which is
of course the best. In short, she has an enormous sense of entitlement coupled
with an equally enormous sense of deprivation; the combination makes her a
constant whiner.

NT: *Runners-up?*

JF: Mrs. Bennet, Mrs. Price. Mrs. Bennet is only a runner-up because, although she has her great grievance—the entail of Longbourn and the probably future poverty of herself and her unmarried daughters—her grievance is

BAKEWELL PUDDING

---

*B*akewell Pudding kept Jane Austen going when she was writing. Although the following recipe is from Mrs. Beeton's book *Modern Household Cookery* of 1861, there is no reason to think that it is a considerably different concoction from the one that Austen enjoyed.

BAKEWELL PUDDING.
(Very Rich).

INGREDIENTS:
¼ lb. of puff-paste [pastry for cream puffs and éclairs]
5 eggs
6 oz. of sugar
¼ lb. of butter
1 oz. of almonds
Jam.

MODE:
Cover a dish with thin paste, and put over this a layer of any kind of jam, ½ inch thick; put the yolks of 5 eggs into a basin with the white of one, and beat these well; add the sifted sugar, the butter, which should be melted, and the almonds, which should be well pounded; beat all together until well-mixed, then pour it into the dish over the jam and bake for an hour in a moderate oven.

Time: 1 hour.
Average cost, 1s 6d
Sufficient for 4 or 5 persons.
Seasonable at any time.

Jane Austen evidently liked almonds, which provide the main flavoring for Bakewell Pudding as well as for the white soup that Mr. Bingley serves at his Netherfield ball.

singular, not multiple like Mary's. Her whines seem always to spring from that great one. Thus, when she blames Mr. Bennet for taking no pity on her poor nerves, she's whining because she thinks he won't help her in disposing of their daughters by visiting Mr. Bingley. Mrs. Price too has just the one great complaint—that everything comes on her at once and that no one helps her— but one feels she doesn't greatly care, that getting things done isn't really of much concern to her. Consequently, she does nothing, whining the while that nothing is getting done.

NT: *Who is your top male whiner?*

JF: A tie between Mr. Woodhouse and John Knightley. As for Mr. Woodhouse, his all-encompassing narcissism means that he can whine not only for himself but for others; he barely distinguishes between his own needs and theirs in any case. He is therefore a vicarious whiner, projecting his sense of threat and deprivation onto others, like "Poor Miss Taylor" or even onto the horses that he does not wish to exercise too much by taking them to Randalls; not the horses' sufferings but his own are his real concern. What is interesting about Mr. Woodhouse's whines, however, is his certainty that others will take care of him, and rightly so—unlike Mary, who is always sure that she will not be taken care of, "always the last of my family to be noticed."

John Knightley's whines to Emma about having to attend the party at Randalls are as empowered as Mr. Woodhouse's. He is quite sure, always, of others' assent to his sense of outrage when his domestic habits are in any way threatened—for example, by going out on a cold night to visit the Westons. What redeems him is that he can later be conscious of his bad behavior. In many ways as a whiner he resembles Mr. Woodhouse, though in every other way they are opposites: John Knightley is certain that no one could enjoy going out on a cold evening any more than he does, just as Mr. Woodhouse is certain that no stomach, like his, can bear roast pork. Irrational as their whines are, however, they are treated with more consideration than those of women. That is, Austen makes clear, I believe, that in her world men's whines will not be disregarded; women's will.

NT: *Runners-up?*

JF: Sir Walter Elliot, more or less. A member of the Jane Austen Society of North America suggested Wickham, but I think his complaints about Darcy are too consciously manipulative to qualify.

Sir Walter Elliot

Sir Walter Elliot is a narcissist of the first order. Not only is his house full of mirrors, but he is interested only in the people who reflect him. His eldest daughter, Elizabeth, is acceptable to him because she is "very like himself" and his youngest daughter, Mary, has "acquired a little artificial importance" because she has married into a landowning family. But "Anne, with an elegance of mind and sweetness of character which must have placed her high with any people of real understanding, was nobody with either father or sister: her word had no weight; her convenience was always to give way;—she was only Anne."

Sir Walter values appearance as much as he values titles, and beyond that he seems to value nothing. He is haughty and dismissive of the ugly and hyperexcited by those whose rank exceeds his.

His cousins the Viscountess Dalrymple and her daughter, the Honourable Miss Carteret, are the only characters that excite him, since their snobbery matches his own and he has the challenge of maintaining his *froideur* while simultaneously courting them. Sir Walter deplores the navy not only because it provides an opportunity for promotion for men not born into the gentry but because seamen are "the most deplorable looking" personages, with faces "the colour of mahogany, rough and rugged to the last degree . . . they are not fit to be seen."

> *T*he worst of Bath was, the number of its plain women. He did not mean to say that there were no pretty women, but the number of the plain was out of all proportion. He had frequently observed, as he walked, that one handsome face would be followed by thirty, or five and thirty frights; and once, as he had stood in a shop in Bond-street, he had counted eighty-seven women go by, one after another, without there being a tolerable face among them. It had been a frosty morning, to be sure, a sharp frost, and hardly one woman in a thousand could stand the test of. But still there certainly were a dreadful multitude of ugly women in Bath; and as for the men! they were infinitely worse. Such scare-crows as the streets were full of!
>
> —SIR WALTER ELLIOT

Class

All of Austen's novels are concerned with class differences and their nuances. Lady Catherine de Bourgh of *Pride and Prejudice*, who easily rivals Sir Walter Elliot as a first-class snob, likes to "have the distinction of rank preserved," according to Mr. Collins, her biggest fan. Elizabeth Bennet will not succumb to Lady Catherine's tirade about the unworthiness of her class and simply retorts that since Darcy is a gentleman and since she is a gentleman's daughter, she would not "quit the sphere" of her own class were she to marry Darcy. Lady Catherine, while forced to acknowledge that Mr. Bennet is a gentleman, goes on to declaim, "But who was your mother? Who are your uncles and aunts? Do not imagine me ignorant of their condition." Sensitivity to class is a marker of snobbery for Lady Catherine and for Sir Walter Elliot, who laments the meritocracy of the navy that can help people ascend into a higher class. The nuances of class are not noticed merely by those who would triumph in their position at the head of the class. Mr. Knightley, for example, is aware of the reality of class differences and therefore is more considerate of characters that are marginalized in the class system. He pays special attentions to Mrs. Bates and Miss Bates, and he warmly recognizes the merit of Robert Martin, the farmer who will marry Harriet Smith. He is aware of an incipient "Lady Catherineness" innate in Emma (Austen does use the word "condescension" in describing both Emma and Lady Catherine) and condemns her excesses of class pride both by chastising her seriously and by laughing at her. "Nonsensical girl!" he exclaims when she makes some observations about the "air" of gentlemen.

One of the anxieties about class is its very instability. The ancient and venerable "Shades of Pemberley" can easily be "polluted" in the view of Lady Catherine by the bloodline's being vitiated by the lower class. Because the system of primogeniture could invest much of the family wealth on one child, members of the same family were not always of the same class. Jane Austen herself was in the very same position as Miss Bates, the unmarried daughter of a clergyman's widow with very little money. Her brother Edward,

> When the celebrated Victorian poet laureate Alfred Lord Tennyson visited Lyme Regis he said, "Don't talk to me of the Duke of Monmouth. Show me the exact spot where Louisa Musgrove fell."

on the other hand, was living in opulence. Older sons had the expectation of inheriting the family fortune, which would put their younger brothers in the financially precarious position of having to find their own way in the world and to establish a career. In most cases in Jane Austen's novels the younger sons, such as Henry Tilney, Edward Ferrars (who has been disinherited and by default joins the financial status of a younger son), and Edmund Bertram, become clergymen. John Knightley, younger brother of the master of Donwell Abbey, works as an attorney. Older sons who are brought up with the expectation of wealth, an estate, and sometimes even a title may fall into idleness and dissipation like Tom Bertram and Frederick Tilney. Characters like Darcy and Mr. Knightley who are occupied with the business of attending to their estates have a sense of vocation that Austen warmly appreciates. Darcy of course needs to rid himself of his "pride" when it comes to class consciousness before he can be a suitable husband for Elizabeth. When Edward Ferrars realizes that he cannot live by being "completely idle" and decides to become a member of the clergy, it should be a signal to the reader that he will become a fit partner for Elinor.

In *Persuasion*, Austen demonstrates that the men of the navy, hardworking and meritorious, are the new, natural "aristocracy." They are the men who can now afford to live in estates like Kellynch Hall, which has been mismanaged by the old guard. Willian Price, of *Mansfield Park*, seems bound for a glorious career and a life far from the stultifying lodging at Portsmouth where he spent his early childhood. While some readers may think that Austen's novels reinforce a class-based system, most think that her novels celebrate the triumph of merit over birth and of generosity rather than stinginess, in words, thoughts, and deeds.

The *Baronetage* and the *Peerage*

O scar Wilde quips in his play *A Woman of No Importance* that the *Peerage* is "the best thing in fiction the English have ever done." Jane Austen would have concurred. She satirized the importance of the *Peerage* and the *Baronetage* in *Persuasion*. Readers are struck by Sir Walter Elliot's addiction to reading about himself and his position in the *Baronetage*. The book, his only reading material, offers him "occupation for an idlè hour, and consolation in a distressed one; there his faculties were roused into admiration and respect, by contemplating the limited remnant of the earliest patents; there any unwelcome sensations, arising from domestic affairs, changed naturally into pity and contempt." The *Baronetage of England*, along with *Burke's Peerage* and *Debrett's Peerage*, outlines the history of the upper crust of England. These books offer a history of each family. The first Sir Elliot of Kellynch Hall, for example, achieved the dignity of baronet in the "first year of Charles II."

Although the Elliots of Kellynch Hall are a fictional creation, the *Peerage*s provide a fascinating (or tedious, depending upon your interest in titled people) glimpse into the history of some of England's oldest families. After the royal family and its royal dukes, a ducal family ranks next in prestige. There are fewer than thirty dukedoms extant.

A duke or a duchess is addressed as Your Grace (along with the archbishop of the Church of England), unless you are yourself a member of the gentry, in which case you may call them Duke or Duchess, rather like addressing a pet!

Next in prestige are the marquesses and the marchionesses, followed by earls and countesses, viscounts and viscountesses. These people are addressed as Lords and Ladies. Barons and baronesses, baronets and their ladies, and knights, knights' ladies, and dames follow. The men are called Sir.

A title is not the entire picture. Darcy of *Pride and Prejudice* is untitled but is deferred to because of his enormous wealth. Also, wealth does not necessarily accompany a title; many peers have had to think of inventive ways to earn money. The Marquess of Bath, for example, has turned his family estate into an amusement park and a "Jungle Safari." The owners of fine estates have been able to earn money by selling filming rights to moviemakers. The Duke of Marlborough, for example, won a small part in Kenneth Branagh's *Hamlet* by renting Belvoir, his historic castle near Oxford, to use as Elsinore.

Perhaps the most famous peerage is *Debrett's Peerage and Baronetage*, a publication that now comes out every five years. John Debrett, whose name is a byword for authoritative genealogies of the aristocracy, was the son of a cook in service to the Countess of Ilchester. He went to work for John Almon's Bookshop and Stationers and eventually took over the business, which included editing *Collin's Peerage*, which had first been published in 1769. Debrett's name appears in the 1784 edition and has continued to be associated with the highest echelons of society for more than two hundred years, Sir Walter Elliot, however, would have snubbed him; Debrett himself never went to the trouble and expense of having a coat of arms granted for his family.

Mrs. Smith

A nne Elliot's old school friend Mrs. Smith is living in severely reduced circumstances in Bath. Anne is happy to renew her acquaintance since Mrs. Smith was kind to her after her mother's death. Mrs. Smith was unlucky in her marriage and is now a penniless widow. One of the charms of Anne Elliot is her insistence on maintaining this old friendship, despite her father's disdain:

> Who is Miss Anne Elliot to be visiting in Westgate Buildings? A Mrs. Smith. A widow Mrs. Smith,—and who was her husband? One of the five thousand Mr. Smiths whose names are to be met with everywhere. And what is her attraction? That she is old and sickly.—Upon my word, Miss Anne Elliot, you have the most extraordinary taste! Everything that revolts other people, low company, paltry rooms, foul air, disgusting associations are inviting to you.

Mrs. Smith has the proof, the "smoking gun," to show that William Elliot is not the worthy fellow that the idealistic Anne has assumed and gives her information that is essential to Anne's seeing Mr. Elliot clearly. In return for her loyalty to Anne and her ability to tell the truth about unpleasant aspects of life, she is rewarded with Captain Wentworth's recovery of some of her husband's property.

Mrs. Smith illustrates the alarming fact that an irresponsible husband could leave a woman destitute. She is powerless except insofar as she uses the traditional feminine weapon of gossip. In refusing to shun the powerless, Anne acquires critical information about Mr. Elliot's sordid background and lack of ethics.

Nobody hears Anne, nobody sees her, but it is she who is ever at the center. It is through her ears, eyes, and mind that we are made to care for what is happening. If nobody is much aware of her, she is very much aware of everyone else and she perceives what is happening to them when they are ignorant of themselves.
—STUART TAVE

Jane Smiley on Jane Austen

The Pulitzer Prize–winning novelist Jane Smiley has a Ph.D. in Old Norse literature. She is the author of Barn Blind, At Paradise Gate, Duplicate Keys, The Age of Grief, The Greenlanders, A Thousand Acres, Moo, and The All-True Travels and Adventures of Lidie Newton.

NT: *When did you first read Jane Austen?*

JS: I read all of the novels when I was a teenager. I think the first one that I really, really liked was *Persuasion*. I had one of the one-volume editions that had all the novels in it, and I read it two or three times. The first time I read the novels I was the same age as the girls, or younger. The last time that I read them I was the same age as the parents, or older. That changes your interpretation over the years.

The first time I read *Pride and Prejudice* I read it as a romantic love story about Elizabeth and Darcy, in which she is not the prettiest girl in the room and he is slightly disagreeable, and they find the other's good qualities and come together. The last time I read it I recognized that there was that romance in it, but I was much more interested in the irresponsibility of the parents and the way that these girls were really on their own, which is why Ly-

TONY HENDRA ON *PERSUASION*

Tony Hendra, a former editor of the *National Lampoon* and *Spy*, is a writer. He played the role of the band manager, Ian Faith, in the film *This Is Spinal Tap*.

I've always thought Jane Austen to be one of the funnier writers England has produced—after P. G. Wodehouse and Oscar Wilde (to whom the English can hardly lay claim). She's beyond question the funniest woman writer that has ever lit up that crepuscular little isle. Take that passage in *Persuasion* where the young party has adjourned to the resort of Lyme and Louisa Musgrove sustains a bad fall on the Cobb while trying to get Captain Wentworth to catch her. The scene of dark comedy is sly enough, but there is then this passage: "The report of the accident had spread among the workmen and boatmen about the Cobb, and many were collected near them, to be useful if wanted, at any rate, to enjoy the sight of a dead young lady, nay, two dead young ladies, for it proved twice as fine as the first report." When I first read those lines thirty years ago, I fell on the floor, laughing. I still do. And for this reason I can safely say that if I were allowed a date with any woman writer in history, alive or dead, my first and only choice would be Miss Jane Austen.

dia is so headstrong and finally runs off with Wickham. The last time I read it more as a sort of an analysis of a certain type of family system, where everybody is kind of disagreeable except Elizabeth and her sister Jane. But even Jane has this problem of being too easygoing. So I was much more interested in the psychology of all the characters than I was in the romantic love story.

The best thing about Jane Austen is how beautiful her style is. It is very clear; it is sparkling and ironic. She gives herself plenty of room to tell the story, but it moves along at quite a smart pace. The thing that struck me when I reread all the novels several years ago was that between her early novels and her late novels she changed from an eighteenth-century mode of narration to a much more sophisticated mode of narration. For example, *Pride and Prejudice* and *Sense and Sensibility* are largely narrated; it's mostly indirect narration. *Emma* is much more dramatic. We see the scenes as they happen in a more dramatic way. I don't mean dramatic in the sense of histrionic; I mean dramatic in the sense that it has a structure like a drama. People appear and they say things; then there's another scene and people appear and they say things. That's very similar to the way most nineteenth-century novels were written. By the time she gets to *Persuasion* she is almost in a stream of consciousness mode because she is much more in Anne's head, and it's not so much the social structure or the drama anymore; it is about the evolution of Anne's state of mind.

NT: *Your works are on a much larger scale, but they also look at what we might call provincial life. Do you think that your own writing has been influenced by Austen?*

JS: Well, of course it has. I couldn't say how, though. But I can say that since I read her books so much when I was a girl and into my twenties and thought about them so much, of course my writing grows out of hers, but I have no idea in what way. There is a kind of precision about her technique that is a good model for anybody. There is also an irreverence in her that is a good model for a girl who wants to be a writer because it is tempting when you're a girl to be romantic, highly romantic, or overly respectful. She manages to be precise and ironic and specific. That teaches you, when you start to write, that you can have your own point of view that is a little bit detached and irreverent. I thought it was great to be able to do both those things: to incorporate both affection and detachment in my work.

NT: *In some ways her novels are portraits of what we might today call dysfunctional families, which reminds me of your work in, say,* A Thousand Acres.

JS: I think that dysfunction is the normal course of events, not a divergence from the norm. One of the nice things Austen does is draw a gallery of characters, and some of them are nicer than others. The climax of the story is where the two nicest ones manage to get together or to get back together, as in *Persuasion*. But just because she manages to bring the two nicest people together, she does not thereby predict that they are going to succeed in some ideal way apart from the network of quirk, let's call it that, in which they live.

She does not have a post-Freudian attitude about family life. Psychology and psychotherapy have implied that if you explore the things that give people the quirks that they have, that if only the techniques in child raising or in education were better, somehow you would get a group of people that were functional rather than dysfunctional. Jane Austen does not have that view. She sees a kind of perennial system where there are nice people and not nice people and angry people, selfish people, vain people, and kind people, and that system just continues. Her characters exist in the context of that system. So I think it is wrong to call the families that she is writing about dysfunctional because that implies that she would think there were other families that were functional.

For people who love Jane Austen, there is nothing more to say. It is a joy to read the novels over and over again because they always have something to offer. One of the main things they have to offer is her quirkiness of personalities, which are so delightful and intelligent. She is so intelligent! It is not a learned intelligence like that of George Eliot. It is very quick and lively and insightful and observant. You feel like it's wonderful to be in her presence.

FINANCIAL FEARS

*D*uring the time that Austen worked on *Persuasion*, she was filled with concern over not only her own failing health but a series of financial devastations that threatened her family. Edward Knight, her wealthiest brother, had to face a lawsuit that might have forced the loss of a large part of his estate. A contested will from more than a hundred years previously was at issue. If Edward were to lose the lawsuit, he would lose Chawton Estate and Chawton Cottage, and the Austen women would once again be homeless. Ultimately he settled and paid a large amount of money to keep Chawton in the family.

In March 1816 Henry Austen's bank collapsed and failed. He went bankrupt, and many members of the family lost money that had been deposited in the bank. Henry, Frank, and Charles lost significant amounts of money, and the Austen women could no longer depend on their financial contributions. More than half their annual income would be gone. The news of the bank failure was compounded by the shipwreck of Charles's ship *The Phoenix*, leaving him without a boat to command and no prospects of getting one in the near future. After all, England was no longer at war. Charles in fact did not receive another command for ten years.

The Austen family made it through these crises with a remarkable amount of sympathetic support for one another. Only Aunt Leigh-Perrot, the possible shoplifter, was vocal and bitter. Jane must have felt even more urgently the need to earn money from her writing.

THE NAPOLEONIC WARS

*T*hese wars were the occasion for much of the good fortune of Captain Frederick Wentworth, William Price, and, in real life, Austen's seagoing brothers, Frank and Charles. Napoleon Bonaparte was emperor of the French from 1804 to 1815. After numerous military victories, he was able to take advantage of his fame to reorganize France during its period of political instability following the Revolution. Realizing that "It is by baubles that men are led," he created the Legion of Honor and other ways of "decorating" citizens who were probably starved for a legal hierarchy in the society that had been leveled by the Revolution.

His grand scheme was to reorder Europe entirely and to make France (and himself) in charge of the balance of power. In his victorious march across Europe, Napoleon called himself, perhaps without irony, a soldier of the Revolution. He and his great armies managed to overwhelm his Continental opponents, but the British controlled the seas after they defeated his plans for an invasion of England at the Battle of Trafalgar in 1805. Because Napoleon understood that until he mastered England, there would be an enormous gap in his power, he declared a blockade against all commerce with Britain. A lively smuggling trade ensued. Napoleon's fall was caused by his 1812 invasion of Russia. His vast army had no supplies because the Russians had abandoned everything in his path. Moscow was deserted (except for Pierre Bezukhov, if we choose to accept Tolstoy's version of the war!). Fewer than ninety thousand of Napoleon's original six hundred thousand troops survived. In Paris conspiracies to unseat Napoleon were under way, and he had to rush back to deal with them while the Russian, Prussian, and Spanish armies combined to defeat him at Leipzig in 1813. The Russian Tsar Alexander entered Paris in March 1814, and Napoleon was forced to abdicate. He was forced into exile at Elba. A year later he returned to France. The Allied armies, led by the Duke of Wellington, lured Napoleon into the final moment of the Napoleonic Wars in the Battle of Waterloo in Belgium. Napoleon was made a prisoner of the British and escorted under guard to the small South Atlantic island of St. Helena, a British possession, where he died in 1821. As Mr. Parker comments in *Sanditon*, "Waterloo is more the thing now" than Trafalgar.

The Famous Final Sentence of *Persuasion*

*T*he final sentence of *Persuasion* refers to Anne Elliot: "She gloried in being a sailor's wife, but she must pay the tax of quick alarm for belonging to

A STOPPAGE to a STRIDE over the GLOBE

that profession which is, if possible, more distinguished in its domestic virtues than in its national importance." At first glance the closing sentence seems to say that Anne was proud and happy to be a sailor's wife, even though she must suffer the "tax" of alarm whenever her husband is called to action. At a second glance, however, the final emphasis on a "profession" that is, if possible, "more distinguished in its domestic virtues than in its national importance" seems to suggest that Captain Wentworth is likely to be so attentive to domestic virtues that he is likely to alarm his wife by discovering failings in her domestic virtues. (But who could doubt that Anne's domestic management would not be superb?) Grammatically, for that matter, "that profession" may not refer at all to Wentworth's military profession but rather to Anne's "profession" as a naval wife, and the "tax of quick alarm" may refer to the frightening possibility of her being hauled off herself to the dangers of battle or of being alarmed by seeing her husband leave quickly. Austen in *Northanger Abbey* pokes fun at the conventionally tidy endings of novels, and now, in her last novel, she seems to subvert the tidy ending by closing with a devilishly ambiguous sentence.

ℋere was a woman about the year 1800 writing without hate, without bitterness, without fear, without protest, without preaching. That was how Shakespeare wrote, I thought, looking at **Antony and Cleopatra;** *and when people compare Shakespeare and Jane Austen, they may mean that the minds of both had consumed all impediments; and for that reason we do not know Jane Austen and we do not know Shakespeare, and for that reason Jane Austen pervades every word that she wrote, and so does Shakespeare. If Jane Austen suffered in any way from her circumstances it was in the narrowness of life that was imposed upon her. It was impossible for a woman to go about alone. She never travelled; she never drove through London in an omnibus or had luncheon in a shop by herself. But perhaps it was the nature of Jane Austen not to want what she had not. Her gift and her circumstances matched each other completely.*
—VIRGINIA WOOLF, on Jane Austen

Sanditon: The Final Year

Sickness is a dangerous indulgence at my time of life.
—LETTERS, MARCH 23, 1817

Sanditon is an unfinished fragment of eleven chapters that Jane Austen worked on during her terminal illness. It is fascinating for several reasons. First, her satire is unleashed on hypochondriacs and medical quackery. In the second place, her topical concerns, her large cast of characters, a certain Dickensian cornucopia of zaniness, a fast-paced, almost manic energy all proclaim that *Sanditon* promised to be more like a typically copious nineteenth-century novel. *Sanditon* is a departure from Austen's typical concept of three or four country families in a small village; its presentation of an ersatz community, dedicated to "the waters" and health, implicitly criticizes the commodification of England's green and pleasant land or at least its sandy shores. Charlotte Heywood promises to be the heroine, but the hero is nebulous at best. Sidney Parker appears to be the most eligible gentleman, but the pages are so packed with characters (and caricatures) that the eleven chapters, despite a great deal of hilarity and pungent satire, remain highly provisional in terms of exactly which characters, aside from Charlotte, would come to the foreground. John Wiltshire writes that *Sanditon* is "concerned with the way that the medical and the erotic are related. One might say that the resort of Sanditon combines the attraction of Club Med and a retirement village."

The fragment opens with an accident: Mr. and Mrs. Parker, out in quest of a surgeon to bring to Sanditon, the resort that Mr. Parker is developing, are overturned in their carriage. They are "rescued" by Mr. Heywood and offer to take his daughter Charlotte, aged twenty-two, to visit Sanditon with them. The rest of the fragment does little more than set up a fascinating cast of characters. Lady Denham is the great lady of the town, who, like old Featherstone in George Eliot's *Middlemarch* later, is busy fighting off the claims of would-be heirs. Lady Denham favors young Clara Brereton, poor, dependent, and beautiful, who seems likely to become friends with Charlotte. Sir Edward Denham, a nephew by marriage of Lady Denham's, is both a rake and a rattle. The Parker family is large and varied, a "family of imagination and quick feelings," Austen says. They include extremes of energy and hypochondria: Mr. Parker and Diana Parker are movers and shakers; their siblings Susan and Arthur are the principal invalids of the tale. Another sibling, Sidney, has "hero" potential; he is introduced as being "very good-looking, with a decided air of ease and fashion, and a lively countenance." The character of Miss Lambe, a "sickly and rich," "chilly and tender," "half mulatto" heiress of age seventeen from the West Indies, premises a multicultural plot line.

Obviously it is frustrating to have this wonderful novel truncated so early, but it is marvelous and witty reading.

Nineteenth-Century Wellville

Mr. Parker is a nineteenth-century British Babbitt, a booster, a promoter, an entrepreneur, a one-man chamber of commerce for an as yet barely existing development. He is obsessed with turning the sleepy village of Sanditon into a seaside spa where people will come and benefit from sea bathing, whatever their ills.

> The sea air and sea bathing together were nearly infallible, one or the other of them being a match for every disorder, of the stomach, the lungs or the blood; they were anti-spasmodic, anti-pulmonary, anti-septic, anti-bilious and anti-rheumatic. Nobody could catch cold by the sea, nobody wanted appetite by the sea, nobody wanted spirits, nobody wanted strength.

Mr. Parker seems only to talk in advertising copy or as if he were delivering a motivational speech to the chamber of commerce. He *is* the chamber of commerce at Sanditon, however, with some help from his sister Diana, a perpetual-motion machine of a woman, who moves wheels within wheels to get patrons for Sanditon, her brother's hobbyhorse. If Mr. Parker anticipates the Babbitt of Sinclair Lewis, Diana anticipates the Mrs. Jellyby of Charles Dickens. These characters are also interesting in that they present obsessive behavior unlike any other we have seen in Jane Austen's work. Mr. Parker admits that Sanditon is a second wife and four children to him: "hardly less dear—and certainly more engrossing." His modernity is inconsonant with so much of what we are accustomed to in Jane Austen's works. For example, he is incorrigibly faddish. Speaking of his new house, he tells Charlotte:

> You will not think it a bad exchange, when we reach Trafalgar House— which, by the bye, I almost wish I had not named Trafalgar—for Waterloo is more the thing now. However, Waterloo is in reserve—and if we have encouragement enough this year for a little crescent to be ventured on— (as I trust we shall) then, we shall be able to call it Waterloo Crescent— and the name joined to the form of the building, which always takes, will give us the command of the lodgers.

It is uncannily prophetic that the names of England's great military victories have been appropriated for real estate. It seems to be a vision of our own time, in which the twin evils of advertising and speculation seem to have reduced everything that is noble to the lowest denominator. How could the dying Jane Austen have been so shrewd about the increasing speed of the mills of publicity grinding away? She had plenty of hints, of course. David Nokes reports that "the name 'Trafalgar' became a sudden fashion" to the point that a "Trafalgar Stitch" was created to embellish the needlework of ladies. At the same time, Wordsworth was lamenting "The world is too much with us; late and soon / Getting and spending, we lay waste our powers." *Sanditon* promises to be a look at the wasting of our powers.

Hypochondriacs

Jane Austen's mother had a well-documented tendency toward hypochondria, especially in her later years. George Holbert Tucker, a major biographer of the family, has called her a *malade imaginaire*. Jane wrote to Cassandra in December 1798: "My mother continues hearty, her appetite & nights are very good, but her Bowels are still not entirely settled, & she sometimes complains of an Asthma, a Dropsy, Water in her Chest & a Liver disorder." Mrs. Austen took her laudanum and seemed at least to have a certain ironic perspective on her hypochondria, composing a verse—not quite doggerel—from 4 Sydney Place in Bath:

DIALOGUE BETWEEN DEATH AND MRS A

Says Death, "I've been trying these three weeks and more
To seize an old Madam here at Number Four.
Yet I still try in vain, tho she's turned of three score;
  To what is my ill success owing?"

"I'll tell you, old Fellow, if you cannot guess,
To what you're indebted for your ill success—
To the prayers of my husband, whose love I possess,
To the care of my daughters, whom Heaven will bless,
  To the skill and attention of Bowen."

Bowen was a doctor whose memorial tablet can still be found in Bath Abbey. Mrs. Austen enjoyed her career as a poetaster; among her verses is "A Receipt for a Pudding," which in seven stanzas innocently delineates an atherosclerotic nightmare of half a dozen eggs, a half pound of butter, and plenty of milk.

Jane Austen's mother, Cassandra

The Circulating Library

The library of course afforded every thing; all the useless things in the world that could not be done without, and among so many pretty temptations, and with so much good will for Mr Parker to encourage expenditure, Charlotte began to feel that she must check herself—or rather she reflected that at two and twenty there could be no excuse for her doing otherwise—and that it would not do for her to be spending all her money the very first evening. She took up a book; it happened to be a volume of **Camilla**. *She had not* **Camilla's** *youth and had no intention of having her distress— so, she turned from the drawers of rings and brooches repressed further solicitation and paid for what she bought.*
—*SANDITON*

Circulating libraries made reading possible at a time when books were costly. Readers paid for subscriptions to circulating libraries that entitled them to check out a certain number of books. Each of Jane Austen's novels mentions a circulating library and their dual attractions as social gathering places and places to procure books. Lydia, in *Pride and Prejudice*, for example, feels drawn to the Meryton library, Clarke's, because she can find some of the military men she dotes on there. Fanny Price, on the other hand, when she returns to her father's impecunious household in Portsmouth, decides that she must subscribe to a circulating library not only because she needs to read but also because she wants to educate her sister Susan,  who "had read nothing, and Fanny longed to give her a share in her own first pleasures, and inspire a taste for the biography and poetry which she delighted in herself."

The libraries catered to the demands for books by people who could not afford to buy them. As Lee Erickson remarks in his 1996 study of *The Economy of Literary Form: English Literature and the Industrialization of Publishing, 1800–1850,*

> [B]ooks were not only luxuries but also rising in price so that to have an extensive library was a sign of great wealth. The average three-volume novel cost a guinea in 1815, or based on the current worth of a guinea's gold content, roughly the equivalent of $100 today; and that does not take into account how much lower the standard of living of the average person was then and so how many fewer people could afford to buy books.

Colonel Brandon's and Mr. Darcy's private libraries may have been part of the attraction that Marianne Dashwood and Elizabeth Bennet feel for these men.

The circulating library also functioned as a shop where "pretty temptations such as gloves, parasols, and brooches could be bought." Additionally, since most specialized in recent fiction, some people thought they were purveyors of low culture. In a lengthy philippic in his *Biographia Literaria* (1817) Samuel Taylor Coleridge fulminates against

> the devotees of the circulating libraries, I dare not compliment their pass-time, or rather kill-time, with the name of reading. Call it rather a sort of beggarly day-dreaming, during which the mind of the dreamer furnishes for itself nothing but laziness and a little mawkish sensibility.... We should transfer this species of amusement . . . from the genus, reading, to . . . indulgence of sloth, and hatred of vacancy. In addition to novels and tales of chivalry . . . this genus comprises as its species, gaming, swinging, or swaying on a chair or gate; spitting over a bridge; smoking; snuff-taking; tête-à-tête quarrels after dinner between husband and wife; conning word by word all the advertisements of the Daily Advertiser in a public house on a rainy day, etc. etc. etc.

Of course Coleridge's horror of novels seems reactionary, but indeed, the novel was a fledgling genre and had not yet achieved intellectual force or authority. Later Coleridge delighted in Jane Austen's novels, staying up two nights in a row to finish *Pride and Prejudice*. Austen's novels were in the circulating libraries, but so were ephemera, such as the worst kinds of Gothic novels. Thomas Carlyle, that energetic dyspeptic, commented on the literary effluvia of the early nineteenth century:

> Ship-loads of Fashionable Novels, Sentimental Rhymes, Tragedies, Farces, Diaries of Travel, Tales by flood and field, are swallowed monthly into the bottomless Pool: still does the Press toil; innumerable Paper-makers, Compositors, Printers' Devils, Book-binders, and Hawkers grown hoarse with loud proclaiming, rest not from their labour; and still, in torrents, rushes on the great array of Publications, unpausing, to their final home; and still Oblivion, like the Grave, cries, Give! Give!

Carlyle's concern that books are becoming commodities, speedily devoured, prognosticates the fast-food mentality of much of today's press. Nevertheless, the circulating libraries, in spite of their pretensions and the bibelots they sold, contributed enormously to the growth of a reading public and to the egalitarianism of literature and literacy. Certainly Jane Austen and her heroines relied on these institutions. In *Northanger Abbey*, especially, Austen instructs readers on how to separate literary wheat from subliterary chaff.

On the Presumed Weakness of Arthur Parker's Cocoa

*A*rthur Parker proclaims: "A large Dish of rather weak Cocoa every evening, agrees with me better than any thing." Charlotte Heywood thinks, "as he poured out this rather weak Cocoa, that it came forth in a very fine, dark coloured stream." This is just one of many instances where Austen exposes the hypocrisy of certain hypochondriacs.

℘ Quiz: Illnesses and Hypochondria ℘

Name the character that is described:

1. Which character from *Persuasion* is crippled by severe rheumatic fever?

2. Who is of the opinion that "In London it is always a sickly season. Nobody is healthy in London; nobody can be"?

3. Whose illness has a "putrid tendency" and consists of fever, a heavy stupor, sleepless pain, and delirium?

4. Who has sore throats that are always "worse than anybody's"?

5. Which character in *Emma* caught a bad cold on November 7 and still suffers from it after the New Year?

6. Whose baby "cried, and fretted, and was all over pimples"?

7. Who has a serious illness brought on by a "neglected fall and a good deal of drinking"?

8. Which character in *Sanditon* habitually suffers from an "old grievance, spasmodic bile" and is hardly able to "crawl from [the] bed to the sofa"?

9. Which character tells his spouse that if her daughter were to die, it would be a comfort to know that the illness was incurred in the "pursuit" of a husband?

10. Which character from *Emma* is "never entirely free" from "those little nervous head-aches and palpitations"?

11. Which character from *Pride and Prejudice* comments: "People who suffer as I do from nervous complaints can have no great inclination for talking. Nobody can tell what I suffer!—But it is always so. Those who do not complain are never pitied"?

Sir Edward Denham, Bart.

Sir Edward's great object in life was to be seductive.—With such personal advantages as he knew himself to possess, and such talents as he did also give himself credit for, he regarded it as his duty.—He felt that he was formed to be a dangerous man—quite in the line of the Lovelaces.
—SANDITON

Jane Austen's first novel, *Northanger Abbey*, defends the novel but also shows that too much indiscriminate reading has potential danger, that of perpetrating and perpetuating silliness, to which Catherine Morland temporarily succumbs. In Austen's last work she depicts Sir Edward Denham, who has been corrupted into imitating the seducers he has read about in sentimental literature.

Sir Edward says to Charlotte, "I am no indiscriminate Novel-Reader. The mere Trash of the common Circulating Library, I hold in the highest contempt." He can quote all the poets of the age, but his superficial thoughts and feelings lead one to think he is a very talented parrot with an incredibly vast vocabulary. He is in some ways the obverse of Catherine Morland, the innocent of *Northanger Abbey*. She would like to be a heroine, and he would like to be a villain, "propelled to say, write or do, by the sovereign impulses of illimitable ardour." Catherine, however, knows that she cannot "speak well enough to be unintelligible," and Sir Edward's conversation provides an example of such unintelligibility: "It were hyper-criticism, it were pseudo-philosophy to expect from the soul of high-toned genius, the grovellings of a common mind.—The coruscations of talent, elicited by impassioned feeling in the breast of man, are perhaps incompatible with some of the prosaic decencies of life." Sir Edward's prolix and absurd defense of villainy as "impassioned feeling" shows Jane Austen's acerbity was not diminished during her terminal illness. His role model, Robert Lovelace (pronounced "loveless"), is not merely a seducer but, more seriously, a man who drugs and then rapes the virtuous heroine of Samuel Richardson's famous novel *Clarissa*. Sir Edward's determination to seduce Clara Brereton appears to be burlesque: "[H]e felt a strong curiosity to ascertain whether the neighbourhoods of Timbuctoo might not afford some solitary house adapted for Clara's reception;—but the expense alas! of measures in that masterly style was ill-suited to his purse, and prudence obliged him to prefer the quietest sort of ruin and disgrace for the object of his affections. . . ." The men in Jane Austen's fragmentary *Sanditon* are for the most part ludicrous and inferior to the women. Sir Edward is silly, a would-be Byronic hero without any strengths at all.

> *B*eing convinced on examination that much of the Evil lay in her Gum, I persuaded her to attack the disorder there. She has accordingly had 3 Teeth drawn & is decidedly better, but her Nerves are a good deal deranged. She can only speak in a whisper—and fainted away twice this morning on poor Arthur's trying to suppress a cough.
>
> —DIANA PARKER

What Jane Austen Earned from Her Books During Her Lifetime

Tho' I like praise as well as anybody, I like what Edward calls **Pewter** *too*
—LETTER, NOVEMBER 1814

1803: 10 pounds from Richard Crosby for the manuscript of *Susan* (eventually *Northanger Abbey*).

1811: 140 pounds from the publisher Thomas Egerton for *Sense and Sensibility*. 150 pounds from its profits.

1812: 110 pounds for *Pride and Prejudice*.

1814: 450 pounds from the publisher John Murray for the copyrights to *Sense and Sensibility* and *Mansfield Park*.

Austen made a total of about 700 pounds in her lifetime. In terms of today's value, that could range from about $14,000 to $35,000 or even up to about $120,000 according to the most generous estimates. For a lifetime of work she was lamentably underpaid.

Jane Austen's Illness and Death

Jane Austen is widely presumed to have died of what is now known as Addison's disease, a failure or insufficiency of the workings of the adrenal glands that can destroy the autoimmune process. Addison, who described the disease only in 1849, wrote: "The body wastes, the pulse becomes smaller and weaker, and the patient at length gradually sinks and expires." Claire Tomalin argues persuasively that Austen's symptoms accord more with "a lymphoma such as Hodgkin's disease."

Although we may never know the diagnosis for Austen's premature death, we know something about the course of her illness. Austen first felt sick in 1815. She was tormented by elusive and inexplicable symptoms, which came

and went. They baffled her with the possibility of imminent death and then tantalized her with respites in which recovery seemed possible. In her last two years she wrote *Persuasion* and made a good start on *Sanditon*. Her own illness may have inspired her to create the comic hypochondriacs of those two novels.

The last two months of her life, however, seem to have been nothing but painful both for herself and for Cassandra, on whom the brunt of the nursing fell. But whenever Austen was strong enough to hold a pen, she would write, and she dictated some light poetry—in six stanzas—about the St. Swithin's Day races at Winchester just two days before her death. The poem, albeit satiric, touches on death and immortality since St. Swithin is determined to curse the races with heavy rain. As Austen claims for him, "When once we are buried you think we are dead / But behold me Immortal." Austen is buried in Winchester Cathedral, and the memorial plaque on her tomb does not mention her writings, but it does engage in the hagiography that Cassandra and other members of the family immediately commenced. Cassandra burned many, perhaps most, of her sister's letters, proceeded to call her a "dear Angel," and turned Chawton House into the shrine that it is today.

Cassandra's Conflagration

With the loss of her beloved Jane, Cassandra faced almost thirty years without a close, loving companion in her life. Their nephew J. E. Austen-Leigh wrote:

> Their sisterly affection for each other could scarcely be exceeded. Perhaps it began on Jane's side with the feeling of deference natural to a loving child toward a kind elder sister. . . . [T]his attachment was never interrupted or weakened. They lived in the same home, and shared the same bed-room, till separated by death. They were not exactly alike. Cassandra's was the colder and calmer disposition; she was always prudent and well judging, but with less outward demonstration of feeling and less sunniness of temper than Jane possessed. It was remarked in her family that "Cassandra had the *merit* of having her temper always under command, but that Jane had the *happiness* of a temper that never required to be commanded."

After Austen's funeral Cassandra wrote to their niece Fanny: "I *have* lost a treasure, such a Sister, such a friend as never can have been surpassed,—she was the sun of my life, the gilder of every pleasure, the soother of every sorrow, I had not a thought concealed from her, & it is as if I had lost a part of myself."

During the following decade Cassandra stayed on at Chawton, looking after her increasingly senescent mother. After Mrs. Austen's death in 1827, and Martha Lloyd's marriage to Frank Austen in 1828, Cassandra lived alone for sixteen years at Chawton, where she "contrived to turn the house into a kind of shrine to her dead sister," according to David Nokes. He goes on to say that for Cassandra, "Jane's writings became a kind of sacred text and her beloved image almost a holy icon."

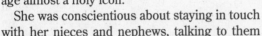

Jane Austen's sister Cassandra

She was conscientious about staying in touch with her nieces and nephews, talking to them about Jane and reading the novels aloud. They were also conscientious about visiting her, although one nephew said that "visits to Chawton, after the death of Aunt Jane, were always disappointments.... All its peculiar charm was gone."

Two or three years before her death in 1845, Cassandra destroyed the bulk of Austen's letters, an act that has occasioned much exasperation from the posterity that craves to learn more and more about Jane Austen. Why did Cassandra selectively destroy so many letters? Most biographers agree that she was thinking not of posterity but of being tactful to the nieces and nephews and also of maintaining a certain delicacy. Much biting malice and mordancy were undoubtedly destroyed, along with physical details of illnesses and jokes that may have been acceptable to Georgian ears but seemed less proper to the Victorian era.

Cassandra was felled by a fatal stroke at age seventy-three, while visiting her brother Admiral Sir Francis Austen near Portsmouth. Her body was brought back to Chawton, and her nephew James Edward Austen-Leigh wrote about her funeral to his sister Anna Lefroy: "The day was fine, but the wind exceedingly boisterous, blowing the pall almost off the coffin, & quite sweeping away all sound of Charles' voice between the gate and church-door. It also struck me as remarkably emblematic of her age & condition that the wind whisked about us so many withered beech leaves, that the coffin was thickly strewed with them before the service closed."

THE KNATCHBULL KINSHIP

*O*ne of Jane Austen's favorite nieces, Fanny Knight, became Lady Knatchbull, the second wife of Sir Edward Knatchbull in 1820. When Lord Byron died at Missolonghi, Greece, in 1824, his body was brought back to England and lay in state at 25 Great George Street, Westminster, the London home of the Knatchbulls. Their son, the first Lord Brabourne, edited Austen's letters in 1884, dedicating them to Queen Victoria. Brabourne's grandson married the oldest daughter of Lord Mountbatten of Burma, a great-great-granddaughter of Queen Victoria's in 1946. Their son Lord Romsey became godfather to Prince William of Wales after his birth in 1982.

Edward Austen Knight, Jane's older brother, posed for a full-length oil portrait in Italy in 1812. The original is displayed at Jane Austen's house, Chawton. Edward's daughter Fanny became Lady Knatchbull.

Some Dissenting Views on Jane Austen

*I*n the interest of impartiality, it must be admitted that certain resistant undergraduate students are not the only ones who fail to be enchanted with Jane Austen.

Getting into her books is like getting in bed with a cadaver. Something vital is lacking, namely, life.
—EDWARD ABBEY

I'm looking at the Multiplex and I'm almost going to go into that movie with Emma Thompson and then right next door there's a movie where Arnold Schwarzenegger crashes a jet ski into a helicopter and I think that's probably more along my line of thinking, so I never quite get to those Jane Austen movies.
—DAVE BARRY

An accurate daguerreotyped portrait of a commonplace face; a carefully fenced, highly cultivated garden, with neat borders and delicate flowers; but no glance of a bright vivid physiognomy, no open country, no fresh air, no blue hill, no bonny beck. I should hardly like to live with her ladies and gentlemen, in their elegant but confined houses.
—CHARLOTTE BRONTË on reading *Pride and Prejudice*

I am at a loss to understand why people hold Miss Austen's novels at so high a rate, which seem to me vulgar in tone, sterile in artistic invention, imprisoned in their wretched conventions of English society, without genius, wit, or knowledge of the world. Never was life so pinched and narrow. . . . All that interests . . . any character is has he (or she) the money to marry with? . . . Suicide is more respectable.
—RALPH WALDO EMERSON

Miss Austen has no romance. What vile creatures her parsons are!
—JOHN HENRY CARDINAL NEWMAN

I have never read anything Austen wrote. I just never got at reading **Pride and Prejudice** *or* **Sense and Sensibility.** *They seemed to be the Bobbsey Twins for grown-ups.*
—ANDY ROONEY

I have now taken to Jane Austen but although the genius of Proust forces me to tolerate a fiction founded upon snobbery, materialism and hypocrisy, her mere sly pokes of humour cannot persuade me to the same enjoyment.
—VITA SACKVILLE-WEST

𝒥ane Austen's books are absent from this library. Just that one omission alone would make a fairly good library out of a library that hadn't a book in it.
—MARK TWAIN

𝒥 could read Poe's work on salary, but not Jane's. Jane is entirely impossible. It seems a great pity that they allowed her to die a natural death.
—MARK TWAIN

It is perhaps more amusing to contemplate the sardonic ripostes with which Austen would have greeted these criticisms. Not, of course, in public, but in a zinger of a letter to Cassandra that, alas, would have ended up consecrated to the flames.

John McAleer
on Ancestry and Biography

John McAleer received his doctorate at Harvard University in 1955. He has spent more than fifty years teaching college. He has written biographies on people as diverse as Theodore Dreiser, Rex Stout, and Shakespearean critics and actors. McAleer, a professor at Boston College, is currently engaged on a new biography of Jane Austen.

NT: *How would you define the biographer's task?*

JM: I always try to know how the writer's life experience influenced his art, what it was in his own personal experience that gave a special quality to his own writing. For example, I was able to procure a copy of the *Collins Peerage*, which was done by Sir Egerton Brydges, the author of a scandalously bad novel, *Fitz-Albini*. It was rather amusing that his nephew Benjamin eventually married Jane's niece Anna. The authors of both the best novel of the era and the worst novel of the era are united in being godparents to the couple.

Sir Egerton was obsessed with family history, and Jane made extensive use of his *Peerage*. It infiltrates all her writing so that virtually every character in her novels is named from her own family tree. She had relatives who were Elliots; she had relatives who were Wentworths and Woodhouses and Dashwoods and just about every name that comes to mind. The only characters that she does not draw from the family tree are people she does not consider of consequence and people she does not really like, like Henry Crawford. There are no Crawfords in the family tree, but there are Darcys and there are Knightleys, there are Brandons, the people that she respects. She also was related to the Ferrars family, even though I am sure that she did not care for either Fanny Dashwood or her mother. Of course she did like Edward.

I think I understand what her pride of heritage meant to her. Jane was descended from three sons of King Edward I, and she was a direct descendant of Owen Tudor, the grandfather of Henry VII. For several generations she was directly related to the ancestors of Edward IV, whose daughter became the wife of Henry VII. So she and Mary, Queen of Scots had many direct ancestors in common, and I think that explains her great partiality for the Stuart cause.

Another branch of her mother's family gave shelter to Charles I at Stoneleigh Abbey when the citizens of Coventry turned him away. During the last century someone observed an eye peeking out through a floral oil painting at Stoneleigh Abbey. Underneath the floral painting was a Van Dyck portrait of Charles I that Jane Austen's relatives had covered up so that it would not be destroyed by Cromwell's men.

NT: *There are still many aspects of Jane Austen's life that I think have left most scholars puzzled or befuddled. For example, that eight- or nine-year period in the first decade of the nineteenth century when she did not do much writing. Do you have any theories about that?*

JM: I think it is not quite as long a period as we think because she was apparently copying over her three little volumes that went back to her childhood. It would also appear that she made at least one good transcript of *Lady Susan* and of course did work on *The Watsons*. I think the fact that she gypsied around from household to household was very unsettling to her because she really liked to strike down roots, and it was only when she got to Chawton in a situation similar to what she had known at Steventon that she really settled down to work in earnest.

NT: *Do you have a title for your biography of Austen?*

JM: I have thought of *The Chawton Benefaction*. R. W. Chapman, who established the authoritative texts of the novels, used that term himself, and he is referring to the benefaction coming from Edward, Jane's brother, that made possible her life there. But I'm using it in the larger sense, that really we owe all the books to those seven years at Chawton. So the benefaction really is Jane Austen's benefaction to humanity, which was achieved at Chawton, when she rewrote *Sense and Sensibility, Pride and Prejudice*, and *Northanger Abbey* and then wrote from scratch the other three novels.

A whimsical illustration
depicting Jane Austen today

PART III

The Legacy

Jane Austen in the Twentieth Century

The Janeites

Jane Austen and Rudyard Kipling would seem to belong to different species. Kipling is the celebrated author of many novels, stories, and poems of manly courage, war, and adventure. Nevertheless, Kipling wrote one of the most interesting of all tributes to Jane Austen, a short story called "The Janeites." The characters and setting are utterly unlike anything in Austen's novels. The characters are Cockneys who have served in World War I and are reminiscing about their experiences in an apparently all-male secret society meeting in the mysteriously named Lodge of Instruction. Jane Austen only comes into the story as a man named Brother Humberstall describes the "secret society" of "Janeites" on the front lines of the British artillery during the First World War. An ability to speak in the language of the Janeites enabled soldiers of any rank or class to enjoy special privileges and a sort of equality with the officers. Humberstall himself has been initiated into the Janeites, who tell him "the Password of the First Degree which was *Tilniz an' trap-doors*."

Of course, as the reference to the Tilneys of *Northanger Abbey* suggests, the "secret" Janeite language consists simply of references to Austen's novels. At first Humberstall is only able to ingratiate himself with the officers by occa-

Jane Austen poolside in Hollywood, with laptop computer and cell phone, was voted one of the ten top entertainers of 1995 by Entertainment Weekly.

sionally dropping references supplied to him by his friend as "passwords." Eventually he reads Austen's novels and masters them sufficiently to name the heavy artillery in the trench after her characters and to defend his choice of names by pointing out the similarities between Reverend Collins, "Lady Catherine de Bugg," and General Tilney and the guns christened in their names.

Even though initiation into the Janeites seems open to all, according to Humberstall, it is still "a very select Society, as you've got to be a Janeite in your'eart, or you won't have any success. An' yet [his friend] made *me* a Janeite! I read all her six books now for pleasure 'tween times in the shop; an' it brings it all back—down to the smell of the glue-paint on the screens. You take it from me, Brethern [*sic*], there's no one to touch Jane when you're in a tight place. Gawd bless 'er, whoever she was."

For the men in the trenches, Austen was "comfort food." The story also suggests her greater ability to civilize and make equal all ranks of English society. Austen's novels epitomize the British culture that makes all equal in the face of struggle and death. Her importance as an emblem of Englishness is further suggested in the poetic epigraph Kipling wrote at the head of the story:

> Jane lies in Winchester—blessed be her shade!
> Praise the Lord for making her, and for all she made!
> And while the stones of Winchester, or Milsom Street,
>   remain,
> Glory, love, and honour unto England's Jane!

Still, Kipling's is a man's world, and despite being a Janeite in his "'eart," Humberstall also provides a characteristically masculine disparagement of Austen and her works:

Jane? Why she was a little old maid 'oo'd written 'alf a dozen books about a hundred years ago. 'Twasn't as if there was anythin' *to* 'em either. *I* know. I had to read 'em. They weren't adventurous, nor smutty, nor what you'd call even interestin'—all about girls o' seventeen (they begun young then, I tell you), not certain 'oom they'd like to marry; an' their dances an' card-parties an'picnics, and their young blokes goin' off to London on 'orseback for 'air-cuts an' shaves. It took a full day in those days, if you went to a proper barber. They wore wigs, too, when they was chemists or clergymen.

Clearly, Kipling has mastered Austenian irony, for even as Humberstall struggles to pin down Austen's greatness—"what beat me was there was nothing to 'em nor *in* 'em. Nothin' at all, believe me . . ."—he manages to put his finger on her ability to capture the human frailty around us:

I mean that 'er characters was no *use*! They was only just like people you run across any day. One of 'em was a curate—the Reverend Collins—always on the make an' lookin' to marry money. Well, when I was a Boy Scout, 'im or 'is twin brother was our troop-leader. An' there was an upstandin' 'ard-mouthed Duchess or a Baronet's wife that didn't give a curse for any one 'oo wouldn't do what she told 'em to; the Lady—Lady Lady Catherine (I'll get it in a minute) De Bugg. Before Ma bought the 'airdressin' business in London I used to know of an 'olesale grocer's wife near Leicester . . . that might 'ave been 'er duplicate.

Humberstall concludes that all of Austen's characters are "on the make, in a quiet way," not so very different from his own family and his own mother. Of Austen's status as a mother herself, Humberstall has been assured that "She *did* leave lawful issue in the shape o' one son; an' 'is name was 'Enery James."

Jennifer Crusie on Jane Austen as the Mother of the Modern Romance Novel

Jennifer Crusie is a celebrated, award-winning romance novelist. Her novels include Manhunting, Getting Rid of Bradley, Strange Bedpersons, What the Lady Wants, Charlie All Night, Anyone but You, The Cinderella Deal, Trust Me on This, *and* Tell Me Lies. *As Jennifer Smith she has written* Anne Rice: A Critical Companion.

NT: *Why do you call Jane Austen the mother of the romance novel?*

JC: Because she set the standard for the genre. She wrote woman-centered fiction set in an emotionally just universe. That is, her stories not only are about women but also focus on women's lives and relationships with other women, not just on women's lives as they intersect with men's. She pointed out not only the economic aspects of the marriage bond but also the political aspects, which women are well aware of, and she always kept her satire under wraps so that it did its work without alarming anyone. She wrote what seemed to be pleasant romantic comedies, but underneath are these hugely subversive ideas, and much of the best romance fiction written today does exactly the same thing.

Finally, Austen's happy endings are earned, and they're not all cream and roses; she writes not of impossibly happy endings but of probable endings, which the heroine has earned by growing, learning, compromising, and ultimately being true to her own sense of self. Elizabeth in *Pride and Prejudice,* for example, does get the fairy-tale ending, but she doesn't get it by being stunningly beautiful or by having the right shoe size or by sleeping until somebody wakes her up; she struggles and grows and earns her happiness. That's a romance novel ending.

I wrote a short story called "I Am at My Sister's Wedding" that was completely inspired by the relationship of the parents in *Pride and Prejudice.* I've responded in my work to Austen's underhanded wit, particularly in the verbal humor she gives most of her heroines, and to her sly political satire that never grows heavy-handed or overwhelms the story and characters. She showed me what a light hand can do with heavy issues, how powerful pleasurable reading can be in communicating anger and injustice. I've also studied her mastery in weaving subplots into the main plot, inextricably united by theme and motive.

NT: *You are known for fusing romance, humor, and mystery in your novels. Don't you think that Jane Austen uses those three elements very well?*

JC: Romance is important because it is still the major human contact we make; it is right up there with the parental bond. It's been sniffed at as "women's stuff" because it's so overwhelming that it scares many male writers who don't like the idea that something as intangible and illogical as romantic love can make chaos of people's lives. That's why the romance is so peripheral in so many male stories; it's seen as just a little something the guy has on the side, easily controlled, especially if the woman dies in the end so he can mourn her in comfort. Austen and those of us still writing romance move that powerful force to center stage and examine it, forcing our characters to deal with it in emotional, physical, and political terms.

Humor is important in fiction because it's such a huge aspect of character. One of the ways we evaluate people is based on what they laugh at and how they use that laughter. Humor is a powerful weapon; if we as writers can, through our characters, make people laugh at something we're criticizing, we've dealt that idea a real blow. That's why satire, when it's well done, lightly done, is so devastating.

The romance novel is subversive; it puts women at the center of their stories and says that relationships are more important than money or status, that connecting with other people is the only ultimately fulfilling act. It undercuts everything that male writers have traditionally emphasized by creating a new sense of reality, and part of that reality is laughing at the male ideas of the world. Books like *Pride and Prejudice* and *Northanger Abbey* blatantly attack patriarchy and make it ludicrous, and the best of modern romance does that too, whether it's romantic comedy or the deeply serious, dark books many romance writers prefer.

NT: *What about the mystery you mentioned. Do you think that Jane Austen wrote mysteries?*

JC: All books are mysteries. All books begin with a problem to be solved, reveal more aspects of the problem as the plot progresses, and finally solve the problem in the last pages. But romances are, again like the best books, not really concerned with the ending, with the right answer, with whodunit. They're concerned with how their protagonists get there; the journey, not the answer, is the interesting part. The great social mystery for women is men because our realms are so different that much of what men do seems utterly inexplicable. Of course men feel the same about women, but they've never had to worry about it much because they ran the world. But up until the last twenty years or so, women have had to understand men completely because they were so much in their power. So Catherine in *Northanger Abbey* has to understand the men in her life because that's the only way she can survive. Of course she does understand them, but she lets herself be gently kidded out of the understanding, and that is how she ends up out in the cold. In modern romance novels, women solve not only the mysteries of the men in their lives but the mysteries of who they themselves are and how they move through the world; their discoveries are often self-discoveries.

NT: *Jane Austen seems to have preferred the fiction of her own time and novels that amuse, rather than instruct, don't you think?*

JC: I think the best novels always instruct by amusing. That is, the best fiction grabs and keeps your attention with character and plot; you have to keep reading to find out what happened to these people you care about. But way underneath the plot of all the best stories is the theme, the controlling idea, the idea that obsessed the writer so much she was driven to write the book. *Emma* is a great love story, but it also teaches the limits of the power the mind has over the human heart.

All great stories both amuse and instruct. The romance novel's great theme is that women can achieve anything through their own resources, intelligence, courage, and faith. They'll have to work for it, and they'll be challenged, hurt, and changed in the process, but they'll succeed because of who they are and what they do, not what they look like or who rescues them. That's a hell of a theme coupled to a hell of a story. Which for me pretty well explains the popularity of the genre.

Soap Opera Divas on Jane Austen

Jane Austen's work is a revelation about the underlying passions of the Romantic era. She's an inspiration for modern drama.
—JEAN CAROL, Nadine in *Guiding Light*

Jane Austen is very funny, but then so is life. At the same time, Jane Austen explores the very heart of women who suffer in love and women who suffer from being more intelligent and perceptive than the men around them. Her characters do not brave the dramatic fates of the soap opera diva: no amnesia, no show trials, no kidnappings, no returning back from the dead, no evil identical twins. But they feel with at least as much intensity, and Jane Austen does not need to stretch her plots at all to captivate my interest.
—MAUREEN GARRETT, Holly in *Guiding Light*

What I love most about Jane Austen's work was that she was a woman who wrote about women. She wrote women in love—and there's nothing more profound. She wrote with a sense of humor—she was detached, which allowed her to write wit; intelligent wit—not neurotic wit. She's timeless.
—NANCY GRAHN, former Julia Capwell in *Santa Barbara,*
now Alexis in *General Hospital*

I've been thinking about Ms. Austen recently with the sudden surge of film adaptations of her work. As I sat with my heart in my throat watching Sense and Sensibility, *praying for two lovers to open up and reveal themselves to one another before their opportunity was lost forever, I realized why it's so hard to write love stories today. Everybody reveals everything! People don't yearn or suffer in silence; they blurt their secrets to complete strangers! Makes it tough to build in longing and suspense.*
—COURTNEY SIMON, writer for *General Hospital*

I'm not surprised at Jane Austen's current popularity. Her novels incorporate the same elements that make good daytime drama: character-driven, romantic story and characters drawn in great detail and with affection. Women love this kind of storytelling. Too bad she's not around today. She'd give "soaps" a run for their money. I'd work for her like a shot!
—VICTORIA WYNDHAM, Rachel in *Another World*

Alton Abbey and
Jane Austen Retreats

Alton Abbey, an Anglican religious community in Beech, near Alton, Hampshire, is a brief walk from Chawton, the Jane Austen home. The abbey was built by its monks near the end of the nineteenth century and includes twenty-three guest rooms, a guesthouse, and cottages. It is a community of Benedictine monks who offer very popular organized weekend retreats dealing with various topics relating to Jane Austen, both spiritual and secular. Other retreats have focused on George Herbert, icon painting, and Charles Dickens, and there has been at least one Charlotte Yonge Study Day.

Dom Nicholas, an Austen expert, runs the Austen retreats; he has also addressed the Jane Austen Society in the United Kingdom and has written an introduction to *Lady Susan,* in which he calls the title character a "glittering serpent, a wily dragon, a fabulous monster."

In an article printed in February 1995, the religious correspondent of the *Times* of London, Ruth Gledhill, praised Alton Abbey and its "youthful charismatic abbot, Dom Giles Hill." She awarded the abbey four stars out of a maximum of five for its architecture, music, liturgy, and spiritual high and five stars for after service care. Spiritual high is not a very explicit criterion, but I assume it is a splendid experience. As for after service care, I imagine monks and abbots sharing cream tea and theology with visitors.

The abbey is open to visitors daily from 5:30 A.M. until 9:00 P.M. Services are open, but are not compulsory.

If you are interested in a schedule of retreats and more detailed information, you can write to Alton Abbey, Alton, Hampshire, GU34 4AP, United Kingdom, or telephone 01-420-562145. Retreat spaces fill up early, so considerable planning in advance is often required.

Elsa Solender on the Jane Austen Society of North America

E lsa Solender is the current president of the Jane Austen Society of North America. She is a journalist and a teacher, and she participates in an impressive range of volunteer activities. In addition, she is a lap swimmer, a cross-country skier, and a frequent worldwide traveler.

NT: *Tell me about your experiences as president of the Jane Austen Society of North America.*

ES: As I have traveled around the continent in my first year as president of JASNA, I have discovered that we have an amazing variety of people as members. Most of them have a very impressive level of knowledge about Jane Austen's novels, life, and era. We are able, though, to accommodate the first-rate literary scholar, the devoted librarian who has memorized virtually every word of the novels, and the retiree or homemaker who has seen a recent film adaptation, read a novel or two, and been intrigued enough to seek us out to learn more. We have attracted a merchant marine who comes to JASNA meetings whenever he is onshore, a recent chief counsel to the State Department, a composer, and a national newspaper columnist, as well as many teachers, lawyers, librarians, homemakers, writers, academicians. They chat happily together about Jane Austen, socialize across all class and geographical lines. Their immense goodwill toward other admirers of Jane Austen cuts across all geographical, ethnic, and economic lines. We are mostly women, but the approximate twenty-five percent of us who are male never feel out of place.

NT: *How was JASNA founded?*

ES: JASNA was created in 1979 by three unusual people who met at the annual British Jane Austen Society meeting on the third Saturday in July. There is a tent set up on the lawn of Chawton House. Women used to wear hats and white gloves, and men were turned out in ties and jackets despite the heat. Sometimes people fainted. They would hear two lectures, eat strawberries

Elsa Solender, president of the Jane Austen Society of North America

and cream, and then mill about. Now the British, like us, have regional branches, but I think our success was what stimulated that development.

The three North Americans wanted to have more activities in the American style. I also think our two gentlemen founders, the late J. David Grey of New York and the late Henry G. Burke of Baltimore, felt more attention should be paid to the third founder, Joan Austen-Leigh, of Victoria, British Columbia, a great-great-great-grandniece of Jane Austen's and herself a novelist.

Jack Grey was a junior high school vice-principal. Henry Burke was an attorney and accountant and had a Ph.D. in political science from Johns Hopkins. His wife, Alberta H. Burke, who died in 1975, had the greatest collections of Austeniana anywhere: every first edition, translation, American editions, all secondary source materials, and some manuscripts. She left the manuscripts to the J. P. Morgan Library in New York and set up the Henry and Alberta Burke Jane Austen Collection at Goucher College.

The first JASNA meeting took place at the Gramercy Park Hotel in New York in December 1979 with a hundred people in attendance.

NT: *How many members does JASNA currently have?*

ES: Our numbers grew steadily from that first hundred in New York to about one hundred sixty at the second conference in Baltimore. They evened out at a nice, manageable twenty-two hundred between 1985 and 1994. Then in 1994, when the Jane Austen feature films and TV miniseries began to be shown, our numbers began to skyrocket. We currently have about four thousand forty members in good standing. We never advertised. Imagine if we had? But every film, every article in the media, and every TV showing brought in new members.

NT: *Why is Jane Austen more popular than ever?*

ES: Everyone has a theory. Let me share a few. One simple answer is that her works aren't under copyright any longer. Thus she's currently the cheapest screenwriter of our era. The columnist Russell Baker at a New York Public Library forum dismissed another theory, which is that people today crave civility and find it in Jane Austen's world. I think he misunderstood the meaning of the word "civility." In the eighteenth century, civility was not simply being polite. It was a code of behavior for citizens, as opposed to "courtesy," the code feudal or courtly code of behavior. Civility was a formula developed so that people of varying backgrounds and classes who lived together in English towns could get along with each other. In that sense I think the civility portrayed in Jane Austen's novels can be very meaningful for our era.

Another theory is that Jane Austen offers a kind of escapism from our world into a kinder, gentler time. Since she does create a complete world in her books, there is an escape into that world for the reader. But it's an escape for which you do not have to park your brains at the door.

Funny thing, when the feminist movement began in the early 1970s, Jane Austen was rejected as too conservative and accepting of her society. When Jane Austen and Sappho were the first women writers whose works were added to the Literature-Humanities curriculum at Columbia University, some people sneered about Austen's being a "safe" choice. Thereafter some feminists—notably Susan Morgan and Deborah Kaplan—noticed that Austen was actually a subtle but truly subversive writer; her protagonists all make the most important decision of their lives—their choice of spouse—for themselves. That was amazing. Furthermore, Austen's portrayal of the patriarchal society is very acute, as is her presentation of marriages in which a pretty face or a fortune was the attraction. Whoever says Jane Austen's novels end with "happily ever after" has not read carefully of the marriage of Mr. and Mrs. Bennet in *Pride and Prejudice* and many another mismatch.

Austen's work also has a universality to it that cannot be underestimated. Her depiction of the psychology of humans is uncannily accurate. Wherever people meet and mate, Austen's work is meaningful. That is why the setting for the novel *Emma* could be transported from a small English village in the early nineteenth century to a somewhat larger American "village" called Beverly Hills for the film *Clueless*. Both the message and the humor were intact, although the satiric bite was much less. Still, both were portrayed from a secure narrative point of view, so secure that the narrator-writer was able to poke fun at the society without destroying its evident virtues.

Finally, Jane Austen is wonderfully rereadable. Each time you read one of her novels, it's a new experience. You bring what you've learned to it, and she has more to teach you, more to amuse you, than you noticed before.

NT: *Can you give me an overview of your job as president of JASNA?*

ES: My job as president is different from my predecessors' role. The volume of work is now too great for a single volunteer to handle. I have a part-time personal assistant and use our database service more heavily than my predecessors. I share presidential responsibilities with our Executive Committee more, I believe, than previous presidents. I am trying to lead the development of a strategic plan for retaining our serious membership constituency as well as for fulfilling our fiduciary responsibilities. I have traveled more than all past presidents combined and will continue to do so in order to strengthen our existing regions and develop new ones. Finally, in the area of public relations, I think I've been on more television shows and spoken to more journalists, everything from *Good Morning America* to whatever. . . .

ALL ABOUT JASNA
(THE JANE AUSTEN SOCIETY OF NORTH AMERICA)

The benefits of membership in JASNA include the annual journal, *Persuasions,* 202 pages most recently. Another is an invitation to the annual general meeting. JASNA publishes a newsletter, *JASNA News,* three times a year, with book reviews, interviews, and lots of news about Jane Austen in the news, among other things. New members also get access to a unique Jane Austen Book Service. The large number of regional groups have many activities. Some have monthly book groups and performance groups. Other have two or three other programs per year. There are large active groups in the New York, Chicago, and San Francisco regions that have four or five major programs each year.

In the dues categories below, a student membership refers to any full-time student. A family membership refers to two individuals living at the same address. Both hold full membership privileges, but they receive only one copy of JASNA publications and other mailings. Life and sustaining members, in addition to other benefits, receive a semiannual president's letter with news of the society between editions of the *JASNA News*. Membership years run from December 16 to December 16.

American membership secretary
(checks should be in U.S. dollars, made out to JASNA):

Barbara Larkin
2907 Northland Drive
Columbia, MO 65202
(314) 474-9682

Canadian membership secretary
(checks should be in Canadian dollars, made out to JASNA-Canada):

Nancy Thurston
200 Kingsmount Blvd.
Sudbury, ONT P3E 1K9
(705) 670-1357

Annual student membership:
United States: $15
Canada: CDN $24
International: U.S. $24

Annual individual membership:
United States: $23
Canada: CDN $32
International: U.S. $32

Annual family membership:
United States: $33
Canada: CDN $42
International: U.S. $42

Annual sustaining membership:
United States: $50
Canada: CDN $59
International: U.S. $59

Individual Life Membership:
United States: $300
Canada: CDN $345
International: U.S. $345

THE ANNUAL GENERAL MEETING OF JASNA

At the opening ceremony of the 18th Annual General Meeting of the Jane Austen Society of North America at the Omni Ballroom in Richmond, Virginia, attendees were presented with little chintz bags (one woman sternly complained, "It is *not* polished chintz") tied by pastel ribbons. Inside each bag was an assortment of letters, just like cardboard Scrabble tiles, and everyone had to unscramble his or her letters; at my table we had Norland Park, John Thorpe, John Knightley, George Wickham, and Philip Elton, in fitting with the year's theme of "Jane Austen and Her Men."

Startled by the solemnity and the quietness of such a large group, I gazed about me; people were focusing as hard on unraveling their anagrams as a child trying to keep within the lines of a coloring book. The crowd seemed older, conservative. I looked in vain for bright colors and spotted no signs of lime green, the "fashion" color of the season. Well, at least they have good taste, I thought as I observed some members putting together anagram after anagram with businesslike alacrity and others stumbling through their task much like Harriet Smith trying to decipher a charade.

The meeting, much like a conference, was wonderfully organized with an assortment of small-group sessions and some fascinating speakers. Although there were well over five hundred people, it felt cozy. One of the local hostesses announced on the loudspeaker that someone had misplaced a copy of *Less than Angels* by Barbara Pym; would anyone who encountered it bring it to the registration desk? As though one heart were beating, the people in the room became vigilant; we were determined that the hapless reader of Barbara Pym would not leave without her tome.

On Saturday night there was a banquet, and many members dressed in Georgian costume. The general air was convivial, so I started to make friends and ask people why they liked attending the annual general meetings. The responses were heartening:

"I feel like I am part of a family; you can talk to anyone."

"I worship the woman."

"It's a big disturbance to leave your house and your pets to go to a convention, but I have done it seven or eight times."

"I think the controversy is fun. Everyone gets so passionate."

"This is less pompous and more broad than academic conferences, and it is fun to have a chance to dress up in period costume."

> ## WHAT IF AUSTEN'S CHARACTERS HAD HAD SUPPORT GROUPS?
>
> ———∞∞∞———
>
> *M*arianne Dashwood could have benefited from membership in the Women Who Love Too Much group; Mr. Grant of *Mansfield Park* would have been a good candidate for Overeaters Anonymous, Sir Walter Elliot for Parents Without Partners, Willoughby for Sex and Love Addicts Anonymous, Mr. Woodhouse for Codependent No More, and Mrs. Norris could have benefited from the Carbohydrate Addicts List on the Internet.

"I come to carry my wife's briefcase."

"I love the people here. I would let any of them into my house. I have belonged to other organizations dealing with Trollope, Dickens, the Brontës, and I assure you that things were stolen there. Nobody at a Jane Austen meeting would steal anything."

"You don't have to wear power clothes, a tiara, or nouveau grunge. As long as it is clean. But don't come barefoot or topless."

"I like meeting intelligent women."

"She wrote only six books, but there is always something new. We will never stop talking."

"Why feel sorry for Charlotte Lucas? Mr. Collins might be great in bed."

"The conversation with literate, interesting people creates opportunities for stimulating interaction not usually found in everyday life. Passion, knowledge, fascination crop up in the hallways, at restaurants, at the sidelines of the meetings, and late at night in the hotel rooms. It is to experience a *world* from the past and relate it to the social structures of today."

Cyber Jane:
Austen Sites on the Internet

The Internet offers an astonishing omnium-gatherum of sites pertinent to Jane Austen. From the sublime to the ridiculous, from the ephemeral to solid scholarship, the World Wide Web provides a daunting, exhausting number of links to material related to Austen. Ken Roberts, of Ontario, who maintains two Web pages dedicated to Jane Austen says: "The texts of almost all of Jane Austen's writing are on-line. . . . If you're interested in movies, there is endless material about films based on Jane Austen's work and on the actors who appear in them."

Dramatizations of the Novels

Jane Austen's works have inspired several dramatists to adapt her works for the stage. A. A. Milne, best known for *Winnie the Pooh,* wrote *Miss Elizabeth Bennet: A Play. First Impressions: A Musical Comedy,* which had a Broadway run of eighty-four performances in 1959, starring Polly Bergen as Elizabeth and Hermione Gingold as Mrs. Bennet.

A South African musical production by Mark Eldon features Elizabeth and Darcy singing "Should I Dance with You, Should I?," "You Should Dance with Me, You Should," and an unlikely duet between Lydia and Mr. Collins entitled "Whom Shall I Ask to Marry Me?" Jane Bennet trills that "It Takes Two to Fall in Love."

There are other adaptations of Austen's works for the stage, of course, but so far none has become a perennial success. The radio has been a congenial medium for Austen's works, and many radio dramatizations were presented, especially in England, during the central third of the twentieth century. Some of the performers are familiar to viewers of BBC television productions, and there is a *Masterpiece Theatre* connection. Rachel Gurney, the actress who played Lady Marjorie in *Upstairs Downstairs,* read the part of Emma in a 1948 BBC radio version while Angela Baddeley, who played Mrs. Bridges, read Elizabeth in a 1945 radio production of *Pride and Prejudice.*

In 1965 Dame Peggy Ashcroft did a dramatic reading of *Persuasion* in fourteen parts for BBC Radio. Two years later Derek Jacobi read the part of Darcy. Those of us who enjoyed Jacobi's depiction of Claudius in the series *I, Claudius* may never have thought of him as a Darcy type!

JANE AUSTEN: THE MUSICAL

Kathleen Glancy, of Edinburgh, Scotland, selected a Jane Austen Top Ten Musical Numbers list for the 1987 issue of *Persuasions*. If each of Austen's characters were to have a "theme song," the selections might include such timeless anthems as "Once I Had a Secret Love," a duet performed by Jane Fairfax and Frank Churchill; "How Do You Solve a Problem Like Maria?," a musical query trilled by Sir Thomas and Lady Bertram; and the premonitory air "Baby, It's Cold Outside," intoned by Mr. Woodhouse, whose encore number echoes "Adelaide's Lament" ("A person can develop a cold") from *Guys and Dolls.* Harriet Smith warbles a charming rendition of "Matchmaker, Matchmaker," to her patroness Emma, as Willoughby serenades Marianne Dashwood with "If I Were a Rich Man."

Tunes by Sondheim, Rodgers, Porter, Berlin, and others provide plenty of melodies of self-expression for characters like Lydia Bennet ("I Cain't Say

CLASS VOTES AT JANE AUSTEN HIGH

BEST-LOOKING

Jane Bennet	John Willoughby

MOST POPULAR

Emma Woodhouse	Charles Bingley

MOST LIKELY TO SUCCEED

Lucy Steele	Fitzwilliam Darcy

MOST INTELLECTUAL

Mary Bennet	Henry Tilney

BEST ATHLETE

Catherine Morland	Frederick Wentworth

BEST SCHOOL SPIRIT

Sophia Croft	William Price

BIGGEST FLIRT

Lydia Bennet	Henry Crawford

WITTIEST

Elizabeth Bennet	Frank Churchill

TEACHER'S PET

Fanny Price	William Collins

PERFECT ATTENDANCE

Anne Elliot	Edmund Bertram

MOST TIME SPENT IN DETENTION

Mary Crawford	Frank Churchill

SNAPPIEST DRESSER

Augusta Elton	William Elliot

No"), Colonel Brandon ("The Sadder but Wiser Girl for Me"), Mary Crawford ("Life upon the Wicked Stage"), Mr. Darcy ("Never Gonna Dance"), Emma Woodhouse ("Cockeyed Optimist"), Willoughby ("There's No Place like London,"), and Frank Churchill ("Hair").

Emily Auerbach: *The Courage to Write* — Women Novelists and Poets

The inspiring principle which alone gives me the courage to write is that of so presenting our human life as to help my readers
—GEORGE ELIOT

Professor Emily Auerbach teaches at the University of Wisconsin at Madison and is also a producer for Wisconsin Public Radio. She directs a series called The Courage to Write *on women writers. She also hosts a talk show called* University on the Air. *She is the author of* Searching for Jane Austen, *scheduled for publication by the University of Wisconsin Press.*

NT: *Tell me about your original* Courage to Write *program.*

EA: My early program, which was just a half hour long, looked at Austen's life, the fact that she hid her writing, and the way her writing is quite unconventional in terms of its portrayal of the heroine. In the four-hour series we were able to go in to much more depth, including looking at her juvenilia. When actors read excerpts from those early sketches and from her letters, listeners encounter the saucy, defiant side of Jane Austen.

Many of the scholars that I interviewed for my four-hour series talk about how much you'll find in Jane Austen underneath the surface. The image that I like to think about when talking about Jane Austen is "Hidden Pictures," as in the children's activity where you see what looks like a charming country scene but the game is to find the hidden hat or knife. You may have to look four or five times before you see this very subtly drawn picture that is hiding in what on the surface looks like just a country scene. I think Austen's novels are like that.

NT: *You look for the comb that's hidden behind the hill with the cranberry bog on the side.*

EA: Right. Because you can be reading along in a Jane Austen novel and miss the fact that there's a minor character, given maybe a paragraph, who introduces startlingly revolutionary ideas. She will add these little touches in her books, such as a fleeting reference to the slave trade.

The four-hour series also features lots of famous guests talking about their reaction to Jane Austen. For fairness, I thought I would include those who do *not* like Jane Austen, and so I did interview the humorist Dave Barry. He said that everyone should read everything that Jane Austen wrote so that he doesn't have to. I also interviewed Andy Rooney of *Sixty Minutes,* who compared Austen's books to the Bobbsey Twins for grown-ups, even though he's never read them. I linked their reactions to Mark Twain, who also seemed to think that the "masculine" thing to do was to hate Jane Austen.

These attacks are balanced of course by Austen fans: Margaret Drabble, who told me that as she writes her novels, she is in a perpetual dialogue with Jane Austen and Carol Shields, whose Pulitzer Prize–winning novel *The Stone Diaries* in some ways harkens back to Jane Austen; and novelist Fay Weldon, who talks about adapting *Pride and Prejudice* for the BBC. What I was struck by when interviewing novelists Reginald Hill, Stephanie Barron, and Kelly Cherry or columnists like Mary McGrory and Ellen Goodman is how many of the people who now consider themselves devoted Janeites started off by really disliking her. I think one of the things I was hoping my series would do would be to encourage anyone who had started a Jane Austen novel and then was turned off by it to try again. In fact I have had wonderful letters from public radio listeners, including one woman who said she had been given the novel *Emma* by her son as a Christmas gift, so she felt that she ought to read it. She said she had tried eleven times and had not made it through, but after hearing the radio series about Austen and realizing how many other people there were who sometimes were initially turned off as they encountered the world of her novels, she has decided she was going to try and make it through this time. I hope she does!

NT: *I think a lot of readers, especially younger ones, fail to pick up on the ironic voice and miss the humor.*

EA: Yes. I have had undergraduates come up to me and say, "You know, I've read three chapters of *Pride and Prejudice,* and nothing is really happening." If you read her novels looking for helicopter chases and battle scenes, you are not going to find it there. It is a world of subtlety and characterization and intricate diction.

NT: *Can you tell me something about your new book on Austen?*

EA: *Searching for Jane Austen* explores parallels between Austen and other women writers and considers how relatives and critics deliberately sweetened and distorted her image and censored her words. I offer an introduction to all six novels and the juvenilia and provide appendices with ideas for burned-out teachers or people wanting to find Austen resources on the Web. The book reprints my article "'A Barkeeper Entering the Kingdom of Heaven': Did Mark Twain Really Hate Jane Austen?" This article includes an unfinished essay by Twain called "Jane Austen."

NT: *Tell me more about the tapes. How can I order them?*

EA: There are whole Austen books on tape, of course, but our documentary programs help people learn more about Austen's life and era and some of the themes running through all her work. The four programs in our Austen series are called "Jane Austen and a Style of Her Own," "For Better or Worse: Jane Austen and Marriage," "Prejudice and Pride: The Legacy of Jane Austen," and "Jane Austen, Janeites, and the Jane Austen Society of North America."

The main source for *Courage to Write* programs and guides is called the Audio Store. Its number is 1-800-327-6986; the address is 821 University Avenue, Madison, WI 53706. Independent Learning through the University of Wisconsin-Extension offers courses in many areas, including the Courage to Write and the English Novel. You can live anywhere in the world and participate. A toll-free number for information about Independent Learning Courses is 1-800-442-6460. You may also E-mail ilearn@admin.uwex.edu for information. I can be reached at 608-262-3733, or by E-mail at emily. auerbach@mail.admin.wisc.edu or 628 Lowell Hall, 610 Langdon Street, Madison, WI 53703.

Tobacco Cards: Jane Austen Is Gaining on Ty Cobb

Jane Austen collector items are proliferating. There are paper dolls, tea towels, rare editions of her books, bookmarks, and calendars. One of the most unusual Austen items is the tobacco card. These were cards that were inserted in packets of tobacco or cigarettes prior to 1940 in order to promote sales. They were often part of a collector's series of sports figures, royalty, musicians, actors, or English authors. Steve Berman, who sells original tobacco cards at Maple Leaf Collectibles in Collingwood, Ontario, reports that competition to purchase a Jane Austen tobacco card has been brisk. He recently sold one depicting the familiar portrait done by Cassandra for $61.03 and reflects that her popularity is indicated by comparable sales. A Shakespeare tobacco card sold for $43.50, Charles Dickens for $14, George Bernard Shaw for $13. Charlotte Brontë's tobacco card went for $7.50, but Berman got less than $3 for cards depicting Tolstoy, Milton, Pepys, and Plato. The price of the Austen card, however, did not astonish Berman, who has sold cards depicting such sports figures as Babe Ruth and Ty Cobb for thousands of dollars.

Jane Austen Books:
A Bookstore

"We are everything Austen—books new and used, entertainment and merchandise." Patricia Latkin, the owner of Jane Austen Books, produces a periodical catalog of her materials. You may get on her mailing list, or place an order for a book, by writing her at

Jane Austen Books
860 N. Lake Shore, Suite 21-J
Chicago, IL 60611-1751

Telephone: 312-266-0080
Fax: 312-266-0081
E-mail: JABooks@aol.com

Film Adaptations

Either you know the story already, or I will risk spoiling your enjoyment of the five movies, three miniseries, two operas, and one ballet-on-ice about to be based on Austen's original.
—BENEDICT NIGHTINGALE

Linda Mizejewski on Austen and the Woman's Film

Linda Mizejewski is a poet who teaches film studies at the Ohio State University. She is the author of two books on film: Divine Decadence: Fascism, Female Spectacle, and the Making of Sally Bowles *and* Ziegfeld Girl: Image and Icon in Culture and Cinema.

NT: *What do you think of the films based on Jane Austen's novels?*

LM: The *Emma, Persuasion*, and *Sense and Sensibility* films do a wonderful re-thinking of what used to be called the woman's film as it's been discussed in recent feminist film criticism. The debate has always been about the "masochistic" position of the woman spectator–heroine, the latter proscribed into her limited domestic space, the former unable to achieve a proper "distance" from the screen. Because these films are 1990s "period pieces" about drawing room rather than bedroom passions, there's a self-consciousness about them (and I would argue it's not true of the Greer Garson film [*Pride and Prejudice*], which occurred in an era of "classic" cinema in which period pieces and costume films were more of what "serious" movies were supposed to be. Garson, Garbo, and other "classy" women stars of the era *often* took up these kinds of costumes and roles).

Today we put Emma Thompson in those hairnets and corsets, and it's obviously Emma Thompson "doing" an Austen character. In this way maybe the relationship of the three period films to *Clueless* is really very direct: If distance, irony, and arch commentary on gender/sexuality are the hallmarks of camp, then all these texts are campy in degrees. I don't think they're set up for the "overidentification" of 1940s melodrama. In fact, no one even thinks of them as melodrama, even though they fit into the women's films paradigm of old. Maybe it's because there's too much cool bite in Austen to be strictly melodrama.

NT: *What else is interesting to you in the films?*

LM: These period films make a strong argument for the women's and sisters' relationships as a primary source of interest and energy. I'd argue it's one of the subtle legacies of feminism and maybe also contemporary voyeuristic curiosity about female eroticism with females. The Hugh Grant character's relationship with Emma Thompson [as Edward and Elinor in *Sense and Sensibility*] paled in comparison with the richness of Emma Thompson and Kate Winslet [as Marianne]. Since the latter made her claim to fame in *Heavenly Creatures,* there's an aura of passionate attachments among women that clings to her stardom.

NT: *Do you have any theories on why Jane Austen was named one of the top ten entertainers of 1995 by* Entertainment Weekly? *Is it a good sign, or do you think it is a part of the "dumbing down" phenomenon?*

LM: That's a gibe that falls back on the cliché "Well, the movie is never as good as the book." More interesting approaches to adaptation simply start in other places. How does "authorship" shift into a different configuration? Austen isn't just novelist here but a cultural sign of a cluster of other things: contemporary curiosity about her era, nostalgia for a certain kind of courtship, stardom (Austen's and Thompson's), et cetera. I would not even argue good-bad, but I'd say that Austen has become a sign for a set of courtship/gender/sexual relations that are now of great interest to us.

Linda Troost and Sayre Greenfield
on *Jane Austen in Hollywood*

L inda Troost is an associate professor of English at Washington and Jefferson College, and Sayre Greenfield, her husband, is an associate professor of English at the University of Pittsburgh at Greensburg. Troost edits an annual, Eighteenth Century Women. Greenfield is the author of The Ends of Allegory. Together they edited Jane Austen in Hollywood, a collection of essays on the film versions of Austen's work.

NT: *The articles in your book,* Jane Austen in Hollywood *often discuss how the movies give us "extra" Darcy or "extra" Brandon and Ferrars. What does that mean?*

LT: The recent films develop the personalities of the men in new ways, giving us "extra" doses of Brandon or Darcy. Interestingly, this change parallels the same development in contemporary romance fiction. Since the late 1980s romance heroes, at least in novels by Americans, have had their points of view included, and many have acquired a set of ideal qualities that the bodice-ripping heroes from the late 1970s might find astonishing: Romance novel heroes now possess and express tender feelings, respect women, show great sensitivity and vulnerability, love small children and animals, and are generally nice and witty.

The Austen films, which are cultivating a female audience, instead of the usual teenage male one, make Austen's men into New Men. The novel's stolid Edward Ferrars is not very attractive to anyone except the novel's Elinor Dashwood; Hugh Grant's Edward, however, is another story entirely! Colonel Brandon is a dull fish in the novel, but not when played by Alan Rickman. In short, the films of the 1990s, like the romance novels of the 1990s, give us the heroes we want in the 1990s, men who feel. We want to feel Darcy's emotion as he, for instance, writes the letter to Lizzy or his anguish as he leaps into that pond to cool his ardor. This desire for open emotions explains the Darcymania that erupted when Colin Firth played the role for the BBC; this production and this actor showed us how our favorite hero felt as he fell in love with one of our favorite heroines.

NT: *Do you have a favorite among the Austen films? Which one? Why?*

LT: Favorite of the films? That's a really hard question because we love them all. Sayre, when pressed, answers *Clueless,* but he admits that is an easy answer. I am particularly thrilled by any adaptation of *Pride and Prejudice* but have a hard time deciding if I like Colin Firth or David Rintoul better as Darcy.

On some days I like Wishbone, the Jack Russell terrier, more than any of them. [The year 1996 saw *Furst Impressions,* a version of *Pride and Prejudice* aimed at children and starring Wishbone. . . . In the 1997–1998 season, the thespian dog starred in a remake of *Northanger Abbey* entitled *Pup Fiction.*]

NT: *Do you have any reservations about the films?*

LT: The problem that film adaptations of Austen's works present to a person already interested in her novels is essentially the fear of success. On the one hand, the Austenites may wish the films good commercial fortunes as a way of seconding their own appreciation, but on the other hand, this very confirmation of their tastes renders their appreciation less exclusive, less a way of marking their superiority.

SG: Insofar as the audience for the films consists largely of those who have already read the novels, we pay the admission, purchase the videotape, or at least turn on the television to see to what extent these new versions of Austen measure up to our standards. For this audience the films complicate the process of reading and do not replace it. The producers and distributors, however, seem to assume that seeing comes before reading, so they picture an audience with less time, less knowledge, and less patience than the reader of

ALDOUS HUXLEY ON ADAPTING *PRIDE AND PREJUDICE* FOR THE SCREEN

*A*ldous Huxley, writer, philosopher, connoisseur of mescalin and peyote, may be best remembered for his novels, such as *Antic Hay, Point Counter Point, Eyeless in Gaza,* and *Brave New World.* He moved from his native England to Italy and finally in 1937 to California, where he augmented his income by writing screenplays. In a letter to Eugene F. Saxton he comments: "I work away at the adaptation of *Pride and Prejudice* for the moment—an odd, cross-word puzzle job. One tries to do one's best for Jane Austen; but actually the very fact of transforming the book into a picture must necessarily alter its whole quality in a profound way. In any picture or play, the story is essential and primary. In Jane Austen's books, it is a matter of secondary importance (every dramatic event in *Pride and Prejudice* is recorded in a couple of lines, generally in a letter) and serves merely as a receptacle for the dilute irony in which the characters are bathed. Any other kind of receptacle would have served the purpose equally well; and the insistence upon the story as opposed to the diffuse irony which the story is designed to contain, is a major falsification of Miss Austen."

Austen possesses. Of course these hawkers of Austen may well be gathering new readers for her too. The films may prepare an audience for reading, intriguing the viewers into a subsequent perusal of the texts.

However, for readers of Austen, a fear remains that these films (and the proliferating Internet Web sites devoted to them) may substitute for the novels.

Instead of reading Austen, Austen film fans of the 1990s may just visit the Colin Firth Web sites and buy CDs of music from Austen's era, thinking that they are participating in high culture. Last year Linda joked that Jane Austen figurines would be the next wave. It turned out to be a reality; the first "limited edition Elizabeth Bennet figurine" appeared in the fall 1998 Past Times catalog. Being an Austenite is becoming less exclusive than it was; fortunately there is still exclusivity to be found in buying a "limited edition" collectible figurine!

Undoubtedly the films and the spin-off products do substitute for the novels for some people, and they certainly provide a different (and complementary) experience from reading. The films are, by necessity, "E-Z Austen," but we need not fear they will replace or degrade the novels. The film and television adaptations are attuned to one cultural moment as Austen's novels have proved themselves not to be. Every generation needs a film or video remake of *Pride and Prejudice,* whereas Austen's novels have fitted a succession of cultural moments for nearly two hundred years, and that is the reason they form part of the literary canon of great works. The films get remade because they do not inhabit a long sweep of time comfortably.

Feature Films and Video Adaptations: A Selection

1940: *Pride and Prejudice,* United States. Directed by Robert Z. Leonard. Laurence Olivier as Darcy; Greer Garson as Elizabeth; Edna May Oliver as Lady Catherine de Bourgh; Maureen O'Sullivan as Jane. Screenplay by Aldous Huxley and Jane Murfin. 114 min. Available on video.

This film had its genesis in 1935 when Harpo Marx saw a dramatization of *Pride and Prejudice.* He sent a telegram to the great movie mogul Irving Thalberg, saying, "Just saw Pride and Prejudice. Stop. Swell show. Stop. Would be wonderful for Norma. Stop." He was referring to Norma Shearer, married to Thalberg and fresh from playing Elizabeth Barrett Browning in *The Barretts of Wimpole Street.* Evidently Shearer was not immediately interested in moving from the role of Elizabeth Barrett to Elizabeth Bennet. In 1940, however, the film was made starring Laurence Olivier and Greer Garson. Watch for the Victorian costumes and the transformation of Lady Catherine de Bourgh into a good egg, who reconciles with Lizzy. At the 1990 Annual General Meeting of the Jane Austen Society of North America an actress who played one of the younger Bennet sisters recalled, "Those of us in our thirties were trying to re-

member what it was like in our twenties, those of us in our twenties were trying to remember what it was like in our teens, and all of us were trying to remember what it was like to be virgins."

The movie opens with the title "It happened in OLD ENGLAND," but as
Laura Jacobs says in *Vanity Fair,* "one glance at Ye Olde sets shows we're in
the glycerin hills of Hollywood. . . . [I]t's Austen in Oz, which is to say, a
hugely entertaining purist's nightmare." MGM promoted the film by describing it as "Five charming sisters on the gayest, merriest manhunt that ever
snared a bewildered bachelor! Girls! Take a lesson from these husband
hunters!"

The Bennet girls all sport very thick mascara and appear to be well into
their thirties. Mr. Collins, oddly enough, appears to be simply a steward for
Lady Catherine; perhaps Hollywood did not want to offend the clergy by presenting such a smarmy one. Because the second half of the book is telescoped
into the last ten minutes or so of this film, the outcomes do not seem to make
much sense. One coincidence: The beautiful Jane Bennet is played by Maureen O'Sullivan, who also portrayed Jane in the Tarzan films from the same
era.

*Slightly superannuated
Bennet sisters, anticipating
Victorian dress by several
decades, from the 1940
MGM version of Pride
and Prejudice.*

1971: *Persuasion,* Great Britain, made for ITV. Directed by Howard Baker. Ann Firbank as Anne Elliot; Bryan Marshall as Frederick Wentworth; Basil Dignam as Sir Walter Elliot; Morag Hood as Mary Musgrove. Dramatized by Julian Mitchell. 225 min. Available on video.

1972: *Emma,* Great Britain, made for BBC. Directed by John Glenister. Doran Godwin as Emma; John Carson as Mr. Knightley; Donald Eccles as Mr. Woodhouse; Constance Chapman as Miss Bates; Fiona Walker as Mrs. Elton; Debbie Bowen as Harriet Smith. Dramatized by Denis Constanduros. 257 min. Available on video.

1982: *Pride and Prejudice,* Great Britain, made for BBC. Directed by Cyril Coke. Elizabeth Garvie as Elizabeth; David Rintoul as Darcy; Malcolm Rennie as Mr. Collins; Sabina Franklyn as Jane; Moray Watson as Mr. Bennet; Priscilla Ogle as Mrs. Bennet. Dramatized by Fay Weldon. 259 min. Available on video.

Widely renowned as one of the funniest and liveliest of the Austen film adaptations.

1983: *Mansfield Park,* Great Britain, made for BBC. Directed by David Giles. Anna Massey as Aunt Norris; Sylvestra Le Touzel as Fanny Price; Nicholas Farrell as Edmund; Robert Burbage as Henry Crawford. Dramatized by Ken Taylor. 261 min. Available on video.

Le Touzel does a fine job as the timid Fanny; the highlight is Anna Massey's depiction of Aunt Norris. The Crawfords are delightfully vulgar.

1985: *Sense and Sensibility,* Great Britain, made for BBC. Directed by Rodney Bennett. Irene Richard as Elinor; Bosco Hogan as Edward Ferrars; Tracy Childs as Marianne; Peter Woodward as Willoughby. Dramatized by Alexander Baron. 174 min. Available on video.

1987: *Northanger Abbey,* Great Britain, made for BBC. Directed by Giles Foster. Peter Firth as Henry Tilney; Robert Hardy as General Tilney; Katharine Schlesinger as Catherine Morland, Googie Withers as Mrs. Allen. Dramatized by Maggie Wadey. 90 min. Available on video.

Not particularly well received; Austen's biographer Deirdre Le Faye says it is "awful" and Jean Bowden, archivist at Chawton, concurs: "They completely missed the joke."

1995: *Pride and Prejudice,* Great Britain, made for BBC. Directed by Simon Langton. Jennifer Ehle as Elizabeth; Colin Firth as Darcy; David Bamber as Mr. Collins; Crispin Bonham Carter as Bingley; Susannah Harker as Jane; Julia Sawhilla as Lydia. Adapted by Andrew Davies. 301 min. Available on video.

This is the famous wet T-shirt Darcy version of *Pride and Prejudice*. Darcy strips off some of his clothing and takes a dive into a pool on his Pemberley estate, thus erotically enhancing him, as Lewis Menand writes in the *New York Review of Books*. In another scene Darcy sits naked in his bathtub, watching from the window as Lizzy plays with a large dog, cheerfully tugging at a stick in the dog's mouth. The sexual overtones in this production launched a thousand Web pages with much focus on the buff physique of Colin Firth.

Colin Firth made his name as Mr. Darcy in *Pride and Prejudice*. He smoldered, he was a master of the moody silence, and he wore trousers so tight that you could count the small change in his pocket. Firth attributes part of his success to the writer Andrew Davies's helpful script. "Darcy looks as if somebody has had a bad attack of wind," the script notes at one point. Another note reads: "Darcy probably has an erection." Not with those trousers, he wouldn't.

—*THE TIMES OF LONDON*, APRIL 6, 1997

1995: *Persuasion,* Great Britain. Directed by Roger Michell. Amanda Root as Anne Elliot; Ciaran Hinds as Frederick Wentworth; Corin Redgrave as Sir Walter Elliot; Susan Fleetwood as Lady Russell; Sophie Thompson as Mary; Phoebe Nicholls as Anne; John Woodvine as Admiral Croft; Fiona Shaw as Mrs. Croft. Screenplay by Nick Dear and Jeremy Sams. 104 min. Available on video.

Jane Austen purists generally find this the best of all the film adaptations. Watch for Sophie Thompson as a particularly querulous Mary Musgrove and Corin Redgrave as a Sir Walter Elliot who is almost Caligula-like in his repul-

In Persuasion, Anne Elliot and Captain Wentworth quickly devise a plan to get help to the unconscious Louisa Musgrove. Her future husband, Captain Benwick, is shocked by the gravity of the situation.

sive self-centeredness. John Woodvine does a nice turn as Admiral Croft. Amanda Root, perfect in the part of Anne Elliot, manages to look and act a pallid thirty at the beginning of the film, yet as it progresses, she comes to life and looks more youthful. Quiet and absorbing, the film is the one that is most like sitting down with a Jane Austen novel. Carol M. Dole points out that this is the one Austen film that most strikingly gives "visual testimony to the workings of the British class system." We see the array of servants at Kellynch Hall, field-workers toiling at Kellynch, and fish cutters at Lyme Regis.

1995: *Sense and Sensibility,* Great Britain. Directed by Ang Lee. Emma Thompson as Elinor; Kate Winslet as Marianne; Alan Rickman as Colonel Brandon; Hugh Grant as Edward Ferrars; Gemma Jones as Mrs. Dashwood; Greg Wise as Willoughby; Imogen Stubbs as Lucy Steele. Screenplay by Emma Thompson. 135 min. Available on video.

Watch for the adroit way that Thompson has found to make Edward Ferrars appealing to the viewer (he is the most cloddish of all of Austen's heroes). In her Academy Award–winning screenplay of the novel, Emma Thompson goes to pains to make Colonel Brandon and Edward Ferrars much more attractive than Jane Austen's originals. Douglas Bush has commented that Austen's Edward Ferrars "displays every attribute of a poker except its occasional warmth (a phrase that applies also to the older Colonel Brandon)." Austen herself states flatly that Ferrars "was not handsome, and his manners required intimacy to make them pleasing" and that though Brandon 's face "was not handsome his countenance was sensible." Edward wins Elinor's heart, in part, by his kindness toward the traumatized and precocious Margaret, who is dismissed in the book as not particularly promising. Hugh Grant, who plays Edward, is, according to Emma Thompson, "repellently gorgeous, why did we cast him? He's much prettier than I am." Rickman makes Colonel Brandon much more exciting than the novel premises. Stubbs is absolutely cunning as Lucy Steele.

Ang Lee states: "Austen is a combination of sharp satire and emotional drama; it's usually seen as sense being Elinor and sensibility Marianne. But I think everybody has both in them. It's an irony that Elinor marries for romance and Marianne for righteousness."

Jane Austen should be required reading for pre-film majors!
—ARMY ARCHERD

1995: *Clueless,* United States. Directed by Amy Heckerling. Alicia Silverstone as Cher; Stacey Dash as Dionne; Paul Rudd as Josh; Dan Hedaya as Mr. Horowitz. Screenplay by Amy Heckerling. 113 min. Available on video.

The very act of rendering Jane Austen's novels on film or video involves interpretive decisions and a transition from the quiet meditations of prose to the spectacle of film and from the private appreciation of a reader to the public responses of an audience. But no other rendering of Austen's work for the screen has been as radical as Amy Heckerling's loose adaptation of Austen's *Emma* into the high school comedy *Clueless.*

Heckerling has astutely updated the various stages in which a presumptuous heroine who seems to have it all and to know it all arrives at a better knowledge of herself and others by eventually realizing that she has been "clueless" all along. In *Emma,* Emma Woodhouse, "handsome, clever, and rich," having foreseen the marriage of her governess to a neighbor, believes she has a gift for arranging other people's lives. Her

> *In Clueless,* makeovers replace Jane Austen's emphasis on learning how to "see life steadily and see it whole."

major project is what the characters of *Clueless* would call a "makeover" of Harriet Smith.

Emma's interference involves raising Harriet's sense of her own value, increasing her expectations

> *Emma*" was a fashionable name in Jane Austen's time, evoking the image of Lord Nelson's glamorous mistress, Emma Hamilton. The name "Cher," in our time, inevitably conjures up the glamorous image of pop stardom.

of a marriage into respectable society, and discouraging her acceptance of marriage from a local farmer. This plot is exactly played out in *Clueless,* in which the Emma character, Cher, sets in motion the courtship and eventual marriage of two of her teachers and then takes on the "makeover" of an obviously "clueless" new student, Tai, whom she compels to overcome an attachment to Travis, a low-caste "loadie" (a heavy marijuana user), and to aspire after the rich and socially prominent Elton. Like Harriet Smith, Tai has her heart broken by Elton, sets her sights higher still, on Cher's stepbrother, Josh, and eventually returns to her appropriate social level with Travis.

In both works a handsome, apparently eligible young man enters the social circle and begins a lively flirtation with Emma/Cher. In *Emma* this young man, Frank Churchill, is sufficiently attractive to warrant a return of Emma's affections and consequently an examination of her own emotions and potential for love. Finally she learns he has been trifling with her while his real love was already committed to another woman. In *Clueless,* the newcomer, Christian, has the same effect on Cher, until she eventually learns that he is gay, an "Oscar Wilde–reading, Barbra Streisand–loving, friend of Dorothy." Both Emma and Cher, then, have the same experience of being apparently wooed and jilted, and both learn to know their own hearts better.

There are other plot parallels: Frank Churchill rescues Harriet from some Gypsies, while in *Clueless* Christian rescues Tai from some rowdies at a mall. The Box Hill picnic episode of *Emma* shows Emma as a social diva with a moment of heartless brittleness in insulting her garrulous but affable neighbor Miss Bates. Emma is rebuked by Mr. Knightley. In *Clueless,* Cher ignorantly insults the good-hearted Hispanic maid, Lucy, and is rebuked by Josh.

Other similar plot elements abound. Emma and Cher are of course leaders of their social set, and both are devoted daughters, conscientiously concerned with the health of their fathers. Most important, both learn their capacity for good and ill by trifling with their neighbors' lives and by being trifled with themselves.

Finally, Emma and Cher realize that in setting other people to rights, they have themselves been "clueless" all along, misreading other people's minds while remaining ignorant of their own.

1996: *Emma,* Great Britain, made for ITV. Directed by Diarmuid Lawrence. Kate Beckinsale as Emma; Mark Strong as Mr. Knightley; Samantha Morton as Harriet Smith; Prunella Scales as Miss Bates; Bernard Hepton as Mr. Woodhouse. Adapted by Andrew Davies. 120 min. Available on video.

A. A. Gill commented of this production that "Emma was the most trippingly tedious Georgian of the lot. Her raison d'être was social woodwork. She was a nuptial joiner, and I desperately, more desperately than I've ever felt anything for a long time, wanted to screw her into a mahogany coffin with scrolled finials, fluted pilasters, bas-relief acanthus and a fold-out bureau. . . . And bury her." Nevertheless, many viewers enjoyed this version of *Emma* and responded to Beckinsale's brunette beauty. Andrew Davies, the dramatist, goes to pains to show the servants and the workers behind the scenes. He is interested in "the fears and evasions of the aristocracy and the gentry, living in such close proximity to the great unwashed." At the end of this version Emma invites Robert Martin and his now wife, Harriet, to visit her at Hartfield, signifying her social acceptance of the farmer and his wife.

1996: *Emma,* United States/Great Britain. Directed by Douglas McGrath. Gwyneth Paltrow as Emma; Jeremy Northam as Mr. Knightley; Toni Collette as Harriet Smith; Juliet Stevenson as Mrs. Elton; Ewan McGregor as Frank Churchill; Phyllida Law as Mrs. Bates; Sophie Thompson as Miss Bates; Greta Schacci as Anne Taylor Weston. Screenplay by Douglas McGrath. 111 min. Available on video.

Douglas McGrath
on His Film *Emma*

Douglas McGrath *is a contributing editor of the* New Republic. *He grew up in Midland, Texas, received his college education at Princeton, and began his career on the television series* Saturday Night Live. *He cowrote the screenplay of* Bullets over Broadway *with Woody Allen and wrote the screenplay and directed* Emma, *starring Gwyneth Paltrow, which appeared in the summer of 1996.*

NT: *What did you find was the greatest difficulty in adapting a fairly long novel to the confines of a film that is not going to last much longer than two hours?*

DM: That is the very challenge. Given that the novel is about four hundred pages and a screenplay for a film of this length can't be much more than one hundred pages, the awful choice is what you leave out. If you love the book, that becomes very painful. You look for places where there is repetition, and then you remove it because in a film you don't have to keep reminding people that certain characters speak this way or that certain people have this problem.

NT: *I imagine, for example, that characters like Mrs. and Miss Bates you can establish quickly in a film, whereas in the novel there is a lot of repetition.*

DM: I love Miss Bates too. In the novel Emma knocks on the door, and then the next twelve pages are Miss Bates saying hello. A lot of what Austen is doing is just dramatizing the loneliness, the garrulousness, the neediness. Seeing it, you don't need as much as you do in the book. Once you have someone saying it out loud and you see what her face is like and see how her voice trembles and hear the excitement and pleasure she takes in being with people, you don't need the same amount as you need in the novel.

NT: *It was a brilliant decision to cast Sophie Thompson and her mother, Phyllida Law.*

DM: I thought so too. Sophie auditioned for us, and I originally turned her down because I thought she was too young, even though I thought she did a beautiful reading and a very delicate, funny reading. She is a young woman, and I thought she was younger than Miss Bates should be. Our casting agents persuaded me that I should see her again. She came in looking quite dowdy; she scooped her hair all over her face, wore some funny little glasses, wore a figure-obscuring dress, and suddenly I could see how she would look spinsterish. Before, she had looked like she just rolled in off her Rollerblades.

Then, when Phyllida Law came in, that's when we knew we wanted the two of them as mother and daughter. I loved them. They're utterly delightful people, and I thought they were just perfection in the movie.

NT: *I also thought that the casting of Juliet Stephenson as Mrs. Elton was magnificent. She does not have a lot of time in the movie to establish her obnoxiousness, and it was done brilliantly.*

DM: Juliet is so precise and vivid an actress that she conveys what she needs to convey as soon as you need her to convey it. She does her work, as our former President Bush would say, with laserlike specificity.

NT: *Did you have any particular difficulties in making the film?*

DM: It was really joyful all the time. In the writing of it you are looking at some of the most wonderfully written dialogue and sentences in literature. As for directing it, the cast brought all of that so effervescently to life and in just the ways that I had hoped. I have to admit I was lucky because it was an enjoyable experience almost all the way through, whether it was working with Rachel Portman, who wrote the Academy Award–winning score and so enhanced what we had by her music or with Michael Howells, who was our production designer and who really was responsible, along with Ruth Myers, the costumer, for the unique period look. Each day was really gratifying to go through because everyone made better what we had on the page. I am really grateful to the actors. They are all smart people and brought something vivid and fresh to the playing of their characters.

I wanted to avoid making an adaptation like some of the television versions, which are so reverential that the air kind of goes out of them. Although I don't think we were an irreverent version, because everyone loved the material, we all felt alive and not like museum figures moving around.

If you analyze the language, it is not the language we speak in today at all. Yet because the actors were so gifted, they really made it sound very light and natural. There was no mustiness in it.

*I love "chick movies" as much as the next queer,
but if you've read one Jane Austen novel or
seen one Jane Austen movie, you've seen them all.
Pretty, sensitive girls in lovely dresses
pining for the love of a good man.
Big deal. Step into any West Hollywood gay bar
and you can see that.*
—HUGO, *GAY DAZE*, AN INTERNET JOURNAL

FORTHCOMING FILMS

1999: *Northanger Abbey,* Great Britain. ITV. Dramatized by Andrew Davies, who promises sex and "one or two scenes in which Catherine will imagine things that should never happen to young girls."

1999: *Mansfield Park,* Great Britain, for BBC. Directed and dramatized by Patricia Rozema. Frances O'Connor as Fanny Price; Jonny Lee Miller as Edmund Bertram; Harold Pinter as Sir Thomas Bertram.

According to the *Spectator,* January 9, 1999, BBC Films admits "that the modern, feminist script will shock many people, including as it does an alleged lesbian scene during which Mary Crawford apparently makes a play for Fanny Price." The *London Mail* says that Fanny Price is a "fast-talking, muscular, modern girl." The BBC Films representative Tracie Scoffield says that "the novel lacks pace and energy for modern filming. The new film is true to the moral temperature of the original, but we have revved up the dynamics of the relationships."

2000: *Sanditon,* Screenplay by Fay Weldon.

Jane Austen has edged up on us as Heritage so gently and steadily we hardly noticed her revival: now she's well and truly established in the televisual Theme Park. Reckoned as a minor novelist at the time of her death—in 1817—she has crept up the list ever since. She made £860 (on my reckoning) from her work during her lifetime, and has made fortunes for others ever since. Though that is ever the fate of writers, who, like criminals, sit at the apex of an inverted triangle of other people's occupations, maintaining on their creative shoulders the weight of all those others who make a good living from their single, desperate, untoward activities, their works of art or criminality; from editors and policemen, to Ministers of Culture and the Home Secretary, and many a business and commentator in between.

—FAY WELDON

Continuations, Sequels, and Spin-offs

*ℐane Austen industries cranks on, and on and on, turning out
products that merge in my mind into* Northanger Sensibility,
or Prejudice Abbey, *or* Pride and Persuasion Park.
—BENEDICT NIGHTINGALE

Probably more than any other author, Jane Austen has given impetus to the creation of sequels, spin-offs, prequels with an abundance that more than rivals the dazzling number of spin-offs that *The Mary Tyler Moore Show* inspired during the 1970s. The eponymous television shows *Rhoda, Phyllis,* and *Lou Grant* each sparked a certain amount of viewer loyalty while some people maintained that they could watch only the original *Mary Tyler Moore Show*. If Jane Austen's novels can be compared with a television show (yes, the comparison will make many readers blanch), their success has obviously galvanized people who wish there were more, people who would like to play tribute to Austen by imitation, a sincere form of flattery. Readers who feel confined by the fact that only six Austen novels are complete do have other avenues to explore.

Julia Barrett on Jane Austen Sequels

Julia Barrett reports that "there are those among us who are quite willing to admit that we prefer the works of Jane Austen above any other. I count myself one of such readers—and they are legion—who find themselves returning to her six novels fascinated, year after year. It is to this lifelong passion that I have addressed myself so far as a novelist. My hope is to pick up Austen's wonderful creations—people so lively and so vivid for us all—just to see if I could extend our encounters with them longer, increase our pleasures in them a touch further yet keep with her own themes, speak in her language, and remain true to her remarkable wit."

Her first attempt was Presumption: An Entertainment, a sequel to Jane Austen's Pride and Prejudice (which she undertook with Gabrielle Donnelly). She wrote The Third Sister, this time a continuation of Sense and Sensibility. She has recently completed yet another continuation of an Austen novel. Her first book of nonfiction was Getting Even with Getting Old, a study of aging in America.

NT: *What inspired you to write sequels to Austen?*

JB: I always noticed that I never put her books down without a question in my head. I wondered what had happened to that enchanting girl in *Pride and Prejudice* who was the sister of the hero. She had been squired away by Wickham. Fortunately she is salvaged and brought home, and there is no injury to her. I was also interested to know what had happened to Margaret, the third sister in *Sense and Sensibility*. Here is a girl who grows up with one inhibited sister, Elinor, and one passionate hysteric, Marianne. Her father is already dead. Her mother is ineffectual. I had to know what happened to her. These were the kinds of questions that were in my head for some years. Austen dropped Margaret very quickly.

NT: *I recall that she said that Margaret did not show much promise.*

JB: She said that Margaret was a good-humored, well-disposed girl. She adds that she had already imbibed a good deal of Marianne's romance without having much sense and did not, at thirteen, bid fair to equal her sisters. Then Austen drops her. We do see her in one scene at table where she spills the beans about Marianne's attachment to Willoughby.

NT: *Why do you think readers are so insatiable when it comes to Austen?*

JB: I think that Austen's books are in such contrast with the vulgarity all around us. In a democracy like ours, where there is so much chaos, the civility and respect that come out of Austen's books give us confidence in human nature and make us feel that we do not live in chaos. Of course I can pick out a Lady Catherine de Bourgh or a Willoughby at a party anytime.

NT: *But your sequels are not modernizations?*

JB: No, not at all. I feel that would be a violation. I think that Jane Austen lived in her period and understood her period, yet human nature does not change that much. So I try to stay as close to her mind and her wit as I can, and sometimes I feel that I am dancing on a pin. Certain things do not fit, and they should not be introduced.

Stephanie Barron on Jane Austen as Detective

*S*tephanie Barron, *a journalist and a former "overt" foreign policy analyst for the CIA, graduated from Princeton with a degree in European history. She is the author of a series of novels featuring Jane Austen as sleuth. The first in the series,* Jane and the Unpleasantness at Scargrave Manor, *was published in 1996.* Jane and the Man of the Cloth *followed in 1997,* Jane and the Wandering Eye *in 1998, and in 1999* Jane and the Genius of the Place *was published. Barron is continuing the series to the delight of Austen enthusiasts and lovers of mysteries. She lives in Evergreen, Colorado.*

NT: *What got you interested in writing a detective series in the first-person voice of Jane Austen?*

SB: I got the idea in 1993 well before I knew that the movies were coming out. It is as though there were serendipitous interest in Austen that was worldwide at that time. I had been reading Austen, as I do every year, since I was twelve, and when I read Austen, I have her voice in my head. I feel as if I am speaking in the language of the early nineteenth century. My husband will come home and say, "How was your day?" and I will say, "Being evident the weather should continue to be fine, Sam and I determined upon a party at the lake." He would say, "I can see you've been reading *Persuasion*." So I wanted to be able to use that extraordinarily rich language with its communicative powers in a book that would appeal to contemporary readers.

I was afraid that the language might be a little bit inaccessible, so I thought if I could give the readers a compelling mystery that might pull them through the story line, they would accept the language almost unconsciously. So it was very self-indulgent on my part. That's one reason I was interested in writing the series.

The second reason was Jane herself. She strikes me as having been extraordinarily perceptive. She lived in an era when there was no police force patrolling the countryside of England and nothing like what we would consider forensic techniques. What you needed for the resolution of crime and serving out justice was native wit and perception about motivation. We see through her novels that extraordinary perception. That is the dynamic that would serve her very well as a detective, so I thought she would be ideal. She was also a single woman in an era that accorded very little social status to single women. She was relegated to the role of observer in a lot of the drama of the day, which made her a consummate writer and a keen detective. She also had a lot of free time for observation.

NT: *How did you come up with the framing device you use in your novels, the explanation for how the manuscripts come to be in your hands?*

SB: I wanted to increase that willing perception we undergo as we read fiction. I wanted people to be susceptible to the idea that this was really Austen's voice, so I wanted to give a measure of authenticity to the manuscript I had written by posing as editor. It heightens the sense of reentering a world that Jane herself might have inhabited.

I chose to "find" the manuscripts in the United States because I am an American and I wanted to have a plausible reason for their discovery here. I have very good friends who live in Baltimore and own a house that is a Georgian mansion dating from pre-American Revolutionary times. They are descendants of signers of the Declaration of Independence, and it seemed plausible to me that they could have intermarried with descendants of Austen's brothers. So I used that as an almost factual frame.

NT: *Why did you decide to bring actual family members into your works?*

SB: I tried very hard to embed the fictional plot in the framework of her life. I tried to follow what I know she did do in life. Happily, in her letters, she is fairly explicit about the people she met. She mentions the Lyme surgeon; it also turns out he was the coroner of Lyme, so he is very useful in any book about a murder in that town. I tried to be credible. My primary source for the books of course is her collected letters. It's an incredibly rich source because she gives so many domestic details. She writes a lot about the servants; she was very aware of them and interacted with them all the time in her own life. For example, she gave her father's discarded newspapers to them to encourage reading. Her letters have an informal, almost a vivacious sense of humor that was so clearly Jane and seeped into the novels but is much more contained in the letters.

NT: *Did you decide to set your mysteries during those years that we don't know a whole lot about what Austen was doing by design?*

SB: Yes. I was looking for interesting moments in her life, and I always do try to work the books around key emotional moments. To me her decision not to marry Harris Bigg-Wither is a pivotal moment in her life because she was choosing to turn her back on security, not only for herself but for her mother and sister. I don't think it is co-incidence that right after she refused him she decided to seek publication of her first novel. The two decisions are linked. She turned her back on marriage and security, and she recognized that she needed some help being self-sufficient monetarily and that she could do this through her writing. She tried to publish *Susan*, which we now know as *Northanger Abbey*. It is an interesting moment in her life when she made the decision, which few women at the time would have had the courage or the support of their family to make. So I wanted to begin my series when she is setting out as an older woman for her time. I do intend to try to take this series up to her later years.

I am also trying to bring out a side of Jane that I think is sometimes over-looked, and that is her awareness of the political and social developments of her time. She has been criticized by various scholars for her lack of attention to political events or some of the changes in society that followed from the Revolution throughout Europe that started around the time of her birth. I think that you can find a lot of signs of those changes in her novels, but they are subtle, and you have to look for them. You certainly find reference to it all the time in her letters and so I am trying to bring out her awareness of naval warfare through her brother and politics in general through her involvement with the fictional Harold Trowbridge.

—⁂—

*T*he runaway hit of the book industry in 1998 was Helen Fielding's book *Bridget Jones's Diary,* which earned Fielding a ranking as the twelfth most entertaining person of 1998 (Leonardo di Caprio was first) by the pundits at *Entertainment Weekly,* who opine that Fielding's book is a "canny retelling" of Jane Austen's *Pride and Prejudice.* Fielding admits that "I just stole the plot from *Pride and Prejudice*. I thought it had been very well mar-ket-researched over a number of centuries." Bridget views a screening of the BBC *Pride and Prejudice* and discusses Colin Firth with her friend. She also meets a Mr. Darcy of her very own.

Sequels and Spin-offs:
A Select List

Aiken, Joan. *Eliza's Daughter*. New York: St. Martin's, 1994. Sequel to *Sense and Sensibility*. Follows the story of the natural child that Colonel Brandon's niece Eliza had with Willoughby. She is a hoyden who hangs out with Coleridge and Wordsworth but thankfully saves Elinor Ferrars's life.

——. *Emma Watson. The Watsons Completed*. New York: St. Martin's, 1996.

——. *Jane Fairfax. Jane Austen's Emma Through Another's Eyes*. New York: St. Martin's, 1990.

——. *Mansfield Revisited: A Sequel to Jane Austen's Mansfield Park*. Garden City: Doubleday, 1984.

Atchia, Paula. *Mansfield Letters*. London: Book Guild, 1996.

Austen-Leigh, Joan. *Later Days at Highbury*. New York: St. Martin's, 1996.

——. *A Visit to Highbury*. New York: St. Martin's, 1995. Joan Austen-Leigh is the great-granddaughter of James Edward Austen-Leigh, son of Austen's eldest brother, James. Austen-Leigh's two Highbury books focus on an epistolary exchange between Mrs. Goddard, who runs the school where Harriet Smith boards, and her sister in London. Focus is on life in Highbury village.

Aylmer, Janet. *Darcy's Story from Pride and Prejudice*. Bath, England: Copperfield Books, 1996.

Bader, Ted and Marilyn. *Desire and Duty: A Sequel to Pride and Prejudice*. Denver: Revive Pub., 1997. Focus is on Georgiana Darcy. Darcy loves his marriage to Lizzy Bennet so much that he is seen "beaming." He presides over alcohol-free banquets.

Barrett, Julia. *Presumption: An Entertainment*. Chicago: University of Chicago Press, 1995. Very well-received continuation of *Pride and Prejudice*.

——. *The Third Sister*. New York: Penguin, 1996. Intriguing continuation of *Sense and Sensibility*. Focus is on Margaret Dashwood. Barrett's style is likely to please Austen lovers.

Barron, Stephanie. *Jane and the Genius of the Place*. New York: Bantam, 1999.

——. *Jane and the Man of the Cloth*. New York: Bantam, 1997. Jane Austen as detective. Elegantly written, excellent historical perspective. First in the series that provides lots of intriguing glimpses at Austen's family as well as her own acumen.

——. *Jane and the Unpleasantness at Scargrave Manor*. New York: Bantam, 1996.

——. *Jane and the Wandering Eye*. New York: Bantam, 1998.

Beckford, Grania. *Virtues and Vices*, New York: St. Martin's, 1981. Warning: This off-color, salacious tale of ribaldry, based on characters from *Persuasion*, is not likely to amuse many readers. Lady Russell is a nymphomaniac, and Wentworth is her boy toy. Mrs. Clay sleeps with *everyone*.

Bedford-Pierce, Sophia. *Jane Austen's Little Instruction Book*. White Plains, NY: Peter Pauper Press, 1995.

Billington, Rachel. *Perfect Happiness*. London: Hodder and Stoughton, 1996. Sequel to *Emma*. Mr. Knightley sings, and Frank Churchill runs mad.

Black, Maggie, and Deirdre Le Faye. *The Jane Austen Cookbook*. London: British Museum Press, 1995.

Corringham, Mary. *I, Jane Austen: A Re-creation in Rime Royal Based on the Letters of Jane Austen, Her Novels and the Comments of Her Biographers*. London: Routledge & Kegan Paul, 1971. Rime Royal, seven-lined stanzas of iambic pentameter, is sometimes called the Chaucerian stanza, since Chaucer used it in his *Troilus and Criseyde* and *The Parlement of Foules*. One hundred sixty-three stanzas purportedly written posthumously by Austen, who traces her life, her death, and her posthumous reputation: "That D. H. Lawrence loathed me, makes me glad / I should so hate to be admired by *him*."

Fenton, Kate. *Lions and Liquorice*. London: Michael Joseph, 1996. Not really a sequel; a novel about a film crew working on a version of *Pride and Prejudice*.

Fielding, Helen. *Bridget Jones's Diary*. New York: Viking, 1998.

Gillespie, Jane. *Aunt Celia*. New York: St. Martin's, 1990. A continuation of *Emma*.

———. *Brightsea*. New York: St. Martin's, 1987. Brings back the Misses Steele from *Sense and Sensibility*. Nancy Steele, at forty, is still unmarried and exasperates Mr. and Mrs. Palmer, whom she visits too frequently.

———. *Deborah*. London: Robert Hale, 1995. A sequel to *Pride and Prejudice*. Anne de Bourgh, frail daughter of Lady Catherine, breaks loose, runs away, changes her name to Deborah Smith, and becomes a plucky governess.

———. *Ladysmead*. New York: St. Martin's, 1982. Spin-off from *Mansfield Park*. Interesting focus on the fate of Aunt Norris and Maria Bertram Rushworth, who are living together.

———. *Teverton Hall*. New York: St. Martin's, 1984. Depicts the ordeals of the offspring of Mr. Collins and Charlotte Lucas. Lady Catherine, in a fit of ire about Darcy's marriage to Elizabeth Bennet, discontinues her patronage of Mr. Collins.

Kirazian, Lisa. *The Visitor*. San Diego: Laurel Co., n.d. This is a play about a graduate student "stuck" on her dissertation; the topic is, not surprisingly, Jane Austen. She receives a "visit" from Austen herself, who plays havoc with the student's boyfriend and professor and teaches her some valuable lessons.

Memoir (pseudonym). *Gambles and Gambols*. Pasadena: Shelter Cove, 1983. Based on characters from *Mansfield Park*. Edmund is the author of sundry books of sermons, including one entitled "Man as an Excretion of the Rotting Rock." Brings in characters from many of the other Austen novels. Mrs. Smith, of *Persuasion*, has taken on George Wickham as her new financial adviser!

Michon, Cathryn, and Pamela Norris. *Jane Austen's Little Advice Book*. New York: HarperCollins, 1995.

Newark, Elizabeth. *Consequences or Whatever Became of Charlotte Lucas*. San Francisco: New Ark Productions, 1997. Twenty-six years after their marriage Mr. Collins has gout and is grumpy. He has given Charlotte five children, and the eldest son is married to one Eugenia Elton. Their youngest daughter, Eliza, has fallen in love with the scion of Darcy and Elizabeth.

Smith, Naomi Royde. *Jane Fairfax*. London: Macmillan, 1940. This novel develops the background story of Jane Fairfax and shows her life with the Campbells. Mrs. Dixon is courted and ditched by Henry Crawford, who appears from the pages of *Mansfield Park*. The final part of this novel brings us to Highbury, and many of the characters and scenes from *Emma* are given from Jane's point of view. Mrs. Elton writes to Maple Grove.

Tennant, Emma. *Elinor & Marianne: Continuing Sense and Sensibility*. London: Simon & Schuster, 1996. An epistolary novel. Marianne wants to set up a utopian commune.

———. *Emma in Love*. London: Fourth Estate, 1996. The notorious continuation of *Emma*: Mr. Knightley is an impotent yenta, Emma's lesbian attraction to Jane Fairfax runs deep, and Miss Bates either is suffering from Tourette's syndrome or has simply decided to abbreviate her loquacity to the use of four-letter words.

———. *Pemberley: Pride and Prejudice Continued*. New York: St. Martin's, 1993. Darcy and Elizabeth fight, and she decides to run off and become a governess. They make up.

———. *An Unequal Marriage or Pride and Prejudice 20 Years Later*. New York: St. Martin's, 1994.

White, T. H. *Darkness at Pemberley*. London: Gollancz, 1932. Reprint. New York: Dover, 1978. A detective story that borrows names but not real characters from *Pride and Prejudice*.

Wilson, Barbara Ker. *Antipodes Jane: A Novel of Jane Austen in Australia*. New York: Viking, 1985.

Bibliography

Barry Roth, Bibliographer of
Jane Austen Studies

Barry Roth, a native of Brooklyn, New York, and a professor of English Literature at Ohio University since 1968, has completed his third annotated bibliography of Jane Austen studies, which covers the years 1984 to 1994. Roth says
that his bibliography "charts the steady growth and enrichment of literary criticism of Austen in the second half of the twentieth century. Thus, where the first
bibliography (published in 1973 and devoted to the period 1952–1972) contained 794 items and the second (appearing in 1985 and treating 1973–83) included over 1,060 pieces, this third work has 1,327 entries."

NT: *Why do you think there has been such a proliferation of Jane Austen studies?*

BR: I think this is owing partly to the growth of women's studies. Austen used
to serve as one of the very few women in European literature who functioned
on an equal level with men in an essentially all-male tradition; now she's seen
in addition as playing a vital part in a women's tradition. Also, like Shake-

speare, she both repays close investigation and is being set more solidly than ever before in her historical context.

Writers used to think that she had no sense of history or politics or public life in general, that she was just a retiring spinster who happened to write six perfect novels. Now she is characteristically studied as aware of her environment, and this insight has led to political, historical, even anthropological investigations. Moreoever, the ambiguities one finds in her work (e.g., is she politically conservative or liberal or radical?) keep on attracting attention and refusing simplistic definition. Less grandly, as you know, publications of all kinds, not just those on Jane Austen, have proliferated in academe in recent decades.

NT: *What would you say is the recent proportion of academic to nonacademic books on Jane Austen?*

BR: I'd say books for the nonacademic reader have been pretty constant in the last forty years or so, in number and content: they treat over and over again the clothes of the period, food in her books, and the Regency period generally—the "Jane Austen and her world" type. But there are very many more academic books than ever before. One source of some of this growth is the fact that there are significantly more doctoral dissertations written on her each year (I record over one hundred ninety in the eleven-year period covered by my last bibliography, and there's no sign of abating).

NT: *Have you read any of the sequels people have written to the Austen novels?*

BR: No, and for the same reason I don't read "modern romances": I'm interested in Jane Austen, not pale imitators lacking her ironies and paradoxes and profound understanding of what makes people go. I am also not attracted to publishing ventures that seek to market her for their own pecuniary advantage. Ditto my sense of the recent film versions of some of the novels. I find these films essentially false costume dramas, limited in scope and meaning, lacking her distinctive voice.

NT: *What caused you to be interested in Austen?*

BR: I started reading her when I was ten or twelve, and I've stayed ever since. I'm continually attracted to her humor, wit, incisiveness, clarity of vision; her keen dramatic sense, the precision of her thinking and diction; her combination of romance and realism, which she balances perfectly; her vision of laughter as healing. I cherish some of her deepest values, including an intelligent and feeling consideration of other people; her lack of illusions.

NT: *Do you have a favorite novel?*

BR: In different ways they're all favorites. For example, I think I like to teach *Mansfield Park* best because it has more problems in it, both ideologically and in terms of its being a novel. I think *Emma* is probably the most complicated, the most polyvocal, of her books. *Pride and Prejudice* is a pure joy to read and to teach, and *Sense and Sensibility* has its own defining difficulties as a novel, but its unique tone and some of the things it has to say seem really important to me, and these aspects make it a great pleasure to read and teach too. All the novels seem to me to be clearly by the same author, yet each is also sui generis.

Select Bibliography

In compiling this select bibliography, I have been ruled more by my own amusements and subjectivities and the propinquity of my bookshelves than by a desire to be comprehensive. The following books have given me sufficient pleasure that I would reread them, and in most cases I *have* reread them. Not all the works cited below are still in print, but all should be available at a decent-size library. Those works prefaced by asterisks have given me the most sustained pleasure, insight, information, or enlightenment. Several of the works I consider important deal only in part with Jane Austen, but that part is significant and illuminating.

As for the biographies of Austen, they are a very mixed lot indeed. Some biographers subscribe to the Gentle Jane school of analyzing Austen's character as unfailingly, graciously happy and Christian, unfailing in her familial duties, and others depict her as angry, sarcastic, bitter, thwarted, or disappointed. All agree, however, that she was a genius of the first order. I assume that Austen was all those things at least some of the time, that she was a complicated, deeply textured, and nuanced woman. The better biographies of Austen do not present conclusions so much as possibilities.

Batey, Mavis. *Jane Austen and the English Landscape*. London: Barn Elms/ Chicago Rev. Press, 1996.

Bloom, Harold, ed. *Modern Critical Views: Jane Austen*. New York: Chelsea House, 1986.

Brown, Julia Prewitt. *Jane Austen's Novels: Social Change and Literary Form*. Cambridge: Harvard University Press, 1978.

Brownstein, Rachel. *Becoming a Heroine: Reading About Women in Novels*. New York: Viking, 1982.

Bush, Douglas. *Jane Austen*. New York: Macmillan, 1975.

Butler, Marilyn. *Jane Austen and the War of Ideas*. Oxford: Clarendon, 1975.

Cecil, David. *A Portrait of Jane Austen*. London: Constable, 1978.

Clark, Rowena. *Hatches, Matches, and Dispatches: Christening, Bridal & Mourning Fashions*. Victoria, Australia: National Gallery of Victoria, 1987.

Collins, Irene. *Jane Austen and the Clergy.* London: Hambledon, 1994.

Copeland, Edward, and Juliet McMaster, eds. *The Cambridge Companion to Jane Austen.* Cambridge: Cambridge University Press, 1997.

Duckworth, Alistair. *The Improvement of the Estate.* Baltimore: Johns Hopkins University Press, 1971.

Erickson, Lee. *The Economy of Literary Form: English Literature and the Industrialization of Publishing, 1800–1850.* Baltimore: Johns Hopkins University Press, 1996.

Fergus, Jan. *Jane Austen and the Didactic Novel.* London: Macmillan, 1983.

***————. *Jane Austen: A Literary Life.* New York: St. Martin's, 1991.

Gammie, Ian, and Derek McCullough. *Jane Austen's Music: The Musical World of Jane Austen Seen Through the Manuscripts and Printed Editions Held by the Jane Austen Memorial Trust at Chawton, with Brief Histories of Contemporary Composers and a Catalogue of More Than 300 Musical Works.* St. Albans, England: Corda Music Publications, 1996.

***Gard, Roger. *Jane Austen's Novels: The Art of Clarity.* New Haven: Yale University Press, 1992.

***Gilbert, Sandra M., and Susan Gubar. *The Madwoman in the Attic: The Woman Writer and the Nineteenth-Century Literary Imagination.* New Haven: Yale University Press, 1979.

Gorman, Anita G. *The Body in Illness and Health: Themes and Images in Jane Austen.* New York: Peter Lang, 1993.

***Gray, J. David, A. Walton Litz, and Brian C. Southam. *The Jane Austen Companion.* New York: Macmillan, 1986.

Grigson, Jane. *Food with the Famous.* London: Seven Hills, 1991.

Halperin, John. *The Life of Jane Austen.* Baltimore: Johns Hopkins University Press, 1984.

Hardy, Barbara. *A Reading of Jane Austen.* New York: New York University Press, 1976.

Honan, Park. *Jane Austen: Her Life.* New York: St. Martin's, 1987.

Jarvis, W. A. W. *Jane Austen and Religion.* Stonesfield, England: Stonesfield Press, 1996.

Johnson, Claudia. *Jane Austen: Women, Politics, and the Novel.* Chicago: University of Chicago Press, 1988.

Jones, Vivien. *How to Study a Jane Austen Novel.* London: Macmillan, 1997.

Kaplan, Deborah. *Jane Austen Among Women.* Baltimore: Johns Hopkins University Press, 1992.

***Kaye-Smith, Sheila, and G. B. Stern. *More About Jane Austen.* New York: Harper's, 1949.

***————. *Talking of Jane Austen.* London: Cassell and Co., 1943. American title: *Speaking of Jane Austen.* New York: Harper, 1944.

Kirkham, Margaret. *Jane Austen: Feminism and Fiction.* Brighton: Harvester, 1983.

Lane, Maggie. *Jane Austen and Food.* London: Hambledon, 1995.

————. *Jane Austen's World: The Life and Times of England's Most Popular Author.* Holbrook, Mass.: Adams Media Corp., 1997.

Lascelles, Mary. *Jane Austen and Her Art*. Oxford: Clarendon, 1939.

Laski, Marghanita. *Jane Austen and Her World*. New York: Viking, 1969.

Le Faye, Deirdre, ed. *Jane Austen's Letters*, 3d ed. Oxford and New York: Oxford University Press, 1997.

Lefroy, Helen. *Jane Austen*. Pocket Biographies. Phoenix Mill, England: Sutton Publishing, Ltd., 1997.

Littlewood, Ian, ed. *Jane Austen: Critical Assessments*. London: Routledge, 1997. 4 vols.

Litz, A. Walton. *Jane Austen's Achievement: A Study of Her Artistic Development*. New York: Oxford University Press, 1986.

McMaster, Juliet. *Jane Austen on Love*. Victoria, B.C.: University of Victoria Press, 1978.

———. *Jane Austen the Novelist: Essays Past and Present*. New York: St. Martin's, 1996.

Marsh, Nicholas. *Jane Austen: The Novels*. New York: St. Martin's, 1998.

Mather, Rachel. *Heirs of Jane Austen: Twentieth-Century Writers of the Comedy of Manners*. New York: Peter Lang, 1997.

***Moers, Ellen. *Literary Women: The Great Writers*. New York: Oxford University Press, 1985.

Mooneyham, Laura G. *Romance, Language, and Education in Jane Austen's Novels*. New York: St. Martin's, 1988.

Morgan, Susan. *In the Meantime: Character and Perception in Jane Austen's Fiction*. Chicago: University of Chicago Press, 1980.

***Morris, Ivor. *Mr. Collins Considered: Approaches to Jane Austen*. London and New York: Routledge & Kegan Paul, 1987.

Mudrick, Marvin. *Jane Austen: Irony as Defense and Discovery*. Berkeley: University of California Press, 1968.

Myer, Valerie Grosvenor. *Obstinate Heart: Jane Austen: A Biography*. London: O'Mara, 1997. New York: Arcade, 1997.

Nardin, Jane. *Those Elegant Decorums: The Concept of Propriety in Jane Austen's Novels*. Albany: State University of New York Press, 1973.

Nicolson, Nigel. *The World of Jane Austen*. London: Weidenfeld and Nicolson, 1991.

***Nokes, David. *Jane Austen: A Life*. New York: Farrar, Straus and Giroux, 1997.

Pinion, F. B. *A Jane Austen Companion*. London: Macmillan, 1973.

Polhemus, Robert. *Erotic Faith: Being in Love from Jane Austen to D. H. Lawrence*. Chicago: University of Chicago Press, 1990.

***Pool, Daniel. *What Jane Austen Ate and Charles Dickens Knew: From Fox Hunting to Whist—the Facts of Daily Life in 19th-Century England*. New York: Simon & Schuster, 1994.

***Poovey, Mary. *The Proper Lady and the Woman Writer: Ideology as Style in the Works of Mary Wollstonecraft, Mary Shelley, and Jane Austen*. Chicago: University of Chicago Press, 1984.

Poplawski, Paul. *A Jane Austen Encyclopedia*. Westport, Conn.: Greenwood Pub, 1998.

Roth, Barry. *An Annotated Bibliography of Jane Austen Studies 1973–1983*. Charlottesville: University Press of Virginia, 1985.

———. *An Annotated Bibliography of Jane Austen Studies 1984–1994*. Athens: Ohio University Press, 1996.

Schor, Esther H. *Bearing the Dead: The British Culture of Mourning from the Enlightenment to Victoria*. Princeton: Princeton University Press, 1994.

Selwyn, David, ed. *The Poetry of Jane Austen and the Austen Family*. Iowa City: University of Iowa Press, 1997.

Shepherd, Patricia. *Come into the Garden, Cassandra*. Vancouver, B.C.: 1983.

Smither, Elizabeth. *The Mathematics of Jane Austen*. Birkenhead, Auckland: Godwit, 1997.

Southam, Brian C., ed. *Critical Essays on Jane Austen*. London: Routledge & Kegan Paul, 1968.

———. ed. *Jane Austen: The Critical Heritage*. vol. 2. Critical Heritage Series. London: Routledge & Kegan Paul, 1996.

Stewart, Maija. *Domestic Realities and Imperial Fictions: Jane Austen's Novels in Eighteenth-Century Contexts*. Athens: University of Georgia Press, 1993.

***Tanner, Tony. *Jane Austen*. Cambridge: Harvard University Press, 1986.

Thompson, Emma. *The Sense and Sensibility Screenplay & Diaries: Bringing Jane Austen's Novel to Film*. New York: Newmarket, 1995.

Thompson, James. *Between Self and World: The Novels of Jane Austen*. University Park, Penn.: Pennsylvnia State University Press, 1988.

***Tomalin, Claire. *Jane Austen: A Life*. New York: Knopf, 1997.

***Troost, Linda V., and Sayre Greenfield, eds. *Jane Austen in Hollywood*. Lexington: Kentucky University Press, 1998.

Tucker, George Holbert. *A Goodly Heritage: A History of Jane Austen's Family*. Manchester, England: Carcanet New Press, 1983.

***———. *Jane Austen the Woman: Some Biographical Insights*. New York: St. Martin's, 1995.

Watkins, Susan. *Jane Austen's Town and Country Style*. New York: Rizzoli International Publications, 1990.

***Weldon, Fay. *Letters to Alice on First Reading Jane Austen*. New York: Taplinger, 1984.

Wiltshire, John. *Jane Austen and the Body*. Cambridge: Cambridge University Press, 1992.

PERIODICALS

Annual Reports, Jane Austen Society, U.K.
Persuasions, Jane Austen Society of North America
Sensibilities, Jane Austen Society of Australia

INTERVIEWS

Auerbach, Emily: June 9, 1997
Barreca, Regina: January 27, 1999
Barrett, Julia: June 27, 1997
Barron, Stephanie: June 25, 1997
Battersby, James: June 8, 1997
Boyle, T. C.: January 17, 1999
Buckley, Jim: January 6, 1999
Conroy, Mark: April 6, 1997
Crusie, Jennifer: August 7, 1997
Fergus, Jan: June 12, 1997
Greenfield, Sayre: February 15, 1999
Lank, Edith: January 8, 1997
Law, Phyllida: January 18, 1999
Leahy, Veronica: June 18, 1997
Longenecker, Marlene: April 10, 1997
Martin, Judith: April 25, 1997
Massey, Anna: January 6, 1999
McAleer, John: June 22, 1997
McGrath, Douglas: June 20, 1997
Mizejewski, Linda: April 4, 1997
Riede, David: June 11, 1997
Roth, Barry: July 5, 1997
Smiley, Jane: February 8, 1999
Solender, Elsa: April 10, 1997
Spinrad, Phoebe: May 27, 1997
Troost, Linda: February 15, 1999
Vredenburgh, Joan: May 18, 1997
Walter, Harriet: January 27, 1999
Weldon, Fay: December 22, 1998
Wolf, Joan: January 27, 1999

Answers to Quizzes

Quiz: Letter Writing in the Novels, page 82

1. Lucy Steele to Edward Ferrars

2. Mr. Collins to Mr. Bennet

3. Mr. Darcy to Elizabeth Bennet

4. Frederick Wentworth to Anne Elliot

5. Willoughby to Marianne Dashwood. N.B.: Later he reveals that the content of the letter was dictated to him by his betrothed.

6. Isabella Thorpe to Catherine Morland

7. Lydia Bennet to Mrs. Forster

8. Mary Musgrove to Anne Elliot

9. Diana Parker to her brother, Mr. Parker, *Sanditon*

10. Mary Crawford to Fanny Price

11. Frank Churchill to Mrs. Weston

Quiz: Who Said That?
Great Lines from Jane Austen's Novels, page 102

1. Marianne Dashwood, *Sense and Sensibility*

2. Caroline Bingley, *Pride and Prejudice*

3. Fanny Price, *Mansfield Park*

4. Captain Harville, *Persuasion*

5. Mrs. Elton, *Emma*

6. Anne Elliot, *Persuasion*

7. Darcy, *Pride and Prejudice*

8. Mrs. Bennet, *Pride and Prejudice*

9. Charlotte Lucas, *Pride and Prejudice*

10. Mr. Woodhouse, *Emma*

11. Edward Ferrars, *Sense and Sensibility*

12. Emma Woodhouse, *Emma*

13. Mrs. Elton, *Emma*

14. Sir Walter Elliot, *Persuasion*

15. Mr. Collins, *Pride and Prejudice*

16. Mr. Woodhouse, *Emma*

17. Lady Susan Vernon, *Lady Susan*

18. Mrs. Elton, *Emma*

19. Anne Steele, *Sense and Sensibility*

20. Elizabeth Elliot, *Persuasion*

21. Mary Crawford, *Mansfield Park*

22. John Thorpe, *Northanger Abbey*

23. Mary Crawford, *Mansfield Park*

Quiz: Do Appearances Deceive?, page 124

1. Elizabeth Bennet, in the first impression of Mr. Darcy, *Pride and Prejudice*

2. Marianne Dashwood, *Sense and Sensibility*

3. John Thorpe, *Northanger Abbey*

4. Jane Fairfax, *Emma*

5. Lady Susan Vernon, *Lady Susan*

6. Henry Crawford, *Mansfield Park*

7. Mrs. Jennings, *Sense and Sensibility*

8. Lady Catherine de Bourgh, *Pride and Prejudice*

9. Anne Elliot, *Persuasion*

10. Mrs. Clay, *Persuasion*

11. Mrs. Croft, *Persuasion*

12. Mrs. Elton, *Emma*

13. Lydia Bennet, *Pride and Prejudice*

14. Anne and Lucy Steele, *Sense and Sensibility*

15. Mrs. Ferrars, *Sense and Sensibility*

Quiz: *Food in Jane Austen, page 151*

1. Mrs. Jennings

2. Fanny Dashwood

3. One of the Misses Steele

4. Fanny Price

5. Aunt Norris

6. Dr. Grant

7. Dr. Grant and Aunt Norris

8. Mary Crawford

9. A roast loin of pork

10. Mr. Elton

11. Mr. Knightley

12. Mrs. Elton

13. Mr. Woodhouse

14. Diana Parker

15. Arthur Parker

16. Green tea

Quiz: *Reading and Readers in Jane Austen, page 204*

1. Fanny Price, *Mansfield Park*

2. Marianne Dashwood, *Sense and Sensibility*

3. This is Laura's judgment of Macdonald in *Love and Freindship*.

4. Captain Benwick, *Persuasion*

5. John Thorpe, *Northanger Abbey*

6. Mrs. Elton, of *Emma*. "Hymen's saffron robe" is the quotation from Milton.

7. Henry Crawford, *Mansfield Park*. The stress is Austen's, not Milton's.

8. Mrs. Dashwood and her daughters along with Willoughby

9. Emma quotes *A Midsummer Night's Dream* regarding her wished-for romance between Mr. Elton and Harriet Smith.

10. Sir Edward Denham of *Sanditon*

Quiz: Illnesses and Hypochondria, page 224

1. Mrs. Smith, *Persuasion*

2. Mr. Woodhouse, *Emma*

3. Marianne Dashwood, *Sense and Sensibility*

4. Mary Musgrove, *Persuasion*

5. Jane Fairfax, according to her aunt Miss Bates.

6. Mrs. Palmer's baby, *Sense and Sensibility*, according to her mother, Mrs. Jennings.

7. Tom Bertram, *Mansfield Park*

8. Diana Parker, *Sanditon*

9. Mr. Bennet, *Pride and Prejudice*

10. Isabella Knightley, *Emma*

11. Mrs. Bennet, *Pride and Prejudice*

Index

Note: Titles of works are by Jane Austen unless otherwise noted.

THE END